Cambridge Studies in Chinese History, Literature and Institutions
General Editors
Patrick Hanan and Denis Twitchett

'THE LAMENT FOR THE SOUTH'

Other books in the series

GLEN DUDBRIDGE: The *Hsi-yu Chi*: A Study of Antecedents to the Sixteenth-Century Chinese Novel

STEPHEN FITZGERALD: China and the Overseas Chinese: A Study of Peking's Changing Policy 1949–70

CHRISTOPHER HOWE: Wage Patterns and Wage Policy in Modern China, 1919–1972

RAY HUANG: Taxation and Government Finance in Sixteenth-Century Ming China

DIANA LARY: Region and Nation: The Kwangsi Clique in Chinese Politics, 1925–37

CHI-YUN CHEN: Hsün Yüeh (A.D. 148–209): The Life and Reflections of an Early Medieval Confucian

DAVID R. KNECHTGES: The Han Rhapsody: A Study of the *Fu* of Yang Hsiung (53 B.C.–A.D. 18)

J. Y. WONG: Yeh Ming-ch'en: Viceroy of Liang Kuang (1852–8)

LI-LI CH'EN: Master Tung's Western Chamber Romance (*Tung hsi-hsiang chu-kung-tiao*): a Chinese *Chantefable*

DONALD HOLZMAN: Poetry and Politics: The Life and Works of Juan Chi (A.D. 210–63)

C. A. CURWEN: Taiping Rebel: The Deposition of Li Hsiu-cheng

P. B. EBREY: The aristocratic families of early imperial China: a case study of the Po-Ling Ts'ui family

HILARY J. BEATTIE: Land and Lineage in China: a study of T'ung-Ch'eng county, Anhwei, in the Ming and Ch'ing dynasties

'The Lament for the South'

YÜ HSIN'S 'AI CHIANG-NAN FU'

WILLIAM T. GRAHAM, JR

Assistant Professor, Department of East Asian Languages
and Literatures, Ohio State University

CAMBRIDGE UNIVERSITY PRESS
CAMBRIDGE
LONDON   NEW YORK   NEW ROCHELLE
SYDNEY   MELBOURNE

Published by the Press Syndicate of the University of Cambridge
The Pitt Building, Trumpington Street, Cambridge CB2 1RP
32 East 57th Street, New York, NY 10022, USA
296 Beaconsfield Parade, Middle Park, Melbourne 3206, Australia

First published 1980

Printed in Great Britain at the University Press, Cambridge

Library of Congress Cataloguing in Publication Data
Graham, William T
The lament for the South — Yü Hsin's Ai
Chiang-nan fu.
(Cambridge studies in Chinese history,
literature, and institutions)
1. Yü, Hsin, 513-581. Ai Chiang-nan fu.
2. China — History — Liang dynasty, 502—557 — Poetry.
I. Yü, Hsin, 513—581. Ai Chiang-nan fu. English.
1980. I. Title.
PL2668.Y8A734   895.1'1'2   79-50503
ISBN 0 521 22713 5

CONTENTS

To J. R. Hightower

PREFACE

I began work on Yü Hsin in 1970 and submitted a thesis on the 'Lament'
to Harvard University as part of the requirements for a Ph.D. degree in
1974. Some portions of that thesis, much revised, are included in this book.
The 'Lament' turned out to be a good deal more difficult than anticipated;
convinced that it must make more sense than it seemed to, I spent the four
years of thesis work, and much of the time since then, reading Six-Dynasties
history and literature. Professor J. R. Hightower, my thesis director, patiently
read and corrected a number of drafts, and Dr. Achilles Fang, who had tried
for years to teach me classical Chinese, also agreed to act as a reader of the
thesis. I would like to record my indebtedness to both of them. Professor
Hightower has also gone over various drafts of this book and suggested many
improvements; to him the work is dedicated. A number of others have
discussed the 'Lament' with me or read the draft in whole or in part, they
include Professors Florence Chao, Francis Cleaves, Patrick Hanan, William
Hung, Yan-shuan Lao, T. Y. Li, Denis Twitchett, J. T. Wixted, L. S. Yang,
and Y. S. Yü. Mr. George Potter and Miss Deborah White of the Harvard-
Yenching Library have very kindly helped me to obtain books.

It seems particularly appropriate that a book on the 'Lament' should
appear at this time; according to the theory of the late Professor Ch'en
Yin-k'o, 1978 would be the fourteen-hundredth anniversary of the writing
of the 'Lament'.

September 22, 1978   W.T.G.

INTRODUCTION

Few Chinese writers have distinguished themselves in as many genres as Yü
Hsin (513–81). Yü's lyric poetry is fully equal to that of Hsieh Ling-yün
(385–433), for example. His parallel-prose writings are considered models
of that form, so much so, in fact, that his name has become more or less
synonymous with parallel prose.[1] Finally, Yü's fifteen surviving *fu*, or poems
in irregular meter, include several works of the first rank, and one of them,
'The Lament for the South' ('Ai Chiang-nan fu'), is probably the finest *fu*
ever written. It is mainly with the 'Lament' that this book is concerned.

After a long period of neglect, there are signs of renewed interest in
fu. Most of the studies have been devoted to the earlier works, but there have
also been occasional forays into the Six-Dynasties period;[2] these later *fu*,
shorter and more accessible than the great showpieces of the Han, are likely
to prove more attractive to the Western reader. Chiang Yen's (444–505)
'Regret',[3] one of the best Six-Dynasties *fu*, is no more difficult than Su Shih's
(1037–1101) 'Red Cliff',[4] for example, and a student in second-year literary
Chinese can read either one with ease. The same cannot be said of the works
of Ssu-ma Hsiang-ju (*c*. 179–117 B.C.).

The 'Lament' is unusually long for its period, about the same length as
Ssu-ma's 'Rhapsody on the Shang-lin Hunting Park'.[5] It is also more difficult
than the 'Regret'; one would not recommend it to second-year language
students. I believe, however, that its difficulties are sometimes exaggerated.
It is remarkably free of the obscure vocabulary that turns the 'Shang-lin'
into a dictionary exercise. There are, to be sure, a good many allusions, and
the subject is an unusually complicated one for a *fu*, but it simplifies matters
if we remind ourselves of the fact that, however atypical of the genre, the
'Lament' remains a *fu*.

Yü Hsin, of course, did not have a monopoly on allusions. Ssu-ma himself
says at one point, in Watson's translation: 'A [coachman as clever as] Sun
Shu grasps the reins; A [warrior as brave as] Lord Wei stands beside him.'[6]
These are allusions of a sort, if only on a very low level. The context tells us
that Sun Shu must have been a famous charioteer, which is all we need to

1

know; in the same way, unless one is compiling social notes, it matters little
what contemporary figure, if any, is presented here in the guise of a Sun Shu.
Ssu-ma's was not a real hunt but an ideal one, one so unreal that the legendary
beasts and even the flight through space seem perfectly appropriate. Yü, on
the other hand, was dealing with real historical events. Here, instead of an
idealized hunt of one day, we have the events of a decade ending in the fall
of the Liang dynasty (502–57), still described in allusions as in the two lines
by Ssu-ma quoted above. There is a temptation in such a case to read the
'Lament' as a detailed history of the Liang, with the minutiae of recent
events lurking behind every allusion.[7] This, I think, is a grave mistake; pursued
too far it makes the work unreadable, if not unintelligible. Yü was concerned
only with the broad outlines of history, and he treats this history with an
idealization ultimately very much like that of Ssu-ma Hsiang-ju.

If we read the work in this spirit, and ignore red herrings, it becomes much
simpler and also much more interesting; Yü was not writing riddles, and he
was not trying to conceal anything.[8] If the allusions are sometimes unfamiliar,
that is because fashions change in these as in other things; we could hardly
expect Yü to use the same allusions as, say, T'ao Ch'ien (?365–427). The
generations of commentators on the 'Lament' have identified most of them,
and in case of doubt one can turn to other writings of the same period. The
'Lament' could only have been directed to an audience of such writers, and
it is reassuring to find even the more obscure allusions appearing regularly
in their works; one can conclude that the 'Lament', though never a simple
poem, would have been quite intelligible to a writer such as Tu Fu (712–70).
Most helpful, of course, are Yü's own works, the largest surviving literary
corpus by a pre-T'ang writer. Yü returns again and again to the same events
and the same allusions; this enables us to explain some otherwise obscure
passages in the 'Lament' with near certainty, rather as in a locus problem in
geometry. Much of the commentary in Chapter 4 deals with parallel passages
in other works, and this book as a whole is devoted to the similar aim of
fitting a masterpiece of Chinese literature back into the setting that produced
it.

Chapter 1 is an account of the author's life and times, with the stress on
the latter. We know little about the details of Yü's biography, except for his
official titles; the same thing is true of most other early Chinese writers.
There is a good deal more information available on the political history of
the period, which was quite complicated; Yü himself lived under four different
dynasties and nine emperors. This chapter is intended to provide the information essential for a reading of the 'Lament'.

Chapter 2 consists of notes on Six-Dynasties *fu* in general. Very little has
been written about this subject; I have here stressed the aspects less familiar

to Western readers, as well as the categories of *fu* represented in Yü Hsin's own works. Some of Yü's writings fit rather neatly into a tradition; others, particularly the 'Lament', fit very badly, since Yü was a most original writer. Still, even the 'Lament' could never have been written without this long tradition behind it, and without some knowledge of the tradition we can neither understand what Yü was doing nor appreciate his originality. This chapter also includes some notes on the critical appraisals of *fu*.[9]

Chapter 3 contains a translation and a paraphrase of the 'Lament', arranged in parallel columns. A non-specialist, after reading Chapter 1, might be well advised to go directly on to Chapter 3, which he should find intelligible even without further notes. For the specialist, there is an extended commentary in Chapter 4.

1
THE HISTORICAL BACKGROUND

Much of Chinese poetry deals with current events. Partly, of course, this was a result of the traditional view that literature should serve a didactic function. Partly it reflects the social situation; until fairly recent times, most Chinese writers were officials, either successful or frustrated, and they were naturally concerned with current events. Such works cannot be understood without some knowledge of the events involved; this additional information does not make them better poems, but it at least makes them intelligible, and without that no literary judgment is possible.

This is particularly true of the 'Lament', which deals with events on a scale never before attempted in Chinese poetry and thus requires a correspondingly greater amount of background information. Much of this would have been familiar to a contemporary audience, but it will have to be supplied to a modern reader of the 'Lament', who is unlikely to know much about sixth-century Chinese history. The following is intended to enable such a reader to make his way through the poem. As usual with early Chinese writers, Yü Hsin's biographies consist almost entirely of lists of official titles. Some information of general interest can be deduced from them; that is given in this chapter. The technical details, such as arguments for dating, are given in Appendix II, which is intended for specialists.

The earliest recorded member of Yü Hsin's family is a Yü Meng, a native of Hsin-yeh *hsien* in Nan-yang *chün*, or, in modern terms, of the southwestern part of Honan.[1] Yü Meng held the second-highest of all government posts, that of Imperial Secretary (*ssu-k'ung*), at some time during the Latter Han (25–220 A.D.), but his exact dates are unknown.[2] Thereafter the family disappears from the records for several generations, a fact which suggests decline; the missing figures in the genealogy (Appendix VII) are not likely to have been eminent officials.

The Yü family reappears only in the early fourth century, when a series of foreign invasions led to the collapse of the Western Chin dynasty. One of the great cataclysms of Chinese history, this resulted in almost three hundred years of foreign domination of North China, ending only in 581. There was

a large-scale flight of Chinese to the South, where the native Chinese Chin
dynasty was restored in a new capital at the present Nanking. Many others
chose to remain in the North under foreign rulers; these included a number
of important Chinese families, who managed to preserve their power in the
chaos and fragmentation which followed. Despite this continued Chinese
presence in the North, and even after the sinicization supported by the
Turkish-speaking Northern Wei dynasty (386–534), the Southern émigrés
considered the North very alien indeed.

The Yü family were divided on the question of emigration. Yü Hsin's
ancestor T'ao (Yü Meng's great-great-grandson) fled to the South, where,
having been instrumental in the restoration of the Chin under Emperor
Yüan (*reg.* 317–322), he was rewarded with a marquisate.[3] He settled
his family in Chiang-ling, equivalent to the modern city of that name in
Hupeh. Like other exiles, the family might continue to feel that they were
really 'from' Hsin-yeh, to the north, but by Yü Hsin's time it had become
possible to call them natives of Chiang-ling.[4] This is a fact of considerable
importance for the 'Lament'. Chiang-ling, under the name of Ying, had been
the principal capital of the ancient state of Ch'u and would serve for a few
years as the capital of Yü Hsin's own dynasty, the Liang. There were obvious
parallels between the fall of the Liang and that of Ch'u, so it is hardly surprising
that the 'Lament' should be filled with references to that ancient state.

It is perhaps misleading to speak of a restoration of the Chin dynasty. A
member of the old ruling family had been put on the throne of a much-
reduced state in the South, but the Yellow River valley, the ancient center
of Chinese civilization, had been lost to foreigners. The new Emperor, and his
successors, could only console themselves with the reflection that they were
the guardians of Chinese culture, threatened in the North with extinction by
the barbarians. They were powerless to reconquer the lost territory, or even
to exercise effective control over their own states. In fact, they were often
little more than puppets, retaining their precarious hold on the throne only
until one strong man or another felt disposed to replace them, either with
another puppet or with his own new dynasty. There were constant civil wars,
in which it might make little difference to the nominal emperor whether the
central government was defeated or victorious. A defeat would only mean
a different dictator; a victory could be even worse, since the victorious
general might feel justified at last in making himself ruler in name as well as
in fact. The intervals of peace were spent in intrigues, not unknown in earlier
periods but now much worse.[5]

It was not an attractive time to hold office. The bureaucracy remained, but
the great families, who held the actual power in the state, also felt themselves
entitled by right of birth to monopolize the higher offices.[6] In the turbulent

political situation, any office was potentially dangerous. Even the obscure ones did not offer enough safety to compensate for their inherent unpleasantness; one could easily become the secretary of the wrong man, for example, and end up involved in his ruin. Understandably, this was the great age of the recluse, the man remembered for his refusal to take public office.[7] The most famous of all recluses was T'ao Ch'ien (?365–427),[8] but even T'ao had experimented briefly with an official career; Yü Hsin's grandfather Yi (d. after 499) never held office at all.[9] Fortunately, this was by his own choice. A generation without official position could be damaging to the prospects of a family, but Yü Yi was on record as having refused at least four positions, over a period of seventeen years (479–495). This made him rather a distinguished figure, too lofty to demean himself with a career, and it also entitled him, like T'ao Ch'ien, to the honor of a biography among the recluses.[10] He seems to have been better able than T'ao to afford a life in retirement, since there is no indication of financial hardship in his case.

The political situation improved considerably in the next generation, under Emperor Wu (*reg.* 502–49), founder of the Liang dynasty. A long reign is generally a good sign; Wu's was the longest and, until its last years, the most stable of the period.[11] The previous dynasty, in contrast, had had six emperors in twenty-four years. Emperor Wu inherited from that dynasty, the Southern Ch'i, a policy of assigning the more important provincial offices to members of the ruling family; the system, now more successful than it had been earlier, meant relative peace within the country.[12] As a result of this, the capital at Chien-k'ang (the modern Nanking) grew larger under Emperor Wu than it had ever been before; we read that the city was forty *li* square, and the population was apparently well over a million.[13] Chien-k'ang reflected in an extreme form the political state of the empire. At the end of the rebellion that put him on the throne, Emperor Wu had evidently found the capital largely in ruins. His long reign was spent in restoring and expanding the city, but by 555 it was again in ruins, with the population not even half what it had been fifty or a hundred years earlier.[14]

The situation abroad also improved temporarily under Emperor Wu. Ever since the fourth century, the native Chinese dynasties in the South had been under more or less constant threat of attack from the North. Initially Emperor Wu had been confronted with the Northern Wei (386–534), the strongest of the alien dynasties. He was able to fend off its attacks until it destroyed itself in a civil war, which led to its partitioning in 534 into Eastern and Western Wei. Each of these was nominally governed by a member of the old ruling family of the Northern Wei, but both in fact were controlled by dictators, Kao Huan (d. 547) and Yü-wen T'ai (d. 556) respectively. The Eastern Wei emerged the stronger of the two states, and probably more than a match

for the Liang. Kao Huan, however, at war with Yü-wen T'ai, had no need of
a second enemy and so in 536 concluded an alliance with the Liang. The
decade that followed was the high point of Emperor Wu's reign.

The changing political situation is certainly reflected in the fact that,
while Yü Yi always avoided taking office, all three of his sons had successful
government careers, especially Yü Hsin's father Chien-wu (487–551).[15]
We need not go into all the details of Chien-wu's career here; Yü Hsin himself, in lines 35–6 of the 'Lament', points out the most important feature of
it, his father's relationship with two of the sons of Emperor Wu. Both were
writers and patrons of literature; Chien-wu, a famous poet, naturally attracted
their attention, and in turn was able to provide his son with two very useful
introductions. The men were Hsiao Kang (503–51), Wu's third son, known
posthumously as Emperor Chien-wen; and Hsiao Yi (508–55), the seventh
son, Emperor Yüan.[16] Yü Chien-wu entered the service of Hsiao Kang about
the time of his own son Hsin's birth in 513, and remained with him for over
twenty years.

Between 537 and 539 Chien-wu left Kang to work for Kang's brother Yi.
As noted earlier, Emperor Wu had had a policy of assigning the major provincial
posts to members of his own family. Hsiao Yi, the most important such figure,
spent almost all his adult life in the provinces, as general, military governor,
and inspector general; for much of the time he was in Chiang-ling, the Yü
family home (526–39, 547–55). During this period with Yi, Yü Chien-wu
was back at home again, apparently for the first extended stay since 515.
His father and both his brothers had been dead for years; nothing is known
of his mother, but his brothers had earlier shown a distinct preference for
posts in Chiang-ling, and their families probably remained there.[17] Hsiao
Yi, on the other hand, was a difficult man to work for. He eventually became
quite powerful, and after 549, when the central government fell under rebel
control, he would be the strongest remaining member of the Liang ruling
family. That, however, was far in the future. In the meantime, Hsiao Kang,
who had been Crown Prince since 531, must have looked more promising;
by about 539 Chien-wu was back in Chien-k'ang working again for the
Crown Prince.

His son Hsin had also begun an official career by this time. Around 535–7
we find him as Acting Military Consultant to a general in the provinces. This
was not very important; it ranked on the third level from the bottom of the
eighteen-level Liang hierarchy.[18] He spent most of the next dozen years in
various offices at the capital, generally under the Crown Prince, like his
father. In 542 he was temporarily back in the provinces as Adjutant to a
military governor, and sometime between then and 547 he was sent as ambassador to the Eastern Wei. The mission would have been largely a ceremonial

one. There had been cordial relations between the two states since 536, and ambassadors were chosen more for their literary distinction than for any diplomatic ability.[19] Since they were intended above all to impress the foreigners, they would of course have had to possess the social graces as well as an ability to think on their feet.

The period of Yü Hsin's early career was, as I have said, the high point of Emperor Wu's reign; there is an idyllic picture of it toward the beginning of the 'Lament'. Things changed abruptly in 547, as a result of a disastrous mistake by the Emperor. He was then 83 and may have been a little senile; Yü, who speaks of him generally with reverence, occasionally hints at that possibility, for example in lines 89–90. Emperor Wu simply overestimated the strength of his own state. The most important Eastern Wei general, a non-Chinese named Hou Ching,[20] offered to come over to the Liang with the territory under his control, theoretically perhaps a third of that state. What this meant was not so much submission as an alliance of sorts. Hou Ching was apparently trying to find some way to save himself; he was in the position, familiar in China as elsewhere, of being too powerful for his ruler to trust him, but not powerful enough to take control for himself. This had not been a major problem under Kao Huan, the dictator; the two had been on good terms. After Kao's death, however, it became necessary to make other arrangements; Kao's heir obviously considered him a dangerous rival.

Hou had originally made the same offer to the Western Wei; when that state proved unwilling to send the reinforcements he needed, he switched to the Liang.[21] Emperor Wu found the proposition more attractive. Though the Liang would not admit it, the Eastern Wei was probably the strongest state in China at that time. Hou Ching, who looked very impressive on paper, might possibly tip the balance in favor of the Liang. This would of course mean war, but it might be the beginning of the reconquest of the North, the heartland of ancient China, whose occupation by barbarians had always been both painful and threatening to the Chinese in the South.

Emperor Wu agreed to the alliance, the Eastern Wei attacked, and within a year Hou Ching had lost all his territory and fled south for refuge. Hou was now in an intolerable position, hated by the Eastern Wei and at best a nuisance to Emperor Wu, who, despite Hou's protests, soon renewed the old treaty with the northern state and seemed likely to hand Hou over as part of the peace agreement.[22] Hou made the inevitable decision and rebelled against the Liang, attacking Chien-k'ang in December, 548. After a prolonged siege, the city fell on April 24, 549; it remained in rebel hands for the next three years.

The earlier defeat by the Eastern Wei had already demonstrated the military weakness of the Liang, but it was only during the rebellion that its

critical defect became apparent. Emperor Wu had placed his sons and nephews
in powerful military positions in the provinces; by this time they were mature,
experienced generals, mostly in early middle age. Most, if not all, of them
now saw the rebellion as their opportunity to gain the throne.[23] Some had
led armies in at least a token effort to relieve the siege, but after Chien-
k'ang fell they returned to the provinces to kill off as many rival contenders
as possible. The court was left at the mercy of the rebels. Emperor Wu
died in captivity sometime before July 7, 549, the date when his death was
announced. As Waley says, one is not likely to know the cause of death in
such cases;[24] it might have been old age (he was 85), or perhaps starvation, as
one popular theory had it.[25] Hou Ching put the Crown Prince, Hsiao Kang,
on the throne as a puppet Emperor and set about extending his control.

Here it becomes necessary to give some account of the political and
military events of the next three years. Fortunately, the 'Lament' itself does
not demand of its readers a detailed knowledge of the period, and we also
need not go too far into the impossible question of the motivation of certain
individuals, since for our purposes it does not matter much whether a given
person meant well or not.

The history of the rebellion shows an interesting geographical symmetry,
with rebels in the East and the Liang forces in the West finally confronting
one another along the middle Yangtze. Hou Ching had certain initial advantages. He could issue edicts in the name of his captive Emperor, thus
gaining a bogus legitimacy. In addition, with most of the Liang court in his
control, he had an almost unlimited supply of hostages related in one way or
another to the provincial authorities. By a combination of force and diplomacy,
he was able by 551 to gain control over the East and Southeast, at least
temporarily.

This was possible only because of the lack of unified action against him;
the same period saw the beginnings of a civil war among the Liang princes
in the West. This war went on for years and finally destroyed the dynasty,
but during a lull, having gained a momentary supremacy, Hsiao Yi was able
to put down the rebellion with relative ease. This was Yü Chien-wu's former
employer, by now back in Chiang-ling as Military Governor, with an office
as Inspector General giving him authority over the others of that rank in
the area. Like most of the others, he had started down the Yangtze at the
beginning of the rebellion, stopped part way, and finally turned back, going
upriver much faster than he had come down. He had received a letter accusing
several of his relatives of plotting against him, and he was, as Yü Hsin observes,
an extremely suspicious man. Conceivably the accusation was true; whatever
the case, none of the plotters seems to have done anything beyond raising
armies and gathering supplies, not unreasonable activities during a rebellion.

After the fall of Chien-k'ang, Hsiao Yi claimed to have received one of those secret edicts which even the most closely guarded emperors manage somehow to send out. This one was supposed to have made him Commander-in-Chief of all Liang armies, with unlimited authority. If there were any lingering doubts among his relatives about Hsiao Yi's intentions, they were removed by his next action, the summary execution of Hsiao Tsao, one of the supposed plotters.

According to the accusation, the principal conspirator was Yi's nephew Hsiao Yü, Military Governor of Hsiang-chou.[26] Even without the secret edict, Hsiao Yi was entitled as a superior to exercise military control over Yü, and now, claiming that Yü had refused to send troops, he sent someone to Yü's capital at Changsha to assume command. Not surprisingly, Yü refused to give it up. Next came an army led by Hsiao Yi's oldest son, Fang-teng, who was killed in battle. His replacement proved incompetent, but a third general finally managed to capture and kill Yü in June of 550. In the intervening months Yü had called for help from his brother Ch'a, Military Governor of Yung-chou. Hsiao Ch'a's capital, the present Siangyang in Hupeh, was only about fifty miles from the northern frontier, and Ch'a soon concluded an ominous alliance with the Western Wei. Hsiao Yi had little reason to congratulate himself on a victory over Yü. The war had made enemies of all his relatives, and Ch'a in particular wanted revenge.

Yi's next target was his own elder brother Lun, Emperor Wu's sixth son.[27] Lun was the eldest surviving son, except for Hou Ching's puppet Kang, and thus the obvious claimant to the throne; the Kao family had recognized as much by allying itself with Lun, and he is supposed to have established his own imperial court. He had, however, done nothing to threaten Yi directly except to write protesting his treatment of Yü, and he seems to have been more concerned with Hou Ching. Lun had been one of the few princes to give effective help to the capital during the siege, and after the fall of the city he had continued to battle the rebels along the middle Yangtze. In September of 550 Hsiao Yi sent down a navy against his brother, commanded by Wang Seng-pien; Wang, who had been responsible earlier for the victory over Hsiao Yü, was equally successful against Lun. The latter, a fugitive, was captured and killed by the Western Wei in February of 551.

Hsiao Yi could now give his relatively undivided attention to Hou Ching. I spoke earlier of the geographical symmetry of the period; Hou by this time controlled the East and Southeast, and Hsiao Yi the West and Southwest. Both men had problems to the North. Yi had been forced to cede land to the Western Wei, allied with his nephew Ch'a. On the other hand, the death of Lun had brought him an alliance with the Kao family, dictators of the Eastern Wei, who had by now founded their own dynasty, the Northern Ch'i.

Their long-term intentions were suspect, but for the time being their harassment of Hou Ching was helpful to Yi. Lun's death also allowed Yi to send reinforcements to his own troops battling the rebels in the middle Yangtze; the latter called for help, and Hou Ching himself set out from Chien-k'ang in the spring of 551 on a major campaign up the Yangtze. After repeated defeats and the capture of several important generals, he was forced to flee back down the river. The rebellion was beginning to collapse; observing Hou's defeats, a number of regional leaders in the East rose against him.

Hou had held the capital for more than two years, but had been willing so far to rule through a puppet. After returning from his disastrous upriver expedition, he seems to have felt the need to act quickly. On October 2, 551, he put a child on the throne to replace Hsiao Kang, whom he murdered along with all Kang's sons still in his power. He then took the throne himself, as founder of a Han dynasty. Wang Seng-pien, leading the Liang forces in pursuit, stopped for the winter at Hsün-yang, the present Kiukiang, about 250 miles upriver from Nanking. It was suggested at the time that Hsiao Yi was waiting for Hou Ching to rid him of his rival Kang. In March of 552, the combined forces of Wang and Ch'en Pa-hsien (later to found the Ch'en dynasty) set out to attack the capital, which they captured on April 28. Hou Ching fled east, and was finally killed by his own followers; the vengeful people of Chien-k'ang are said to have eaten his corpse when it was returned there.

Both Yü Hsin and his father Chien-wu had been at Chien-k'ang when it originally came under rebel attack late in 548, and we are told that Hsiao Kang had sent Hsin to break up the pontoon bridge outside the great south gate of the city in an attempt to hold off the attackers.[28] Nothing more is known about Hsin from then until 551, when he reappears travelling up the Yangtze toward Chiang-ling; the sources are more complete for his father. Chien-wu continued in the service of Hsiao Kang, now puppet Emperor, and rose to his highest position yet, that of Minister of Finance (*tu-chih shang-shu*, on the thirteenth level). In 550 he was sent to placate one of Kang's sons, Hsiao Ta-hsin, who as Military Governor of Chiang-chou had been opposing Hou Ching. As mentioned above, Wang Seng-pien's army would later spend the winter of 551—2 in Hsün-yang, the capital of Chiang-chou. In the meantime, like many cities along the middle Yangtze, it changed hands repeatedly. Ta-hsin surrendered it to the rebels on August 25, 550; Chien-wu fled, and eventually made his way to Chiang-ling to join Hsiao Yi.[29] Yü Hsin had also managed to escape from Chien-k'ang, perhaps on the pretext of a mission like his father's to Hsiao Ta-hsin, as he implies in lines 231—2 of the 'Lament'. Reaching Chiang-ling about the autumn of 551, he was reunited briefly with his father, who is said to have died 'not long' after his own arrival there, and almost certainly by February 10, 552.[30]

Hsiao Yi postponed assuming the title of Emperor until December 13 of that year, but in the meantime still claimed the right to appoint officials on the basis of the secret edict. On reaching Chiang-ling, Yü Hsin was made Vice Censor-in-Chief (*yü-shih chung-ch'eng*). He apparently resigned this position because of his father's death; a period of mourning is mentioned in the 'Lament' (lines 283–6) though not in any of his biographies.[31] Normally this would have meant twenty-seven months out of office, but he seems to have been called back by Hsiao Yi before the completion of the full period. This would have been justified only by a military emergency; there were, however, many of those in the next few years.[32]

The suppression of Hou Ching's revolt did not bring peace; the civil war continued and in some ways even worsened. In May of 552, learning of the recapture of Chien-k'ang, Hsiao Chi assumed the title of Emperor. Chi was the eighth son of Emperor Wu and, by this time, Yi's only surviving brother. As Military Governor of Yi-chou (which had its capital at Chengtu in Szechwan), Chi had been able to avoid involvement in Hou Ching's rebellion. He had made occasional feints at his harried older brother during it, but had been restrained to some extent by his own problems with the Western Wei, who were expanding their territory at his expense. His claim to the throne now meant a declaration of war on Hsiao Yi, and the latter was forced to piece together an army to send against Hsiao Chi when he headed down the Yangtze that fall. It was getting more difficult all the time to find troops, since Yi had managed by then to precipitate yet another rebellion in the Changsha area and was also trying to hold off his nominal allies of the Northern Ch'i. They had been moving steadily southward against Hou Ching and seemed little moved by protests that their help was no longer needed.

The campaign against Hsiao Chi was the most bizarre series of events of an extraordinary period. As one would expect, Yi's make-shift army almost immediately required reinforcements. Running short of generals, Yi hit on the remarkable expedient of releasing one of Hou Ching's old followers from prison and sending him up the Yangtze with troops.[33] Another of his generals was reputed to possess magical powers,[34] and Yi himself is supposed to have resorted to sorcery, driving nails into a wooden image of Chi.[35] The story is perhaps apocryphal, but Chi was a formidable enemy. The war against him lasted almost a year before he was finally captured and beheaded in August of 553.

Hsiao Yi had refused for years to assume the title of Emperor; in December, 552, he had finally done so, perhaps in response to Chi's own claim. His empire was only a fragment of his father's, since much had been lost to rebels and invaders; it is said that the new Emperor actually controlled only a thousand *li* of territory and thirty thousand households.[36]

Yi's most dangerous enemy now was a foreign one, the Western Wei, which had taken advantage of his war with his brother Chi to annex most of Szechwan. It is difficult to tell whether Yi recognized the danger of his situation. On the one hand, the official histories show him ignoring the clearest warnings of Wei plans against him. Such behavior, however, is expected of 'bad last Emperors'. Yi, like his father, Emperor Wu, had been cast in that role by traditional historians, and very similar stories are told of both of them.[37] Such blind trust would go very much against Yi's normal practice. He had always suspected the worst of his relatives, and a remarkable number of his closest followers seem to have spent intervals in prison on one charge or another.[38] Of course, paranoia or some other form of insanity is also characteristic of bad last Emperors, so we are back very near to where we started.

One action of Yi's suggests at least temporary misgivings about the Wei. On September 4, 553, he ordered a return downriver to the old capital at Chien-k'ang (or Nanking). He had already had difficulty defending Chiang-ling against his various relatives, and the new proximity of the Western Wei, together with Liang weakness after all the wars of the past five years, would have made a move desirable. Chien-k'ang was a larger city, and a stronger one, with the major obstacle of the Yangtze protecting it against attack from the North. Chiang-ling, on the north bank, lacked this natural defense. Chien-k'ang was moreover a long way downriver from the Wei armies, and the important fortresses along the middle Yangtze that had earlier served as buffers against Hou Ching's attacks from downriver should logically serve the same purpose now against an attack from the opposite direction.

It should be recognized that by moving to Chien-k'ang, Yi would be exchanging one enemy for another. The Northern Ch'i, because of its own expansion south, was now within striking distance of that city, and it was stronger now, and the Liang weaker, than in 547—8 when it had been able to defeat the combined armies of the turncoat Hou Ching and the Liang. Besides that, Chien-k'ang was largely in ruins, having been looted and burned after its recapture from Hou Ching. Chiang-ling was at least intact, and Yi had spent much of his life there. After some vacillation, he decided against the move.[39] This is considered his greatest mistake, and it is true that the consequences were disastrous for him.

Yi was by this time on diplomatic terms with both states to the north. Relations were somewhat better with the Northern Ch'i; the same had been true ever since 536 except for Emperor Wu's ill-advised war of 547—8. The Western Wei, on the other hand, had long been encouraging Yi's enemy Hsiao Ch'a, and their greed for Liang territory was more blatant than the Northern Ch'i's. Ambassadors were not then permanent residents abroad; one state would send someone for a stay of a few weeks, and the other state

would respond in the same way. As it happened, both the northern states
had embassies in Chiang-ling in May of 554. Hsiao Yi apparently demanded
that the Western Wei return to their former boundaries, and he may have
made a point of his better relations with the Northern Ch'i. At all events,
on returning home, the Western Wei envoy is supposed to have complained
of the greater courtesy shown his Northern Ch'i counterpart.[40] This diplomatic affront served as a pretext for a Western Wei invasion.

Diplomacy being what it is, it is not surprising that we should have so
little information about Hsiao Yi's meetings with the Western Wei representative; it is, however, frustrating, because the ambassador sent in response
was Yü Hsin. We are told nothing about his instructions, only his rank at the
time, Grand Counselor, and the date, May 27, 554.[41] In the 'Lament' he
describes his mission as one of preventing an invasion. If that was the case,
he failed disastrously. The Western Wei armies were sent out against the Liang
in November of that year, and Yü Hsin was detained for the rest of his life
in the North.

On many earlier occasions Hsiao Yi had been slow to react to new crises,
probably because he had been fighting on too many other fronts to spare the
troops. Things had always worked out satisfactorily; Wang Seng-pien, responsible in whole or in part for almost all Yi's great victories, would finally
appear and rescue the situation. This time Yi waited too long; it was November
28 when he sent word to Wang to return from Chien-k'ang. The armies of the
Western Wei and their ally Hsiao Ch'a reached Chiang-ling on December 14,
and the city fell long before Wang or any of the other reinforcements could
arrive. Hsiao Ch'a, who had been waiting since 550 to avenge his brother Yü,
now murdered his uncle Yi and a number of Yi's sons, his own cousins. This
was a fitting conclusion; as Yü Hsin says, it may have involved a few outsiders,
but basically the Liang ruling family had destroyed itself. The invaders set
up Hsiao Ch'a as puppet ruler of a Liang state, known historically as the
Later Liang, with its capital at Chiang-ling; his only function was to legitimize
their conquests. Most of the inhabitants of Chiang-ling, including a large part
of the old Liang court, were carried off into a Babylonian captivity in the
North. One finds references in the histories years later to some of them
being ransomed or freed from slavery.[42] Eventually most of the court were
allowed to return to the South; Yü Hsin, one of the few exceptions, speaks
in lines 463—4 of the 'Lament' of his longing to go home alive or even dead.

Yü's poem disposes of the last period of the Liang in a few words, and we
may do likewise. Wang Seng-pien and Ch'en Pa-hsien, the generals who had
recaptured Chien-k'ang from Hou Ching, now moved a surviving son of
Hsiao Yi back there as Liang Emperor. The Northern Ch'i also proposed
their own puppet candidate for the throne, a nephew of Emperor Wu whom

they had captured during the 547–8 war. Wang found his forces no match for those of the Ch'i and was forced to accept their candidate. Ch'en Pa-hsien, seizing this pretext to dispose of a powerful rival, killed Wang in a surprise attack and 'restored' Hsiao Yi's son. Finally, in 557, Ch'en forced this last Liang Emperor to abdicate in his favor and founded the Ch'en dynasty.

The timing of Yü Hsin's embassy had been unfortunate. With the outbreak of hostilities, he found himself in 554 a prisoner in the Western Wei capital at Ch'ang-an, the modern Sian in Shensi. This must not be confused with the great metropolis of the Sui and T'ang, an entirely new construction twenty *li* southeast of the old city, built in the years after 590.[43] In 534 Yü-wen T'ai, a Hsien-pei general, had brought the last Northern Wei Emperor to Ch'ang-an and installed him there as a puppet. At that time, the only apparent advantage of Ch'ang-an was the natural defenses that made it perhaps the strongest city in China; these were important, since Yü-wen was in a position rather like that of the Confederacy during the Civil War. He had great generals. but economically and militarily he was no match for his rival Kao Huan, nor could his court compare with that of the old Wei capital at Loyang, or even with Yeh (in northern Honan), where Kao soon established his own puppet. Both courts naturally claimed to be the real Wei, but Yü-wen's is known historically as the Western, and Kao's as the Eastern Wei.

The disparity was even greater in cultural terms. The late Northern Wei had had a highly developed civilization, though we may sometimes ignore this in literary history, and this was inherited by the Eastern Wei and its successor state the Northern Ch'i. The writers of these states could produce perfectly respectable parallel prose, to give only one example, and this is an art that cannot be learned overnight. They were perhaps inferior in number of writers and in technical brilliance to the South, but when the Liang sent one of its writers on an embassy, the Eastern Wei had no need to feel ashamed of the man they sent to meet him. The contrasting situation in the West is best illustrated by an anecdote; it is surely apocryphal, but it involves only a slight exaggeration of the actual state of affairs. Reportedly Yü Hsin was asked by another Southerner after arriving in Ch'ang-an what he thought of the literary men there. He replied that with few exceptions they could only bray like donkeys and bark like dogs.[44]

By this time Yü-wen T'ai had discovered a new, rather unexpected advantage of Ch'ang-an in addition to its natural defenses. However poor and backward Shensi might be in the sixth century A.D., it had once been the cradle of the Chou, the most sacred of Chinese dynasties (traditional dates 1122–256 B.C.). Unable to compete by other means, Yü-wen set out to give his own court associations with the ancient Chou dynasty. It is very important to remember that this was only a veneer. There was no real attempt to revive ancient Chinese customs; in the civil war leading to the breakup of the Northern Wei, Yü-wen had in fact belonged to the side opposed to siniciz-ation, and he now made considerable efforts to reverse that process.[45] In externals, where it mattered less, he made two token gestures designed to present any apparent backwardness as a deliberate return to the archaic simplicity of the ancient Chou. First, he imitated the *Officials of the Chou* (*Chou kuan*) in certain official titles; second, he encouraged the use of *Classic of Documents* (*Shu ching*) style in writing.[46] This had a striking effect on the histories of the period, filled with strange official titles and unusual vocabulary even in the narrative passages. However conspicuous the change may be, it was only a matter of externals; only the names were changed, not the real institutions. The system was mixed to begin with, the archaic titles being given only to high civil officials of the central government; as time passed even these were gradually changed to less archaic ones. The attempt to imitate *Documents* style, a strange aberration, was even shorter-lived. Su Ch'o himself (498–546), the most famous figure in the movement, used elaborate late-Six-Dynasties parallelism in his *Shu ching* imitations,[47] and subsequent imperial edicts, theoretically the most archaic of all works, gradually lost their archaic vocabulary and grew indistinguishable from contemporary parallel prose. What would nowadays be considered purely literary works, such as poems, were always modeled on the highly developed style used by the contemporary Chinese dynasties, at least to the extent that the authors could approximate it. The only lasting effects of the archaizing movement of the sixth century were philosophical and political rather than literary ones. Confucian polemicists at the beginning of the T'ang used it as a stick to beat the Southern literature of the late Six Dynasties, as ex-plained in Chapter 2; and late-T'ang writers, experimenting with a very different and much more manageable kind of 'archaic prose' (*ku wen*), thought of Su Ch'o's works as a precedent.

Despite this pretense at archaizing, the Western Wei was starved of the high culture of the contemporary South. Understandably, Yü Hsin was lionized by his captors; he had already gained a considerable reputation by that time, and in retrospect must be judged the greatest writer of that century. His captivity, of course, did not mean anything like imprisonment. The preface to the 'Lament' speaks of three years of house-arrest, but that cannot be literally true; probably, like much else in the work, it is intended only as a metaphor, here referring to the absolute prohibition against his return to the South.[48] His position was not unique; all three courts had a certain number of refugees or detainees, often in high office. We must be careful not to judge such people according to moral standards developed only much

later. At that time it was considered almost inevitable that they should take
office under their new rulers. Even the surrender of a city or service under
a rebel, much graver matters, could be excused if done under extreme pressure.[49]

Yü Hsin was nevertheless reluctant to take office under the Western Wei,
who were not only aliens but, judging by their conduct after the capture of
Chiang-ling, savages. His feelings at this time are described in the short *fu*
'The Bamboo Cane',[50] one of the few works by Yü that can be dated even
approximately. Like many Six-Dynasties *fu*, it is an example of prosopopoeia
but here the personal reference is unmistakable. It is based on a story in
Liu Hsiang's (77–6 B.C.) *Hsin hsü*:[51] the seventy-year-old Master Ch'u-ch'iu
('Hills of Ch'u') came to see Lord Meng-ch'ang, who commented that such an
elderly guest must surely have something to teach him. Master Ch'u-ch'iu
replied that, if asked to perform feats of strength, he was not merely old,
he was dead. If, on the other hand, he was needed as a diplomat or adviser,
in that respect he had barely reached his prime. This story is scarcely recognizable in Yü's version. Master Ch'u-ch'iu, the author's persona, goes to see
the Eastern Chin strong man Huan Wen (312–73); the latter represents
Yü-wen T'ai, the corresponding Western Wei figure. Huan Wen, commenting
on his guest's age, presents him with a bamboo cane, the traditional sign of
a ruler's esteem for an elderly minister, and hints at the possibility of a
position for him. Master Ch'u-ch'iu replies that he is not even sixty, but that
his grief has made him old; by the end of his discussion of that grief and its
effects on him, it is clear that he has no intention of accepting office.

Such arguments were more effective on paper than in real life; by the end
of the Western Wei in 557, Yü had been given four titles. If he was reluctant
to accept them, it is quite possible that the bestowers felt more admiration
than trust for this native of an enemy state. The titles were quite distinguished,
but none involved any real power. It is noteworthy that the 'Lament' mentions
neither these nor any other offices he held in the North, while it dwells at
some length on much lower positions during his earlier years under the Liang.
The last specific event in the 'Lament' is the forced abdication ending the
Liang; of his later years Yü tells us only that he was unhappy in the North,
despite the great honor shown him there, and longed to go home.

His biographies, on the other hand, provide a long list of official positions
he held, though little else. Based on these, and the scanty information available elsewhere, one would judge that he was admired more for his writings
than for anything else. He had a distinguished career, though he never came to
hold great political or military power. In the same way, he was befriended
by various members of the Yü-wen family, particularly by Yu, the Prince of
T'eng, who was responsible for the first collected edition of Yü Hsin's works
in 579, and who himself contributed a preface, the earliest source for Yü's

biography. However, as well as one can tell, he never became a real intimate of the family.[52] In this, as in his lack of great power, he was ultimately fortunate. Since he was not a threat to anyone, he survived a series of purges to die a natural death.

The Western Wei dictator Yü-wen T'ai died in 556, a few months after naming his third son, the fourteen-year-old Chüeh, as his heir. To do so he had passed over his eldest son, the twenty-two-year-old Yü; the reason given was that Chüeh's mother, a Wei princess, was of better birth than Yü's. Whatever the reason, the choice was unfortunate; Chüeh was far too young to take over the government of a state. T'ai, on his deathbed, was supposed to have asked an obscure nephew of his, Yü-wen Hu, to assume actual control of affairs.[53] Such dying wishes are always suspect, particularly when, as in this case, the death occurs away from the capital. If this conversation actually did take place, the choice of Hu as regent was even more unfortunate than that of Chüeh as heir.

In 557, Hu forced the Western Wei puppet to abdicate in favor of Chüeh, who thus became the first monarch of the Chou dynasty. Following the practice of the ancient Chou, Chüeh was called, not Emperor, but Heaven [-Appointed] King (*T'ien wang*).[54] The deposed Emperor was made Duke of Sung, like the descendants of the Shang kings, but almost immediately murdered. Yü-wen Hu, acting as regent for a young kinsman, made every effort to appear as another Duke of Chou; he would surely have assumed that title if circumstances had not ruled it out.[55] The resemblance, however carefully cultivated, was limited. Within a year Hu deposed and murdered his young cousin and replaced him on the throne with Yü-wen T'ai's eldest son Yü, who had originally been passed over for the succession. Yü, unlike Chüeh, was an adult and capable of independent thought, but when he took steps to rid himself of his unwanted regent, Hu had him poisoned.

His replacement, T'ai's fourth son Yung (*reg.* 560–78), was more discreet. Taking the throne at seventeen, he managed to avoid rousing his murderous cousin's suspicions for years. Finally, in 572, he hit upon the perfect solution, a bit of black comedy ideally suited to Hu's Duke of Chou pretensions. The Dowager Empress, he told Hu, was drinking too much. Would Hu be willing to speak to her about it? He could use as his text the Duke of Chou's 'Announcement about Drunkenness'.[56] Hu agreed, of course. It being a family gathering, Hu was seated during the lecture. The Emperor, who remained standing near him, took a jade scepter and knocked Hu unconscious. After some fumbling, he was finally beheaded, and the Emperor, whose posthumous title is Wu ('Martial'), became ruler in fact as well as name.

Sometime during the regency, probably in the early 560s, Yü Hsin was sent out to the provinces as Prefect of Hung-nung *chün*. This was an important

position; Hung-nung, on the eastern frontier, guarded the capital against a
Northern Ch'i attack. The rest of the period he spent mostly at Ch'ang-an,
holding a series of extremely high honorary military titles but apparently
engaged in literary work. In 560, for example, he had been assigned to col-
late texts.[57] By tradition, each new dynasty was expected to create a set
of ritual hymns, like those in the *sung* section of the *Classic of Songs*. This
was particularly important for a dynasty which claimed to have resurrected
the ancient Chou; work on these hymns was begun at least as early as 566[58]
and completed in 573.[59] Yü Hsin also had a hand in this, writing some of
the hymns and presenting a congratulatory memorial to Emperor Wu when
the complete series was performed late in 573.[60] It is fairly certain that he
also would have drafted official documents for the regent, such things as
edicts; a number of them resemble his known writings. However, it is almost
impossible to prove authorship in such cases; traditional attributions are
normally based on the shaky evidence of a statement in someone's biography
that he was the actual author of all the official documents of Emperor So-
and-So, or General Such-and-Such. Even if the attribution were certain, it
would add little to Yü Hsin's reputation.

Two more important works, definitely by Yü, date from about this time.
These are his two ceremonial rhapsodies, written as showpieces for important
state occasions. Such things are quite common throughout the history of the
fu, but only two such works by Yü survive. Possibly he did not care for this
kind of *fu*; most modern readers would be likely to agree. As such things go,
both are brilliant display pieces; Suzuki Torao considers the preface to the
second a masterpiece of parallel prose.[61] The first is the 'Rhapsody on
Cosmological Chess' ('Hsiang hsi fu'), written to celebrate Emperor Wu's
own 'Cosmological Canon' ('Hsiang ching') of 569.[62] The second is the
'Rhapsody on the Mounted Archery Contest in the Hua-lin Park on the Third
Day of the Third Month',[63] probably written in 573. This is reminiscent of
some of the old Han rhapsodies on hunts, for example works by Yang Hsiung
(53 B.C.–A.D. 18), except that it lacks the constant binomes of the earlier
works. *Fu*, incidentally, were traditionally given the place of honor at the
beginning of an author's collected works; as the most 'imperial' of Yü Hsin's
fu, this piece appears first among them.

The period when Emperor Wu had actual control of government (572–8) is
remembered chiefly for two events: the persecution of Buddhism and Taoism,
and the conquest of the Northern Ch'i. Wu carried traditional Confucian
practices to an extreme. He lectured frequently on the *Record of Ritual*
(*Li chi*), insisted for a few weeks on observing the full mourning rites for
his mother, however impractical they might be for a sovereign,[64] and issued
numerous edicts calling for economy.[65] In 572, soon after assuming control,

he went so far as to burn down a palace which he thought ostentatious. Confucianism had always asked frugality of a ruler, but this was an extreme step. He may have repented of it later, because he thereafter ordered only that palaces be torn down and the pieces used to relieve the poor.[66] With such devotion to Confucianism, it is not surprising that Wu was hostile to the other two teachings. In 574 he proscribed both Buddhism and Taoism, and ordered the burning of their images and scriptures, and the return to lay status of their monks and priests.[67]

The persecution had only a temporary effect; far more important was the conquest of the Northern Ch'i in 577. This united North China for the first time since 534, when Emperor Wu's father, the dictator T'ai, had moved his puppet west to Ch'ang-an. T'ai, a better man in most ways than any of his sons, had never been able to achieve this. The reason was that the situation had changed in the meantime; the Chou was somewhat stronger and the Ch'i a great deal weaker than twenty or thirty years earlier. The victory marks the high point of the Chou dynasty, which hereafter declined rapidly.

The year 577 was also the high point of Yü Hsin's career; he had by that time become Military Governor of Lo-chou.[68] Any military governorship was important, especially this one; Loyang, the capital of Lo-chou, was one of the greatest cities in China and a model for the later Sui capital at Ch'ang-an. Sometime after August of 578, Yü was summoned back to the capital to take up a much lower post, in the first real demotion of his career. He retired in 579, pleading illness. It may have been genuine, since he died two years later. It is possible, on the other hand, that he saw in his demotion a hint of things to come. Yang Chien, father-in-law of the Chou Emperor and himself founder of the Sui in 581, was already in control of the government by that time; Yü-wen Yu, who edited Yü Hsin's works in 579, would be executed in 580 as part of Yang's massacre of the Chou ruling family. Yü was fortunate enough to die of natural causes; his family were less fortunate. He had lost two sons and a daughter during Hou Ching's rebellion, another daughter and her son died sometime later,[69] and finally Yü's son Li, his only known surviving descendant, was killed by a rebel during the Sui.[70]

2

THE *FU* IN THE SIX DYNASTIES

Tradition has always been a powerful force in Chinese literature; there was a tendency to think of contemporary works in comparison with those of some classic age in the past. For the *fu*, the classic age was the period from the third century B.C. through the Han. The writers of that age were looked on as patriarchs of the genre, and the literary theories of the time have also had a profound influence. For that reason, it is useful to begin with a discussion of the early period; that is the one most likely to be familiar to the Western reader, so it can be kept quite brief.[1]

What are called *fu* actually began as two separate genres: the elegy or *sao*, and the rhapsody. The former, as its name implies, is derived from the 'Li sao' ('Encountering Sorrow') by Ch'ü Yüan, whose dates are traditionally given as 323–277 B.C. Like their prototype, elegies are subjective and personal, sometimes insistently so. They tend to be complaints about the author's position in a hostile world; they also tend to favor allegory. Rhapsodies, on the other hand, are impersonal descriptions, characterized during the early period by wild hyperbole and bizarre vocabulary. When one thinks of the Han *fu*, it is generally in terms of these rhapsodies, such as Ssu-ma Hsiang-ju's 'Rhapsody on the Shang-lin Hunting Park'. It would be convenient if one could restrict the Chinese term *fu* to the rhapsody, but the elegies were also sometimes spoken of as *fu* by Han writers.[2] Thus, however different the two genres might be, the theoretical distinction between them was already blurred, with important consequences.

The elegy and rhapsody did at least have something in common;[3] the next extension of the meaning of *fu*, less justifiable, had even greater consequences. These were new genres, totally unlike anything earlier. It was therefore necessary to find a place for them in the Chinese poetic tradition and, more important, to justify their existence, since the didactic theory of literature dominated the Han. The most admired didactic poetry was, of course, the *Classic of Songs* (*Shih ching*). Nothing much could be done about the form; the 'Rhapsody on the Shang-lin Hunting Park' could not be called a ballad. For the didactic theorists, however, form was much less important than content and purpose.

Parts of the 'Li sao', for example, were clearly devoted to criticism of a ruler, in the best tradition of the *Classic of Songs*, and both works had used political allegory.[4] The 'Li sao', therefore, was in a didactic sense 'derived' from the *Songs*, and this rather tenuous derivation was supported by a series of plays on the word *fu* itself, which had earlier appeared in connection with the *Songs*. There the word had had entirely different meanings, but the fact that the same word was applied to the *Songs* and to this new genre meant that they were somehow all the same.[5] It was now possible to speak of the *Songs* themselves as *fu*, thus giving the best possible ancestry to the Han *fu*. If a given work by Ssu-ma Hsiang-ju did not seem to serve a didactic purpose, then that did not discredit the genre. It had simply had the misfortune to produce a black sheep, as can happen in the best of families.

From then on, the elegy and rhapsody, now theoretically merged, were ideally to serve the same purpose as the *Songs* themselves. That purpose could be defined in different ways; put in the crudest didactic form, it was to 'embody moral and political aims and values'.[6] Another, more sophisticated theory stressed the importance of feelings: to be acceptable, poetry should arise out of genuine and legitimate personal feeling, and express this feeling with appropriate restraint.[7] The latter theory became the dominant one only in the Six Dynasties,[8] but one occasionally runs across it in surprisingly early sources. Ssu-ma Ch'ien (*c.* 148–*c.* 90 B.C.), for example, combines the two theories and praises the 'Li sao' for both didactic value and expression of legitimate feeling.[9] For the most part, however, Han critics could be satisfied only by obvious didactic value; *fu*, like other forms of writing, were expected to persuade the ruler to mend his ways. Given the circumstances, this normally meant telling him how he could become even better than he was already.

The infant genre was judged by this extremely crude standard and found wanting. A number of Former Han *fu* had concluded with a gesture toward didacticism; Ssu-ma Hsiang-ju, for example, stuck on a token plea against hunting at the end of his 'Rhapsody on the Shang-lin Hunting Park'.[10] Such things were never convincing. The theoretical justification was that the writer could teach only after he had captured his subject's attention, or, in other words, that the rhapsodic description of the hunting park and hunt was intended only to sweeten the cup for the medicine at the end. The problem was that, having reached that point, the reader would already be too dazzled to notice the concluding moral. This problem was pointed out by Yang Hsiung (53 B.C.–A.D. 18), an orthodox Confucian and a reformed *fu*-writer, who branded the whole genre as useless for didactic purposes and, most damaging of all, 'excessively adorned'.[11] The latter phrase, which has haunted *fu*-writers ever since then, is undeniably true of some works but overstated; a similar idea was better expressed by Yüan Huang (16th century): 'The greatest danger in lyric poetry (*shih*) is shallowness; the greatest danger in *fu* is obscurity.'[12] *Fu* sometimes do make difficult reading; the same thing can also be true of lyric poems, of course.

The genre of *fu* changed a good deal in the centuries following Yang Hsiung's judgment; critical standards also grew more sophisticated, though theory always lingered behind practice. It is possible that even Yang himself would have felt differently about the genre if he had lived in the late Six Dynasties. Unfortunately, with the revival of Confucianism in the T'ang, *fu* in general became suspect. Yang's remarks were eminently quotable, and dogmatic and militant critics, who had perhaps not read many Six-Dynasties *fu*, nevertheless used Yang as a stick to beat the *fu*. Worst of all, Yang had defined the limits of the debate, so that even later admirers of *fu*, placed on the defensive, were forced to waste their time in pointless arguments about whether Ssuma Hsiang-ju's rhapsodies were genuinely edifying.

Yang himself had experimented in writing didactic *fu* before abandoning the genre as useless, and the most immediate effect of his remarks was to spur further efforts. Imperial hunts were not very promising subjects, since Confucians traditionally looked on hunting as dangerous and also wasteful of manpower and land better devoted to agriculture. Pan Ku (32–92) chose to write instead on the imperial capital, which offered more variety and did not restrict him to a sport of dubious value. Han *fu*-writers had tended to favor a debate format, with spokesmen arguing the merits of rival hunts, etc. They were, after all, trying to persuade, and it is easy to win an argument if one is writing both sides; for the same reason, the hypothetical debate was popular with philosophers. Pan imitates this format, and opens with a description of the magnificence of the Former Han capital at Ch'ang-an. In the second part, instead of trying to give an even more splendid picture of the Latter Han capital at Loyang, he speaks of the moderation and restraint of that city, the progress of classical studies, and so on. The work ends with the Confucian virtues triumphant, at least on paper, but even didactic theorists sometimes admit that Pan Ku's 'Rhapsody on the Two Capitals' is not a success. Virtues such as moderation do not lend themselves to this kind of grand display rhapsody; they fare much better in the more personal *fu*, such as the works on living in retirement, and even there the author needs a more delicate touch than Pan Ku possessed.

Pan's rhapsody is, however, quite important because of its influence. It inspired innumerable imitations, by the end of the Six Dynasties there must have been well over a hundred. One of these, by Chang Heng (78–139),[13] is a great poem, interesting both in itself and as a reminder that an imitation can be far superior to its model. Tso Ssu's (d. *c*. 300) rhapsody on the capitals of the Three Kingdoms,[14] though of less value as literature, is of particular importance for our purposes. Pan Ku had extended the scope of the rhapsody from the hunting park to the imperial capital. Tso took this even further; despite his title, he was writing, not about capitals, but about nations. One of these, the Three Kingdoms state of Wu, would automatically suggest the Liang; it is thus not surprising that there are so many borrowings from the 'Wu Capital Rhapsody' in the 'Lament'. Yü's work is not an imitation; he was writing about the fall of a dynasty rather than the glories of a geographic region, but in passing he gives a highly compressed version of Tso Ssu.

Most of the other rhapsodies on capitals survive at best only in fragments, and the reasons are obvious. These things were of staggering length. Mei Sheng's 'Seven Stimuli',[15] the earliest typical Han *fu*, had devoted about 2400 words to a whole series of pleasures, only one of them a hunt. Ssu-ma Hsiang-ju's 'Shang lin' is about 3600 words long; Pan Ku's 'Two Capitals', 4700; Chang Heng's, 7700; and Tso Ssu's 'Three Capitals', 10,100. The 'Lament', incidentally, is about 3400; the 'Li sao', about 2500.[16] The typical 8-line lyric poem of the T'ang, in comparison, is either 40 or 56 words! In an age of manuscripts, the odds were against survival unless these long *fu* happened to be included in the *Wen hsüan* or a standard-history biography. Historiographers have often protested against the quoting of *fu* in biographies, but a literary historian has reason to be grateful for the practice.

Perhaps uncharitably, one does not much regret the loss of so many capital *fu*, though this has probably deprived us of a good deal of information on folklore and some clues on the layout of cities. The surviving fragments do not invite close stylistic analysis or comparison; they do, however, show the continuing tradition of the rhapsodist as poet laureate. This began at least as early as the second century B.C., when the presentation of a suitable *fu* might gain the writer an official position − not as poet laureate, since the position did not exist, but perhaps as attendant or drafter or something of the sort. Thereafter he would continue to write *fu* on the side, whenever the emperor commanded it or the occasion suggested it. The subjects might range from the founding of a dynasty to a flower that had caught the ruler's fancy. In the former case, the writer could consider himself a direct heir of the authors of the *Classic of Songs*.[17] In the latter case, where he was placed in a less dignified position, his *fu* might be flattering or contemptuous, or anything in between; these works will be treated later.

An imperial capital was an obvious subject for a quasi poet laureate, and some late works on the subject demonstrate well the sinicization of the Northern and Eastern Wei Dynasties. There was, for example, a rhapsody on the fifth-century Northern Wei capital at Tai.[18] When the capital was moved to Loyang at the end of that century, the move inspired a pair of rhapsodies on the old and new capitals, demonstrating, we are told, the extravagance of the old one and the decorum and moderation of the new.[19] This was apparently a real imitation of Pan Ku; the few surviving fragments of other works show less didactic intent. The later move to the Eastern Wei capital at Yeh, which involved the actual transporting of some buildings from Loyang, prompted a rhapsody on 'The Transfer of Capital'[20] as well as one on 'The New Palace'.[21] The latter survives in a fragment of about 175 words, and there is nothing about economy; it should be remembered that both Loyang and Yeh were magnificent cities, later to be models for the Sui capital at Ch'ang-an.

Other subjects resemble more closely the traditional ones of the Western poet laureate. The founding of the Three Kingdoms state of Wu inspired a 'Rhapsody on the Great Yellow Dragon Banner',[22] and its extinction by Chin occasioned another work, 'The Conquest of Wu'.[23] When the Chin was driven out of North China in the fourth century, its almost miraculous survival in the South was celebrated in 'The Restoration'.[24] As a rule any military engagement would call for a rhapsody, such as 'The Southern Campaign'[25] of 303. Oddly enough, there is very little similarity between such things and the 'Lament' except for an occasional phrase or two;[26] there are probably two reasons for this: such works would have seemed quite hackneyed by Yü Hsin's time, and Yü could not afford to imitate their stately, processional pace without losing the reader's interest. Naturally, there would be *fu* on the birth of a Crown Prince,[27] and there was at least one 'In Praise of the Crown Prince'.[28] *Fu* are often criticized as flattering, generally unfairly, but the charge does apply to the last-mentioned work, apparently on the subject of Ts'ao P'i (later Emperor Wen of the Wei, *reg.* 220–6). The regular ceremonies at court, such as 'The New Year's Day Assembly',[29] all called for *fu*, as did sacrifices[30] and hunts.[31] Yang Hsiung had written a number of works on the last two subjects, and his writings became a standard source of inspiration. As time passed it grew ever more difficult to think of anything new to say about such a topic; on encountering Yü Shih-chi's (d. 618) rhapsody on a Ch'en dynasty hunt,[32] one suspects that the author was as bored with the subject as the reader is likely to be. To some extent that may be the fault of this particular author; Watson singles out a lyric poem by Yü Shih-chi to illustrate the decline of that genre in the late Six Dynasties.[33] Yü Hsin's rhapsody on an archery contest, already mentioned in Chapter 1, is unusually good as such things go, but it is not an important work. It should be mentioned that it is in such ceremonial *fu* that the didactic heritage of Yang Hsiung is most apparent. One would expect this in *fu* on sacrifices, but most other ceremonial *fu* include at least a gesture toward didacticism; Yü Hsin, for example, says that the archery contest is important as a ceremony, not as a display of prowess.

This whole category, what one might call rhapsodies of the poet laureate, tends toward the mechanical; quite often the authors possessed no literary talent, and even a capable writer might find such assigned topics uncongenial. The same problems can plague works where the assigned topic was less grand; paradoxically, these *fu* are often more interesting, and sometimes even surprising. For example, the son-in-law of a Chin emperor, having built a splendid palace, invited a number of officials to write poems of praise on a painting in one of his reception rooms. The subject was the famous scene of Chuang tzu fishing in the P'u River; offered a position by the king of Ch'u, he replied that he preferred, like the tortoise, to drag his tail in the mud.[34] Hsi Han (263–306), a grandnephew of Hsi K'ang with some of the family traits, commented that this was a very odd choice of subject for a room filled with people seeking office. Instead of the expected piece of flattery, he wrote a *fu* 'Condoling with Chuang tzu' for appearing in such a place.[35] Such people seldom live long; Hsi Han survived this escapade but was killed at forty-three.

Mi Heng's (173–98) rhapsody 'The Parrot'[36] expresses a similar attitude rather more subtly. Like many others during that period, Mi found himself forced to take office under men he despised. He made no secret of the fact, and thus offended one prominent figure after another. Since none of them wanted to take the blame for killing him, he was sent off to the man thought most likely to do the job. There, he was commanded by the man's son to write a *fu* on a parrot to entertain the guests at a party. The work opens with an elegant description of the bird itself, but as it progresses the bird sounds more and more like a caged human being, and at one point the parrot is specifically compared to an official doing his ruler's bidding. As the commentator Li Shan says,[37] Mi is clearly using the bird as a symbol of his own plight; like the bird, he is even forced to entertain his captors. He was killed not long afterward, at twenty-five. Allegory is, of course, the mode most favored by Confucian critics, and all educated Chinese from at least the Han dynasty on were brought up to look for it everywhere. Undoubtedly such interpretations could be carried to extremes, but writers trained in that tradition inevitably thought of allegory as at least a possibility for their own compositions. There are a great many Six-Dynasties *fu* on things such as plants and birds; some of them, though only a small minority, are unquestionably allegories. They were recognized as such by contemporaries, since biographies often point them out. Not all are great works of literature; Mi's 'Parrot' stands out as an unusually fine example. Still, it is one of the curiosities of literary history that later Confucian critics, capable of perceiving allegory even in erotic songs (or *tz'u*) should ignore it here. The Six-Dynasties *fu* on things are almost always dismissed as 'mere description'.

Some works are purely descriptive, of course, though it is difficult to see why that should necessarily make them inferior, at least by literary rather than philosophical standards. Before dealing with such things, it should be noted that Mi Heng's 'Parrot', like the much later 'Condoling with Chuang tzu', is presented in his biography as an improvisation.

We read of impromptu rhapsodies being composed before this, but apparently none of those survive. What remain from the earlier period are the long, elaborate pieces that occupied the writer for months or years. It is impossible, for example, to imagine Pan Ku sitting down at a party and dashing off the 'Two Capitals'. Mi Heng's work is a marginal case, but other, more convincing impromptu works appear fairly regularly from Mi's time on.[38] Some were written on command, and many more at parties among friends, like the lyric poems that Chinese scholars still compose on such occasions. The growth of improvisation is one sign of a basic change taking place in the *fu* itself. The long showpieces in the Han manner continue to be written, as in the endless series on capitals, but that is not the inevitable model for the rhapsody writer; in fact, the imitations of Han rhapsodies begin to look anachronistic, for several reasons.

First, Six-Dynasties rhapsodies tend to be rather short, unless they deal with a really grand subject such as a palace or capital. One thinks of the Han rhapsodies as exhaustive, with Ssu-ma Hsiang-ju, for example, compiling long lists of exotic flora and fauna. There is much less of this in the major Six-Dynasties works, which gain their effects more economically; the 'Lament' compresses into four lines (67–70) what would have filled pages in a Han *fu*. This compression is sometimes achieved through the use of allusions, which enable the writer to suggest a great deal in a small space. This was, of course, the age of allusions, in all forms of literature, and a writer who chose to do so could supply a whole catalogue of past references to a single plant. Fortunately, this was not the general practice; more often he would limit himself to a reference or two, to texts which were appropriate but not too obvious. Fu Hsien (239–94), for example, concludes a basically descriptive rhapsody on 'The Fan'[39] with a few lines about the famous lyric poem on the same subject attributed to Lady Pan, a concubine of the Han Emperor Ch'eng (*reg.* 32–7 B.C.).[40] The poem had almost certainly been written not long before Fu's own time, so that this allusion had not yet become hackneyed; a later writer might hesitate to use it.

Second, the vocabulary of *fu* was beginning to change. The most striking feature of the 'Shang-lin', aside from the outlandish plants and animals, is the succession of obscure descriptive binomes. These appear less often in Six-Dynasties works, even in those written in conscious imitation of Han *fu*, and by the end of the period they are generally lacking. Chiang Yen

(444–505) is one of the rare exceptions, and even he uses an array of binomes only once in all his twenty-eight *fu*. That is in his 'Imitation of the Rhapsody on the King of Liang's Rabbit Park',[41] inspired by a piece attributed to Mei Sheng; Chiang Yen, famous for his imitations, was aiming here at the old-fashioned style of the earlier poet. Binomes, of course, are characteristic of the Chinese language in general, but long series of rare binomes occur so seldom in late Six-Dynasties *fu* that they give an antique quality to any work where they do appear. Chang Jung (d. 497) uses a great many of them in his 'The Sea', perhaps because Mu Hua (*c.* 300) had already done so in his own work of the same name.[42] Chang's poem, as a result, appears in his biography equipped with phonetic glosses.[43] There is a Chinese joke about this kind of thing: It is easy to write a rhapsody on the sea or the Yangtze, since all you have to do is to add a water radical to every character in the language and you can use them all.[44]

While on the subject of language, one curious feature should be mentioned, the occasional use of colloquial language. This is quite rare, but one finds it in unexpected places. Parts of Ts'ao Chih's (192–232) *fu* 'The Sparrow-Hawk and the Sparrow',[45] for example, sound very much like the roughly contemporary ballad 'Southeast Fly the Peacocks'.[46] Ts'ao Chih is probably the most elegant writer of his age; the surprisingly colloquial language used here may arise from the popular nature of the work, a conversation between two birds where the sparrow manages to save itself by its quick wits. *Fu* could be written on all sorts of subjects, some not very elevated. Hsiao T'ung, the compiler of the *Wen hsüan*, had conservative and rather conventional tastes, and his selection gives one little idea of the whole range of *fu*, though it should be recognized that he did include 'The Lechery of Master Teng-t'u', an amusing but unrefined work.[47] As examples of the sort of thing he omitted, one might mention two other humorous *fu*, by Shu Hsi (261–300): 'Cakes' is in places almost like a cookbook, except that recipes are seldom so inviting; Waley has translated part of it.[48] Shu's 'Encourager of Agriculture'[49] is a crude but effective satire on a corrupt tax-collector. The author, who elsewhere provides a graphic picture of the poverty of his early years,[50] was apparently writing from the heart, but contemporaries found both works vulgar.[51] There were a number of humorous *fu*, particularly in the early Six Dynasties, but they were not admired in the highest circles. Someone once showed a friend a work in the manner of Shu Hsi, laughed uncontrollably while the friend was reading it, and was bitterly disappointed at his total lack of response.[52] Humorous *fu* are much less common in the later period. One exception is the *fu* on 'Fleas and Lice' by Pien Pin (445–500),[53] a deliberate attempt to shock in the tradition of Hsi K'ang's (223–62) letter to Shan T'ao.[54] As a description of personal squalor it far outdoes its model;

at the end Pien's stunned biographer comments that it was all more or less accurate.[55] Pien Pin, famous for his pointed wit and tolerated as a court jester, was really a third-century man born out of his time, and his work seems anachronistic in the fifth century. The humorous *fu* have mostly been lost, like the joke books of the same period, but the occasional surviving works serve as a useful reminder that the *fu* was not necessarily characterized by high seriousness.

Fu could be written on all kinds of subjects, and for almost every imaginable purpose, even the everyday social activities. The Liang Emperor Chienwen's 'Bronze Bell Rhapsody',[56] for example, was written as a thank-you note for a gift of an ancient bell, instead of the customary parallel-prose letter. It is unlikely that Ssu-ma Hsiang-ju would have written a *fu* on such an occasion, unless perhaps a particularly auspicious object had been presented to the emperor. The *fu*, less exhaustive and reduced to manageable proportions, had become an attractive alternative to the social letter; it also sometimes replaced the traditional lyric poems on parting with a friend.[57]

In short, the *fu* and *shih*, though separate genres, were beginning to overlap in the Six Dynasties, both in content and social function. Occasional passages in *fu* were written in *shih* meter.[58] These are interesting, but not terribly important; more important are the cases where rhapsodies were written *instead of* lyric poems. There are, for example, many Six-Dynasties *fu* 'Celebrating Rain' or 'Rejoicing at Clearing Weather'. Some of them are very grand pieces, written as part of the national thanksgiving at an averted famine. Others are more personal works, by an author who disliked the heat or had been depressed by a long overcast period, and the content can be very much like *shih* on such standard themes. Fu Hsien's (239—94) 'In Gratitude for Cool Weather' is of this type; it is only about a hundred words long, including the preface.[59] Hsi Han, author of the 'Condoling with Chuang tzu', wrote what seems to have been an equally individual *fu* on 'Suffering from the Heat'.[60] In the preface, the only surviving part, he explains that he was living in cramped quarters without a breath of air and thinking with envy of the rich, who were presumably suffering less. Even Hsi Han's rhapsodies on medicines (he was a famous herbalist) take on a certain personal quality; read together, they begin to sound like chapters in a serial. In one, he recommends a certain plant, apparently the tawny daylily, for women unable to bear sons.[61] In another, he explains that the son finally born to him almost died in infancy but was saved by a mixture of drugs.[62]

The last two *fu* by Hsi Han bring us from the quasi-*shih* back to the descriptive rhapsody. This was a favorite genre in the Six Dynasties, and it must be admitted that they are seldom so personal. Almost anything could provide a topic, even commonplace household articles; one can lay

down a general rule that the lower the subject was, the loftier its treatment
would be. Fu Hsien's (239–94) 'Comb', which 'hates disorder, loves order',
is a symbol of government officials.[63] Fu's 'Mirror' is equally improving,
devoted almost entirely to the morals to be drawn; the mirror is impartial,
truthful, useful as a warning, and so on.[64] His 'Firefly', 'advancing, does not
compete with the lights of the heavens; withdrawing, gives light in darkness:
truly this is like a worthy minister'.[65] There are fifty-three surviving *fu* by
Fu Hsien, almost all of this type. Read in quantity, they begin to sound like
parodies ('life is like a football game'), but I do not think it is intentional;
Fu is simply determined to write edifying rhapsodies. Other people were more
successful; Sun Ch'u's (d. 293) 'Boats' possess all possible human virtues;
the work is saved by the implication that the same is not always true of
humans.[66]

Handled properly, this sort of thing could develop into real philosophical
fu; for the most part, however, writers were content to mention the philosophical associations of an object only in passing, like an allusion, and for much
the same reasons: it stressed the dignity and importance of the subject, and
it also satisfied a lingering desire for completeness in *fu*. Writers no longer
attempted to exhaust their subject, but they tended to feel the absence of at
least some suitable reference or association; it left a kind of vacuum. As
time passed, almost every conceivable subject acquired overtones, so that it
became practically impossible to describe something entirely in itself and
without associations. One such work is Shu Hsi's 'Cakes'; another is Fu Hsüan's
(217–78) 'Melons'.[67] In both, the topic is capable of standing alone, and
there are no inevitable associations. It is probably no accident that both
rhapsodies deal with food, a major Chinese interest. The editor Yen K'o-chün,
who normally confines himself to recording variants and sources of texts,
was interested enough in the 'Melons' to add a note complaining that he
had never encountered one variety despite having been in eleven provinces.[68]

Hunting, because of the didactic tradition, almost had to be accompanied
by at least a token moral; one interesting exception is Wei Tan's 'Falconry',
which confines itself to practical advice on picking and training a bird.[69]
Rhapsodies sometimes have a strong smell of books about them, but this
one seems based on first-hand experience. Wei, a Northerner, was a younger
contemporary of Yü Hsin and wrote the first commentary on Yü's works,
now unfortunately lost.

Games in particular, because they might seem a waste of time for the
Confucian, had long tended to be described as improving. The ancient game
of pitchpot, where short, blunt arrows are thrown into a container, almost
always was made more edifying than enjoyable.[70] *Wei-ch'i*, the Japanese *go*,
would suggest military strategy.[71]

Understandably, writers of rhapsodies tended to favor the exotic; such things, however free of associations otherwise, automatically reminded one of the greatness of the empire which contained them or received them as tribute. Yin Chü's 'Rare Fabric' thus combines description with an expression of national pride.[72] The fabric, sent by 'Great Ch'in' (the Roman Empire) in 281, seems to be asbestos, but if that is so the author was given a very fanciful account of the 'plant' that produced it. Grapes generally aroused the same kind of pride, as did parrots. The latter could talk, of course, so writers were also likely to see something human in them, even if they did not go so far as Mi Heng. The local flora and fauna generally had associations of their own. Chrysanthemums, for example, reminded writers of immortality, wine-drinking, parties, and strength in adversity, the last because they bloomed so late and endured frost. Any *fu* on chrysanthemums was likely to combine all these associations with a description of the flower.

Flowers in general might remind poets either of mortality or more specifically of the fleeting beauty of women. The Liang Emperor Chien-wen, for example, concludes both his 'Plum Blossoms'[73] and his 'Gathering Lotuses'[74] with the latter comparison. Sometimes an association was so automatic that it can be considered a stock response. Mandarin ducks were always connected with conjugal fidelity. There are very few *fu* that simply describe mandarin ducks; the works on the subject almost invariably deal with a woman who has been rejected or who fears rejection by her husband or lover, for example one by Emperor Chien-wen[75] and another by his brother Emperor Yüan.[76] Yü Hsin has his own *fu* on the subject.[77] Quite short (about 120 words), it gives the standard theme a historical setting. Lady Yü, who had been the consort of the Wei Emperor Ming when he was a prince, had been sent away in disgrace after his accession in 227.[78] Yü's 'Mandarin Ducks' describes her feelings on seeing a pair of the birds; it is a conventional work, of course, but quite good of its kind — certainly better than the two Emperors' compositions.

This leads us to a kind of writing particularly associated with Emperor Chien-wen during his days as Crown Prince. The subject is always love, almost always frustrated love, with rejected women languishing away in their deserted quarters. One thinks of this mostly in lyric poetry, and it therefore is traditionally called 'Palace-Style Poetry' (*Kung-t'i shih*). There are also a good many *fu* on the subject, for which the term 'Palace-Style *Fu*' has been coined. Chien-wen did not invent such poetry; it had been written for hundreds of years before him. He was, however, very fond of it, and his position as Crown Prince meant that a good deal of it was written, some perhaps by writers who would not otherwise have done so. Yü Hsin wrote several such things, presumably during his early period in the South, such as the 'Mandarin Ducks'. Another work, to the classic title 'The Wanderer',[79] also contains the classic couplet:

'Floating dust covering the bed, useless to brush it away; fine grass encroaching on the steps, growing where it will.' Livelier than most, this ends with a hope of the wanderer's return. Optimism and, indeed, joy are quite rare in Six-Dynasties literature. It is depressing to find a modern critic willing to accept 'The Wanderer' (unlike all the other supposed early works) because of its social realism, who rejects the ending as unrealistic.[80]

Yü's 'Mirror' opens with a classic palace-style scene: dawn, birds singing, a woman getting up and beginning to apply her make-up. This in itself is a good sign; in the sadder love poems there is no reason for makeup, since no one will see it, and the mirror can be packed away. Compare Yü's conclusion: 'She cannot even for a moment put it away in its box; if she goes out for a little while into the garden, she takes it along with her.' Yü's 'By the Candle'[81] begins with another typical scene, a woman making winter clothes for her husband away at the frontier. The latter part, however, is devoted entirely to descriptions of candles and incense and allusions to old anecdotes about lights of various kinds. The above *fu* are all to some extent in the palace style, as strictly defined. Confucian critics have tended to use the phrase very loosely as a pejorative term for any poem about women or even flowers; they would include in that category three other *fu* by Yü Hsin: 'Spring',[82] 'Seventh Night',[83] and 'The Lamp'.[84]

'Spring' is a description of palace women going on a holiday outing. 'Seventh Night', quite short, with only fourteen lines, is again a description of women; this time they are celebrating the festival of the seventh night of the seventh month with a custom supposed to assure skill at needlework. 'The Lamp' is set in the women's quarters, but the women are barely mentioned. All these supposedly early works by Yü are anathema to Confucian critics. It must be agreed that they are not among his major works; on the other hand, they seem unlikely to endanger the morals of even the most impressionable, and they are often quite elegant. 'The Lamp', for example, has a famous couplet: 'When moths flutter near, broken flowers drop in confusion; When the wind comes up, shooting stars delicately fall.' Another, in 'The Mirror', shows Yü experimenting with the kind of paradox he uses in line 447 of the 'Lament': 'When it overlooks the water, the moon rises in the pond; when it reflects the sun, water chestnuts grow on the wall.' It is, of course, a round mirror of metal, the 'moon' of the first line. The physics of the second line is clarified by the 'Discussion of Mirrors'[85] of Li Yung of the Chin dynasty: 'When the sun glances off it, its light illumines the wall; if it is placed opposite water, they can only reflect one another.' The water chestnuts are apparently the design on the back of the mirror, and the sunlight glancing off it onto a wall transfers the design there. This may be clearer if one imagines placing a hand between a projector and a screen, the outline of the hand would appear dark on the screen, just as a raised or lowered design on the mirror itself would.

Two special categories of *fu* on things remain to be discussed, the philosophical poem and the allegory. I have already mentioned the tendency to conclude a rhapsody with a moral of some kind. Generally this would arise more or less naturally from a given subject; for Fu Hsien, for example, jade, which is as hard and as pure as the heavens, naturally suggests the Confucian gentleman.[86] Sometimes the moral arises less naturally; an extreme case is the 'Snow' by Hsieh Hui-lien (394–430),[87] which draws a Taoist moral: the snow, 'When the warm sun shines . . . no longer strives to guard its virtue'. It is thus superior to white jade, which 'stubbornly guards the chaste hardness of its form'. This was, of course, offensive to Confucian readers; even worse was a later passage: 'I'm white when that which I touch is so, Grimy when surroundings stain me.' The fact that the 'Snow' appeared in the *Wen hsüan*, the standard anthology of early literature, made it particularly conspicuous. A surprising amount of philosophical debate was carried on in *fu* on things. This is quite obvious in Chia Yi's (201–169 B.C.) 'Owl',[88] where there is no description at all, only a series of Taoist reflections inspired by the appearance of an ominous bird. It is less obvious in the *descriptive* rhapsodies, but that is where some of the major battles were fought. I know of no replies to the 'Owl', at least none in *fu*, but one is frequently told in a preface that a given author's *fu* description of a bird or tree is a rebuttal of someone else's description of another bird or tree; that at first is surprising. Sun Ch'u (d. 293), for example, says in the preface to his 'Solitary Wild Pear Tree'[89] that his brother had shown him a rhapsody on a pear tree. The earlier writer had mistakenly thought that the pear tree should be valued for its usefulness, the wild pear, being useless, therefore being of no value. Sun wrote his reply to demonstrate that uselessness was the best way to stay out of trouble. The title 'Solitary Wild Pear Tree' comes from the *Songs* (119, 169), but the work is entirely Taoist.

Chang Hua's (232–300) 'Tailorbird',[90] also Taoist, is more famous because of its inclusion in the *Wen hsüan*. It is based on a parable in the first chapter of *Chuang tzu*: 'When the tailorbird builds her nest in the deep wood, she uses no more than one branch';[91] in the same way, a man has no need to possess the empire. Chang Hua, praising the tailorbird for staying out of trouble, makes a point of how unattractive and insignificant the little bird is. Literary men tended to question whether such a subject was worthy of a rhapsody, and for Confucians the combination of a low subject and a Taoist moral was doubly offensive. There were thus a long series of replies, mostly Confucian, the earliest apparently being Fu Hsien's (239–94) 'Majestic Phoenix'.[92]

From the philosophical rhapsody it is only a short step to the allegory, and the same topics could be used in both. Evergreen plants had always suggested steadfastness in adversity; Confucius, for example, had said, 'Only when the year grows cold do we see that the pine and cypress are the last to fade.'[93] Because of this, it was almost impossible to write even a descriptive rhapsody on these trees, or on bamboos, chrysanthemums, or other evergreen or late-blooming plants, without at least a passing reference to the implied moral of steadfastness. Such works no one would call allegories, for example the rhapsody 'Pines and Cypresses'[94] by Tso Fen, a younger sister of Tso Ssu and a concubine of Emperor Wu of the Chin (reg. 265–89). This is not even a philosophical work, merely a description. Toward the end the author mentions that the trees are evergreen, adds immediately that they are much more luxuriant in spring, and then moves on to their Taoist associations. This concluding section is nothing more than the typical Six-Dynasties gesture toward completeness already mentioned above, with the author mentioning an appropriate reference or allusion. Compare another rhapsody, 'The Tall Cypress',[95] by the Southern Ch'i prince Hsiao Feng (475–94): As he says, the tree has no flowers in spring, but it is evergreen, unaffected by wind and snow. There is not even a pretense of description, nothing about the magnificence of the tree's surroundings or any of the other traditional touches. The poet here is not talking about a tree at all, but about himself, with one eye on the Analects passage. His biography[96] points out the obvious political reference of the fu, and the fact that he was killed at nineteen should not pass unnoticed. The next example is almost as obvious, the 'Evergreen Plant',[97] by another member of the Southern Ch'i ruling family, Hsiao Tzu-hui (b. after 486). The plant is described as green and pure despite all that winter can do to it, and the allegorical intent is announced in the opening line, where the plant is introduced in exactly the same way as a speaker in one of the debate rhapsodies, in terms that could only apply to a human being: 'There is a creeping plant living in retirement' (hsien chü).

Both the above make agreeable reading; the next allegory is less agreeable, 'The Fly',[98] by Yüan Shun (?487–528), a member of the Northern Wei ruling family. According to the rather disingenuous preface, the author at home one day on leave was annoyed by a bluebottle buzzing around him; therefore, 'hating the way it changes white [to black]', he wrote a fu on it. The quoted passage, taken from the Ch'u tz'u piece 'Embracing the Sand',[99] is fair warning that the literal fly is not the occasion for the fu. This fly is simply the Ch'u tz'u and Songs figure for a slanderer,[100] and the fu itself is pure political invective, filled with all the disagreeable stories about flies that the author can remember. Yüan Shun's biography is detailed enough to leave no doubt about the actual identity of the fly;[101] that is fortunate, because with his work we move into a special kind of allegory. General complaints about a hostile world are intelligible in themselves, even if it does help to have an idea of the author's political situation; some might even feel that Hsiao Feng's 'Tall Cypress' is too general to deserve the name of allegory. Yüan Shun's fly, on the other hand, represents a specific historical figure, like Orchid or Pepper in the 'Li sao', and to understand that sort of allegory we need a detailed knowledge of the background; that we generally lack. What, for example, are we to make of another *fu* on 'Bluebottles'[102] buried among all those edifying works by Fu Hsien? It was, he says, inspired by a passage in the *Songs*,[103] and it deals with the harm that slanderers can do. There is simply no way to tell whether Fu had specific people in mind.

Sometimes we can tell with reasonable certainty that a given work is an allegory, but still be unable to go beyond that. There can, I think, be little doubt that Juan Chi's (210–63) 'Doves'[104] is about murdered human beings rather than doves, even if it is impossible to identify the victims. Juan's 'Macaque' or 'Monkey',[105] also probably allegorical, is even more difficult to interpret, though the monkey may well symbolize the author himself. It is not surprising that this sort of problem should arise. Allegories are written at least partly in order to avoid a more direct statement, and a writer who wants to conceal his true subject usually succeeds, Li Shang-yin (813–58) being a famous example. Juan Chi's allegorical lyric poems are also notoriously difficult to interpret.[106]

The *fu* tradition had always been associated with imitations, or at least with works inspired by earlier *fu*. The *Ch'u tz'u*, for example, had consisted largely of such things, and these in turn provided favorite models for Six-Dynasties writers; we shall return later to these works. Also very popular were the *fu* attributed to Sung Yü (third century B.C.) and the 'Seven Stimuli' by Mei Sheng (d. *c*. 140 B.C.).[107] The latter inspired innumerable imitations, which were commonly treated as a separate genre of 'Sevenses', distinct from the *fu*.[108] The practice was not limited to the most famous works; in fact, any *fu* believed to date from the classic age was more or less sure to find an imitator in the Six Dynasties. The later works were not necessarily very good; imitation is often called the last refuge of the unoriginal writer, sometimes with justice. One sixth-century pedant fills the preface to his 'Rhapsody on the Huai River'[109] with seventeen precedents for poems on bodies of water, from the *Songs* on down, and concludes with the gleeful observation that no one had ever written a *fu* on precisely the same subject as his. One seeming exception, he explains, was not actually about the Huai River itself; by this time the reader is unlikely to care much, or to regret the *fu* proper survives only in a fragment much shorter than the grotesque preface.

Fu, as noted earlier, were often written as a social pastime, like the familiar lyric poems on assigned topics, and many of the shorter imitations seem to belong to this category, written in competition by a group of friends. If these are not generally of the highest quality, neither are the corresponding lyric poems; they were, after all, written only for entertainment. As in other genres, an imitation of an earlier *fu* could also serve as camouflage for a writer who wanted to conceal his real purpose, or at least to present a relatively personal work as a literary pastiche; that is certainly true of many of the *Ch'u tz'u* imitations.

The most popular topics inevitably grew shopworn, and imitations of famous works invited comparisons perhaps unfavorable to the later author.[110] The best Six-Dynasties imitations were done more indirectly, for example with a famous technique applied to a new subject. Sung Yü's 'Winds'[111] had described the totally different winds of the king and the common man. Chiang Yen's (444—505) 'Lamps',[112] a literary fiction, has the Prince of Huai-nan, or Liu An (d. 122 B.C.) commanding an attendant to write a *fu* on lamps; the result is a contrasting pair on those of the prince and the ordinary man. Chiang Yen was one of the greatest *fu*-writers, and his 'Lamps' is fully equal to Sung Yü's 'Winds', probably because Chiang here chooses a different subject. Prosopopoeia, or literary fiction, was a favorite device of Six-Dynasties writers, not only in the *fu*. It could take several forms; in the most basic, a famous writer (or group of writers) is introduced as a character and made to write a *fu* on a new subject. The style of the *fu* produced may or may not resemble the actual style of the historical figure, but in these works he is important only as a famous *writer*. In other cases the stress is on the personality of the ancient writer. Sung Yü and Ssu-ma Hsiang-ju, as romantic figures, inspired a great deal of legend, and there was a natural tendency for later *fu*-writers to introduce them as characters in anecdotes. If the actual author's name somehow got detached from such works, the *fu* would almost inevitably be attributed to the figure in whose name it had been written, and the anecdote would become part of the growing legend surrounding him. That is probably the case with all the rhapsodies which introduce Sung Yü as a *character*; the *Ch'u tz'u* pieces attributed to him, which have no internal evidence of authorship, might as well be attributed to 'Anon.' Ssu-ma Hsiang-ju's 'Ch'ang-men' and 'The Beauty' are also probably literary fictions, as are a number of other supposedly early *fu*. The third category, more common in other genres than in the *fu*, consists of works written to fill a gap. Here we are no longer dealing with famous writers but simply with historical figures who *should* have written a poem (or letter, etc.) on some important occasion but had failed to do so; in that case, someone in the Six Dynasties was sure to remedy the deficiency. The same thing is familiar in the West, from classical times at least through the eighteenth century. It has caused a great deal of confusion in early Chinese literary history, with Li Ling writing a sophisticated Six-Dynasties prose, Li Ling and Su Wu both capable of an equally sophisticated and anachronistic verse, and so on.

These works illustrate Six-Dynasties writers' interest in individual psychology. During the early period it was concerned mostly with the manifestations in eccentric behavior; this results in the Ssu-ma Hsiang-ju apocrypha and some of the *Shih-shuo hsin-yü* and *Chin shu* anecdotes, often very improbable. Later writers no longer limited themselves to the eccentric; they could feel empathy for anyone and, indeed, almost anything. There are innumerable *fu* (and lyric poems) about the hypothetical feelings of a rejected woman, and a writer such as Pao Chao (d. *c.* 466) could even try to see into the mind of a captive wild goose.[113] It is perhaps misleading to speak of individual psychology, since the writers throughout this period thought only in categories: the typical rejected woman, for example. We never feel that any of the subjects is a real individual; the treatments are successful to the extent that they capture the general features of a given category. This constant hypothesizing about other people's feelings, and the fondness for the general, have one rather curious effect: even the personal poetry, whether *shih* or *fu*, is sometimes rather abstract. Pao Chao's *fu* 'A Wanderer's Thoughts'[114] has no preface, and one has to read a good deal of it before concluding that it is about an actual journey rather than a hypothetical one.

Feelings become quite important in the *fu* of the late Six Dynasties, and this can be true even of *fu* on things. Fu Hsien (239–94) had considered a work incomplete without some indication of the moral lesson to be drawn from an object, even a comb. A late Six-Dynasties writer would be more likely to think of the mood the object evoked, normally one of melancholy; this tendency parallels the shift in critical theory from didacticism to feeling. For example, Chiang Yen's 'Rhapsody on Green Moss'[115] mentions its prevalence on 'fallen moats a hundred feet deep, ruined graves ten thousand years old'. Nature itself was responsive to human emotions, as in lines 431–2 of the 'Lament', and the seasons were seen in terms of the feelings they aroused. The most famous *fu* on this subject is P'an Yüeh's (d. 300) 'Autumn Thoughts',[116] but there were innumerable others. The feelings inspired are generally melancholy, natural enough for autumn, but it does seem excessive when Chiang Yen insists on the sadness of all four seasons.[117] Writers quickly discovered that it was much more effective to show rather than tell in such cases, in other words, to describe a setting and let that description suggest the mood rather than filling their works with sighs and tears. The most famous examples of this kind of writing are a pair of *fu* by Chiang Yen, his 'Regret' and 'Separation'.[118] Each is a series of illustrations of the theme, some specific historical cases, some more general, with the emotions more often suggested by the setting than stated. The author is not personally involved in any of this; in his preface to the 'Regret' he says that he was moved to write by his own melancholy nature and his vision of a world filled with the graves of unhappy people.

Pao Chao's 'Ruined City'[119] is rather similar, in using a scene to produce the maximum emotional impact on the reader. Pao's subject automatically reminds one of the 'Lament', but the two works are actually quite different. Pao Chao was no more involved in his subject than Chiang Yen had been; he can therefore indulge in lines like the following: 'Lurking tigers, crouching cats Suck blood and dine on flesh.' This sort of thing was unthinkable for Yü Hsin, who had lost three children during Hou Ching's rebellion; his picture of the ruins of Chien-k'ang in lines 309–18, though no less effective than Pao's, is more restrained and much less blood-curdling. The affinity between the two writers is more apparent in Yü's 'Dead Tree',[120] the best of his display pieces and the closest of his *fu* to Pao Chao's. A dead tree in a court-yard is transformed into all trees, in one of the longest sentences in Chinese literature: 'Of the ancient . . . [there follow 141 words on the more famous trees in Chinese history and literature] none but are moss-buried, fungus-covered, bird-pecked, worm-eaten.' Finally, after some more on the death of trees, the work concludes with a comment by one of the characters, 'If this is true even of trees, how can man endure?' It does contain a philosophical idea of sorts, that of mortality, but this *fu* definitely belongs with the works intended to create a mood; like the rest of them, it is successful precisely because it remains purely descriptive down to the final comment.[121] The 'Dead Tree' is supposed to have been written shortly after Yü reached Ch'ang-an, and according to legend it established his reputation in the North.[122] The work does seem at all events to have been extremely popular.[123]

I said at the beginning of this chapter that the *fu* had begun as two separate genres, the elegy and the rhapsody. The two overlapped to some extent, as shown in the allegorical and philosophical *fu* on things, but most of the works discussed so far are definitely rhapsodies. The *fu* could also be used for more personal subjects, in the elegy tradition. These grew more and more common with passing time, and they constitute the great majority of the really long *fu* surviving from the late Six Dynasties; this comes as rather a surprise. Probably the longest *fu* ever written were those on capitals; almost without exception, the late Six-Dynasties works on the subject survive only in fragments. The ceremonial *fu* (on hunts, sacrifices, etc.) had always been shorter; Yang Hsiung's longest is just over 1700 words.[124] The Six-Dynasties imitations of Yang are mostly about 1000 words long; understandably they were more likely to survive intact than rhapsodies on capitals. The personal *fu* can be quite short, as in works on the death of a friend or relative,[125] but they can easily reach 4000 words.

These long works tend toward the apologia, and they are likely to show at least indirect influence from the 'Li sao'. One possible exception is the series of *fu* on life in the country; these are in fact sometimes as impersonal as the rhapsodies, with catalogues of plants and birds very much like the rhapsodies on imperial hunting parks, the main difference here being the stress on economy and the simple life. For the educated Chinese who wrote *fu*, however, life in the country was equivalent to life *in retirement* from public office, and they generally felt obliged to give at least some explanation of what they were doing out of office. Holzman[126] writes of

> what was perhaps life's greatest moral problem to countless generations
> of Chinese of the ruling class: should they serve in government or
> should they, when the men in power were lacking in virtue, hide away
> in private life and take no part in the direction of state affairs? It is
> difficult for us to realize the importance of the moral choice involved.
> Chinese society was, and probably still is, much more 'monolithic'
> than anything ever known in the West, and a failure to serve in the
> government meant a failure to serve mankind, a failure to realize one's
> life as a moral being.

Not all writers chose to explain their retirement in such Confucian terms; it was, after all, awkward to announce that the state was in disorder, that being the only justification for a Confucian to refuse office.[127] Whatever the actual reason might be, most writers pleaded an irresistible attraction to the bucolic life together with personal unsuitability for an official career; unless the dynasty in question had already fallen, it was more tactful to explain this unsuitability in terms of incompetence rather than distaste. P'an Yüeh (d. 300), for example, in the preface to his *fu* 'Living in Retirement',[128] presents a thirty-year government career as proof of his hopeless ineptitude. For our purposes, aside from any literary merits, these *fu* on life in the country present two features of interest: First, the authors generally feel obliged to explain or justify their retirement, and this leads eventually to long autobiographies in elegy form. Second, despite all their humorous protests of incompetence, the authors tend to write with one eye on the 'Li sao'. This can be seen even in T'ao Ch'ien's 'The Return', the most famous of the *fu* on living in retirement but, like most of T'ao's better poems, a work too original to fit neatly into any category. One line of 'The Return', obviously modelled on the 'Li sao', identifies T'ao as another Ch'ü Yüan: 'After all I have not gone far on the wrong road.'[129]

Ch'ü Yüan, next to Confucius himself, was the patron saint of Chinese officials, particularly of frustrated ones, and any bureaucrat whose career was going badly tended to see parallels with Ch'ü. The 'Li sao' was the most venerated poem in Chinese literature except for the *Songs* themselves, and the association with Ch'ü Yüan also hallowed the other works in the *Ch'u tz'u*. This meant, for example, that the often erotic 'Nine Hymns' were interpreted as allegories of Ch'ü's longing for an understanding ruler. Other *fu* might be suspect as insufficiently edifying, but the 'Li sao' was acceptable to even the most dogmatic critics. In purely literary terms, of course, the *Ch'u tz'u* also had an imaginative power almost totally lacking in other early works; this made it as appealing to the writer as to the moralist. As a result, the *Ch'u tz'u*, and particularly the 'Li sao', have had an influence on later Chinese literature which the Western reader can hardly imagine.

The 'Li sao' is a complicated and rather confused poem; depending on their inclinations, writers might choose any of a number of aspects for imitation, and this has resulted in an extraordinary diversity of works all in one way or another modelled on the 'Li sao'. The most conspicuous feature of the original is the spirit-journey through space. This is basically a shamanistic concept,[130] associated in the 'Li sao' both with the quest of immortality and also with the search for an understanding ruler. The imitations of the spirit-journey may thus be Taoist or Confucian, or even non-philosophical. The Taoist imitations include one in the *Ch'u tz'u* itself, 'The Distant Wandering' (or 'Far-off Journey'[131]); Ssu-ma Hsiang-ju's 'The Great Man';[132] Chiang Yen's *fu* 'On the Desirability of Studying the Cinnabar [Technique for Prolonging Life]';[133] and Sun Ch'o's (4th century) more terrestrial but still imaginary '[Spirit-] Journey to Mount T'ien-t'ai'.[134] The original 'Li sao' flight through space had ended in a curious anti-climax:[135]

> But when I had ascended the splendour of the heavens,
> I suddenly caught a glimpse below of my old home.
> The groom's heart was heavy and the horses for longing
> Arched their heads back and refused to go on.

Inspired by this passage, a number of writers introduced an imaginary flight through space only to prove that 'there's no place like home';[136] these works illustrate a common feature of 'Li sao' imitations, the tendency to alter the original almost beyond recognition. The 'Li sao' itself, however much admired, was rather inaccessible. There are, of course, notable linguistic problems in it, but probably more important are the psychological obstacles it presented. The elaborate allegory, of a kind not at all common in Chinese writing of any period,[137] made the work seem vague and unreal. Besides that, the author's rather shrill insistence on his own purity and rectitude went far beyond the restraint characteristic of most Chinese writers, whatever Ssu-ma Ch'ien might say in Ch'ü's defense. As a result, there was a tendency to approach Ch'ü's work indirectly, through the biographies and commentaries; it was easier to understand and identify oneself with the Ch'ü presented there. In the same way, imitations of the 'Li sao' tend to be more concrete and less vague than the original.

For example, the flight through space inspired innumerable *fu* on real rather than imaginary journeys, and in these the traveler remains firmly earthbound.[138] These are immediately recognizable; the authors stress the 'Li sao' origins, as if to compensate for the more pedestrian subject. The works are in 'Li sao' meter, though mostly with some passages in shorter lines, and they tend to open with a brief autobiography, a glimpse of current events, and a statement of the reason for the journey. During the account of the trip itself, the author will list sites visited along the way, and he will almost certainly pause to reflect on historical events and people associated with a given place; even the historical reflections are inspired by the 'Li sao'. These travel *fu* were extremely popular;[139] Yü's account of his journey up the Yangtze (following line 231) clearly belongs to the category, but this section is only a minor feature of the work.

The 'Lament' is always paired with the 'Li sao', for the best of reasons; the opening genealogy alone would be enough to place it in the 'Li sao' tradition.[140] Yü's real indebtedness to Ch'ü Yüan is at once more general and less obvious. As mentioned earlier, there was a common tendency among 'Li sao' imitators to transform the original in one way or another; as a result, the more remote descendants have very little in common. This makes it difficult to deal with the 'Li sao' tradition as a whole, particularly because of the numerous mutations. Besides that, the 'Lament' itself resists categorization, there is nothing else quite like it in Chinese literature. One can however note certain tendencies in some of the 'Li sao' imitations; these do not lead directly to the 'Lament', but they may help to explain how the work could be produced.

Writing a century or so after the 'Lament', the historiographer Liu Chih-chi (661–721) classifies the 'Li sao' as an autobiography, along with the final chapter of Ssu-ma Ch'ien's *Shih chi*.[141] Ssu-ma Ch'ien's work obviously belongs there, but it is at first surprising to find the 'Li sao' in such a category. Liu Chih-chi's classification is actually very instructive, since Yü Hsin himself certainly thought of the work in the same way. Writers had always chosen from the 'Li sao' the feature that suited their purposes, whether a parallel with their own homesickness or a precedent for versified travel diaries. It was not, however, these features that attracted them to the work in the first place. The 'Li sao' was admired as the allegorical complaint of a devoted minister, rejected by his ruler because of slander, who was thus powerless to avert the fall of his state. The autobiographical elements were already present in the 'Li sao' itself, though only in sometimes maddeningly vague form.

This vagueness had its uses, of course; writers did not call their own rulers misguided, or, if they did so in private, they were generally wise enough not to publish their views. They might, on the other hand, write close imitations of the 'Li sao' deliberately made as vague as the original; an example of this is Chang Heng's 'Meditation on Mystery'.[142] One might take this to be a literary exercise except for the assurance of Chang's biographer that the work was in fact inspired by slander.[143] Alternatively, disgruntled officials might write bitter complaints about government life, such as T'ao Ch'ien's 'Lament for Gentlemen Born out of their Time'.[144] The authors of these would be careful to confine themselves to the general, avoiding first-person pronouns, for example, but at least here we are dealing with the real problems of an official trying to make his way at court, rather than with other women jealous of Ch'ü Yüan's beauty.

Finally, in the Six Dynasties, we begin to get genuine autobiographies in *fu* form, clearly inspired by the 'Li sao'. Of course, they are not complaints about slanderers and incompetent officials, with the contemporary Orchid and Pepper given their real names. They all involve a process of adaptation rather like the one that transformed the 'Li sao' spirit-journey into a travel diary, and, as in the *fu* on journeys, the authors stress certain mechanical features of the 'Li sao', the meter, the opening genealogy, and so on, as if afraid that the reader might otherwise not notice the connection. These autobiographies generally appear in *fu* on life in retirement, or on the author's desire for such a life. They include more or less detailed accounts of the author's career and any periods out of office, all set against a background of current events. Understandably, the discussions of politics are handled very tactfully. The author may dwell at some length on the unpleasant aspects of life under the preceding dynasty, but he will hasten to explain that the current political situation is ideal; it is only personal incompetence, or something of the sort, that makes him want to retire. One example of these works is Shen Yüeh's (441–513) 'Living in the Suburbs'.[145] This is a curious hybrid, apparently one of the first experiments at writing an autobiographical *fu* in imitation of the 'Li sao'. It contains, for example, a flight through space, a feature not at all typical of later works of the type. It is also only partly autobiographical, but the author does devote several hundred words to his family, career, and current events before settling down to a description of his garden and his scholarly activities. Shen Yüeh was, of course, one of the most famous literary figures of his generation, though

perhaps more important as a theorist than as a practitioner. Yü Hsin almost
certainly knew this work, Shen's description of the ruined state of the Broadview Park in his time[146] is remarkably similar to lines 313–15 of the 'Lament'.

Two later works show the autobiographical 'Li sao' imitation in a more
coherent form: 'Explaining My Feelings'[147] by Li Ch'ien (b. 508) and 'Account
of Myself'[148] by Li Hsieh (496–544). The two authors were not related,
despite their common surname, but there is a strong resemblance between
the two works, which deal with much the same events. Both writers had been
officials at the late Northern Wei court and, having gone through the civil
war that led to the partitioning, were composing their *fu* under the Eastern
Wei; this dynasty, we should remember, had a much more highly developed
civilization than its western rival. Li Ch'ien's work is about 1250 words long;
Li Hsieh's, about 1750. They are in 'Li sao' meter and are marked as imitations of that work by the traditional genealogy. As in the 'Lament', the
genealogies are relatively long and contain at least a sketch of earlier history.
These are followed by rather complete accounts of the authors' lives and
careers, set against a background of political chaos; understandably, both works
dwell a good deal on the pleasures of life in the country and the advantages
of retirement from government office. There is every chance that Yü Hsin
knew Li Ch'ien (and possibly Li Hsieh), and he may well have seen the
'Explaining My Feelings'. Yü went as ambassador to the Eastern Wei, and
Li Ch'ien to the Liang, during the decade of peace between the two states.
Ambassadors during this period were chosen for literary ability, and embassies
involved a good deal of passing around of literary works for inspection.
According to his biography,[149] Li Ch'ien wrote this *fu*, his magnum opus,
before going on the embassy to the Liang.

The 'Lament' contains no obvious borrowings from either of these Eastern
Wei *fu*, as opposed to the 'Living in the Suburbs'. Lines 283–6 are vaguely
similar, but that sort of thing is typical of the many *fu* on life in retirement.
I have gone into all these works, not to propose any single one as a model
for the 'Lament', but to show that autobiographical imitations of the 'Li
sao' were rather common by Yü's time. This is important to remember, since
a modern scholar has suggested that the 'Lament' was modelled on a specific
fu, the 'Returning Soul'[150] by Shen Chiung (d. 559). The only thing that
makes Shen's work significant is the subject, the final years of the Liang
dynasty. The 'Lament' in a very few places uses similar phrasing, but these
are clichés common in all the writing of the period. Whether Yü saw it or
not, it is impossible to tell, but it seems unwise to exaggerate the importance
of Shen's very minor work.

The 'Lament' is actually not very much like any of these things, though
it has some of the stock features of a 'Li sao' imitation in common with them:

the genealogy, the list of titles as in the autobiographical *fu*, the journey up
the Yangtze as in the travel diaries. These sections, with the exception of
the journey, must be considered the dullest parts of a great poem. The major
difference, the thing that makes the 'Lament' unique in Chinese literature,
is that Yü gives the work a new focus. The 'Li sao' had been obsessively self-
centered, and the autobiographical imitations of it were only slightly less so.
Li Hsieh, for example, tells us something about current history, but only as
a setting for his own life. Yü Hsin, on the other hand, mentions himself only
in passing; even including the long genealogy at the beginning, only about a
fourth of the work is connected in any way with the author or his family.
Yü in fact apologizes in lines 33—4 of the preface for the intrusion of these
personal matters on a greater theme: the fall of a dynasty. There had never
been a *fu* on such a subject before; the only things even remotely comparable
were the short works 'lamenting' emperors of the Ch'in dynasty.[151] The
authors of these had never made any pretense of dealing with the history of
the Ch'in, but had contented themselves with general reflections on the wicked-
ness of its rulers. Yü here covers the events of a decade, and does so in a form
still recognizable as a *fu*, however new the subject might be. The result has
long caused problems for cataloguers, who normally wind up grouping the
work with other *fu* expressing sorrow for any cause.[152]

As explained earlier, the lexical difficulties of Han *fu* are mostly absent
from Six-Dynasties works; the problems for readers of the latter arise from
the unusual syntax, particularly in the 'Lament', and the allusiveness characteristic of almost all Six-Dynasties writing. Description tends to be selective
rather than exhaustive; as a result, the late *fu* are for the most part relatively
brief. A number of long *fu* were written during the period, but (aside from
imitations of Han *fu*) these long works are personal and autobiographical
rather than impersonal descriptions. The short *fu* may be either lyrical or
descriptive; they tend to fall somewhere between the two extremes. The
shorter length now favored meant that *fu* could be used on occasion for the
same purposes as *shih*; they were no longer necessarily great showpieces,
and the showpieces, which would continue to be written long after the Six
Dynasties, were already beginning to look anachronistic.

The early Han *fu* were often extremely irregular in meter and rhyme, with
rhymes in odd places and prose mixed with verse. By the first century A.D.
the rhymes were regularized at the ends of even-numbered lines, as in *shih*,
with an optional rhyme in the first line after a rhyme-change. A rhyme-
change, of course, always indicated a new subject. By the end of the Six
Dynasties, the prose sections interrupting verse disappeared almost completely,
along with the old prose introductions setting the scene and introducing the
speakers. The reason is that the debate *fu* was much less common than earlier;

when such works were written they were normally in imitation of Han *fu*
or placed in a historical setting, and they seemed definitely old-fashioned.
Otherwise the prose introduction was replaced by an author's preface, and
even this was omitted as often as not. There was a tendency to regularize
the meter somewhat, partly as a result of the favor shown the 'Li sao' meter.
The 'Li sao' itself had had somewhat irregular lines, and the early Six-Dynasties
works still imitated this irregularity in 'Li sao' imitations. Oddly enough,
late Six-Dynasties *fu*, while generally regularizing the 'Li sao' line,[153] tended
not to use that line throughout. There are a few exceptions, such as Pao
Chao's 'Mourning the Dead',[154] written entirely in 'Li sao' meter, but it was
more common to interrupt it occasionally for a section of shorter lines
(typically four-word, sometimes three-word), or else to write in a mixture
of the related 'Li sao' and Ch'u song meters. A regular meter works satisfactorily for *shih* but can get very monotonous if used for the entire length
of a *fu*. Besides that, the light beat in a 'Li sao' line tends to impose a fixed
grammatical structure: 'Admiring *A* who did *X*, Sympathizing with *B* who
suffered *Y*.' This repetitive grammar, combined with metrical regularity,
makes a long succession of 'Li sao' lines dangerous for anyone but a real
master. Yü Hsin himself left no *fu* in any single meter; in fact, he varies
the meter so often that one cannot even identify a dominant meter in a
given work.

The late Six Dynasties *fu* are almost invariably written in the antithetical
style characteristic of parallel prose; they are thus habitually called parallel
fu. The two genres grew up together, and works in the two sometimes resemble
one another so much that one is forced to make rhyme or its absence the
distinguishing feature. Parallelism was a characteristic of the *fu* from the third
century A.D., and it grows more dominant and elaborate throughout the Six-
Dynasties period. The 'Lament', though basically in the antithetical style, is
somewhat unusual even among Yü's own *fu* in its occasional deliberate
avoidance of parallelism, as in lines 315—16.

The Southern dynasties of the period of division had claimed to be the
custodians of Chinese civilization, and most of the literature of the period
was written either in the South or by Southerners who, like Yü Hsin, found
themselves in exile in the North. After the reunification in 589, these Southern
writings, especially the later ones, were admired in fact but condemned in
theory; this is the result of historical accident. The unification had been
imposed from the Northwest, the old area of the Northern Chou, culturally
the most backward section of China. The early T'ang ruling class came almost
entirely from that area. Regionalism, always a significant factor in Chinese
history, seems to have been particularly strong at that time; until recently, of
course, the South had been enemy territory. The Northwest had also seen the

beginnings of the Confucian revival, from the Northern Chou on, and Confucians believed in a causal relationship between the culture of a state and its
political fortunes. The Southern dynasties, always rather weak, had finally
been conquered; this must surely have something to do with the favor they
had shown to Buddhism and Taoism. Emperor Wu of the Liang was the
classic example of a devout Buddhist who had come to a bad end, and it did
not pass unnoticed that he, and the equally ill-fated Emperors Chien-wen and
Yüan, had all been writers and patrons of literature. It was concluded that
an emperor who dabbled in literature (this meant any writing not purely
didactic) was in grave danger of destroying his dynasty. This might well
give an emperor pause, particularly when this philosophical argument was
stated by the very men who formed the power base of the dynasty. Li Shih-
min (temple-name T'ai-tsung, *reg.* 627–49), second emperor and real founder
of the T'ang dynasty, was forced to give way. Himself very fond of the
Southern style of writing, he nevertheless condemned it in all his public
utterances, and in 643 he even abandoned his plan to name a favorite son as
Crown Prince, apparently because that son was too closely identified with
men and literature from the South.[155]

This political situation had lasting consequences, since most of the standard
histories of the period of division were compiled at this time and in this
atmosphere. Even historians originally from the South hesitated to defend
Southern writings, and Northerners dismissed them as 'the music of a doomed
state', perhaps the most damning phrase in the Confucian repertory of
invective. *Fu* were viewed with particular disfavor, and Yü Hsin fared worst
of all. He was the most famous of the Southern writers, admired and imitated
by Emperor Yang of the Sui (*reg.* 605–17), the classic bad last emperor,
and also by T'ang T'ai-tsung himself; he thus became the symbol of the
enemy. Ling-hu Te-fen, the most important historian from the Northwestern
faction, concluded his *Chou shu* biography of Yü Hsin with one of the
most hostile assessments to be found in the official histories. He criticizes
Yü's writings as 'licentious' and 'more corruptive than [the airs of] Cheng
and Wei'; quoting Yang Hsiung on the excessive adornment characteristic
of *fu*, he brands Yü Hsin as 'a criminal even among *fu*-writers'.[156]

This extraordinary attack did not prevent people from reading Yü's
works; almost every major T'ang writer, including Yü's most bitter critics,[157]
shows familiarity at least with the 'Lament'. Tu Fu (712–70) speaks of Yü
with great admiration;[158] this is particularly interesting since Tu was a Confucian as well as a good judge of literature. Unfortunately, not all later
Confucians were equally perceptive; from the Sung on, with the old *fu*
unquestionably in decline, the T'ang historians' views of the genre gained

widespread acceptance. Particularly in the Ming, there was a general feeling that *fu* represented a steady decline from their supposed source in the *Songs*; the only real question was the point when acceptable works ceased to be written. One late Ming critic even suggested that Yang Hsiung had been referring to the 'Li sao' itself when he spoke of 'excessive adornment'.[159] This was, however, an extreme view, and the same critic defends the 'Li sao' as a didactic work expressing genuine feeling, despite its excessive adornment.

The antithetical writing of the late Six Dynasties had aroused particular hostility, and Ming critics often fixed the cut-off date at the point where parallelism grew dominant in *fu*. Yü Hsin's name was more or less synonymous with parallel prose, and the renewed interest in that genre in the Ch'ing naturally helped to restore him to favor; this can be seen in the steady stream of commentaries on his works produced from the seventeenth century on. It was still necessary, however, to deal with the received opinions about the licentious Southern literature of the Six Dynasties. The solution was to divide Yü's life into two periods, abandon the Southern works as indefensible, but stress the totally different kind of poetry Yü wrote in the North. The *Ssu-k'u* catalogue editors suggested that Ling-hu Te-fen's condemnation had been intended to apply only to the Southern works. As Mou Jun-sun says, however well-intended, this is simply not true;[160] the T'ang historians had been thinking of Yü Hsin's entire output, as well as practically all the literature of the period of division, Northern or Southern. This kind of rationalization did, however, make the late works acceptable, and a new 'Lament for the South', with the same title and the same rhymes, was written on the subject of the T'ai-p'ing Rebellion.[161]

The early T'ang attacks have had a lasting effect; one can still see traces of it today, in writers perhaps not fully conscious of the sources of their views. Even admirers of *fu* have sometimes been rather defensive; Chang Hui-yen (1761–1802), for example, protests that Pao Chao and Chiang Yen 'wrote in the wrong genre but had the right ideas',[162] and Hsü Lien says in a preface dated 1825 that he discovered a taste for Hsü Ling and Yü Hsin in his youth but was forbidden by his teacher to read their works. He pursued his studies in secret, and finally compiled the most popular anthology of Six-Dynasties literature, the *Liu-ch'ao wen-chieh*.[163]

More recently the *fu* has found an important supporter in the late Mao Tse-tung. In the year 1959 alone, Mao devoted a letter and a long paper to the contemporary relevance of Mei Sheng's 'Seven Stimuli' and based a parable on 'The Lechery of Master Teng-t'u'.[164] Mao's interest in *fu* was presumably the reason for the 1958 selections from Yü Hsin[165] and the

1964 anthology of Han, Wei, and Six-Dynasties *fu*.[166] The latter, it should be remembered, was one of the last books printed before the Cultural Revolution.

3
'THE LAMENT FOR THE SOUTH'

A note on the Chinese text

The text is that of Ni Fan, with the following exceptions: In lines
125, 128, 141, 160, 185, 255, 260, 368, 380, 389, and 391 I have followed
the *Chou shu* text; in most of these cases the majority of editions agree with
the *Chou shu*. In line 265 I have adopted an emendation by Ku Yen-wu.
In line 429 the reading is that of the *Yi-wen lei-chü*.

庾信　　哀江南賦并序

粵以
　戊辰之年
　建亥之月
　　大盜移國
　　金陵瓦解
余乃
5　　竄身荒谷　公私塗炭
　　華陽奔命　有去無歸
　　中興道銷
　　　窮於甲戌
　　三日哭於都亭
10　　三年囚於別館
　　天道周星
　　物極不反
　　傅燮之但悲身世　無處求生
　　袁安之每念王室　自然流涕
昔
15　　桓君山之志事
　　杜元凱之平生
　　　並有著書
　　　咸能自序

Preface[1]

1 In the year *wu-ch'en*,	In December, 548, the rebel
2 The month when the Dipper points northwest,	Hou Ching attacked the Liang capital at Chien-k'ang, which
3 A great thief stole the state;	fell to him.
4 The defenders of Chin-ling scattered like tiles.	

I then

5 Hid myself in Huang-ku, where all were in mud and fire;

6 And went on a mission through Hua-yang, from which there was no return.

Yü Hsin fled to the court of Hsiao Yi in Chiang-ling; he was sent from there to the Western Wei, which detained him and destroyed Hsiao Yi.

7 The restoration faltered,

8 And failed in *chia-hsü*.

9 I mourned three days in the city hostel,

10 Was imprisoned three years in a detached lodging.

Yü, the subject of a fallen dynasty, was to spend the rest of his life in the North.

11 The stars are completing their cycles,

12 But the course of events moves on.

Now, at the end of the year, the heavens are demonstrating their cyclical nature, but there is no hope either for a restoration of the Liang or for his own return home.

13 Like Fu Hsieh, I can only lament my fate, I cannot save myself,

14 Like Yüan An, thinking of the royal house, I spontaneously shed tears.

Grief, both for his misfortunes and for the fall of the Liang, forces him to express himself in writing.

Already before me

15 The career of Huan T'an

16 The life of Tu Yü

17   Both were recounted

18   Both were retold.

There are respectable precedents for autobiographies

潘岳之文采　始述家風

20　陸機之辭賦　先陳世德

信

　年始二毛　即逢喪亂

　貌是流離　至於暮齒

　燕歌遠別　悲不自勝

　楚老相逢　泣將何及

25　畏南山之雨　忽踐秦庭

　讓東海之濱　遂餐周粟

　下亭漂泊

　高橋羈旅

　楚歌非取樂之方

30　魯酒無忘憂之用

　追為此賦

　聊以記言

　不無危苦之辭

　惟以悲哀為主

35　日暮途遠

　人間何世

　將軍一去　大樹飄零

　壯士不還　寒風蕭瑟

　荊璧睨柱　受連城而見欺

40　載書橫階　捧珠盤而不定

　鍾儀君子　入就南冠之囚

19 P'an Yüeh was first to tell his family's acts in poetry;	and for poems about the history of one's family (such as the beginning of the 'Lament' itself).
20 Lu Chi was first to describe his ancestors' deeds in *fu*.	
21 Hair just turning gray, I encountered death and disorder;	He himself suffered during the fall of the Liang and now finds himself a captive in the North.
22 Far off in exile I remain in my twilight years.	
23 With a song of Yen I set out, my grief unbearable;	Trying to save his dynasty,
24 If I met the old man from Ch'u, he would shed no tears for me.	he only disgraced himself,
25 I feared the rain of South Mountain, but soon walked in the court of Ch'in;	consenting, though reluctantly, to take office
26 I declined the shore of the Eastern Sea, and in the end ate the grain of Chou.	under the conquerors of his own state.
27 Homeless at Hsia-t'ing,	He still considers himself an exile, and nothing can console him.
28 A wanderer at Kao-ch'iao,	
29 Ch'u songs could not make me happy;	
30 Lu wine was useless in dispelling cares.	
31 So looking back I wrote this *fu*	Therefore he has written the 'Lament', which contains some references to his own misfortunes
32 That it might serve as a record;	
33 Not without words of fear and suffering,	
34 It is still, at the core, a lament.	but is basically a lament for a fallen dynasty.
35 The sun is setting, my road is long;	Its writing is made doubly urgent now by the fact that the author, an old man who must soon die, can find no other compensation either for the fall of his state or for his own captivity.
36 How long have I left among men?	
37 When the general went away, the great tree withered;	
38 The hero would not return: the cold wind whistled.	
39 Holding the jade I eyed the pillar, but was cheated of the cities;	He failed in his mission to arrange a treaty with the Western Wei.
40 With the text of the treaty I encroached on the steps, presenting the pearl basin without success.	
41 A gentleman Chung Yi, I went to prison in my southern cap;	He remained loyal even in captivity,

季孫行人　留守西河之館
申包胥之頓地　碎之以首
蔡威公之淚盡　加之以血
45 釣臺移柳　非玉關之可望
華亭鶴唳　豈河橋之可聞
孫策以天下為三分　眾纔一旅
項籍用江東之子弟　人惟八千
遂乃
分裂山河
50 宰割天下
豈有
百萬義師
一朝卷甲
芟夷斬伐
如草木焉
55 江淮無涯岸之阻
亭壁無藩籬之固
頭會箕斂者　合從締交
鋤耰棘矜者　因利乘便
將非江表王氣
60 終於三百年乎
是知
并吞六合　不免軹道之災

42 An ambassador Chi-sun, I was detained in a lodging west of
   the River.
43 Striking the ground like Shen   but his grief could not save his
   Pao-hsü, I broke my head   state,
   against it;
44 Tears running dry like Wei-kung
   of Ts'ai, I wept tears of
   blood.
45 The willows transplanted at the   and he found himself merely
   fishing terrace cannot be seen   a helpless captive in the
   from Jade Pass;   North.
46 The cranes crying at the Flower
   Pavilion — how can I hear them
   from River Bridge?
47 Sun Ts'e divided the empire into   Men from the South had earlier
   three, with scarcely a bat-   gained astonishing victories
   talion for army;   with tiny armies.
48 Hsiang Yü had used the youths of
   the South, barely eight thousand men.
   And yet they
49 Split apart mountains and streams
50 And carved up the empire.
51 How could a hundred myriad loyal   How could the enormous Liang
   troops   armies have been defeated so
52 All at once discard their armor,   easily?
53 To be moved away and chopped
   down
54 Like grass or trees?
55 Yangtze and Huai posed not the   The Liang was militarily
   obstacle of a cliff;   weak,
56 Fortresses lacked the strength
   of a hedge.
57 Payers of head taxes joined to-   and its bad government had
   gether and formed alliances;   alienated the people.
58 With hoe-handles and thorn-tree
   staffs, they made use of advantages and seized opportun-
   ities.
59 Wasn't the royal aura of the South The fall of the Southern dynasties
60 To end in three hundred years?   had also been predicted.
   This would explain why   Either fate or mistakes
61 Swallowing up the world could not   in government could explain
   prevent the tragedy at Chih-   the destruction of a mighty
   tao,   empire.

混一車書　　無復平陽之禍

嗚呼

山嶽崩頹　　既履危亡之運

春秋迭代　　必有去故之悲

65　　天意人事

　　　可以悽愴傷心者矣

況復

舟楫路窮　　星漢非乘槎可上

風飆道阻　　蓬萊無可到之期

窮者欲達其言

70　勞者須歌其事

陸士衡聞而撫掌　　是所甘心

張平子見而陋之　　固其宜矣

我之

掌庾承周　　以世功而為族

經邦佐漢　　用論道而當官

稟嵩華之玉石

潤河洛之波瀾

5　居負洛而重世

邑臨河而宴安

逮永嘉之艱虞

始中原之乏主

62 And standardizing axles and
        script could not avert the
        disaster at P'ing-yang.
        Alas!   However, the author himself
63 When mountains crumbled, I passed   suffered through the fall of the
        through danger and destruction,   Liang, and the coming New Year
64 And now, as the seasons pass, I   intensifies the grief he feels
        always grieve for what is gone.   because of it, whether its fall was
65 Whether it was heaven's will or   caused by fate or human conduct.
        man's doing,
66 It breaks my heart,
        Especially since   The fact that he cannot return
67 The boat's way is blocked: I   home makes matters worse.
        can't go up the Milky Way by
        raft;
68 Whirlwinds stop me: there's no
        hope of reaching P'eng-lai.
69 An unhappy man will express   Therefore, he cannot help
        himself in words,   writing the 'Lament'.
70 As the weary must sing of their
        toil.
71 If Lu Chi laughs on hearing of   He has no right to complain
        it, I shall be content;   if better writers than he think
72 If Chang Heng looks on it with   the work contemptible.
        disdain, that is only right.

The 'Lament' proper

1 We aided the Chou as Director of   Origin of the surname Yü
        Granaries, for generations of   ('granary')
        service being granted that name;
2 And assisted the Han in govern-   Yü Meng, an ancestor, was
        ing the state, holding a post   Imperial Secretary under
        as discusser of the Way.   the Latter Han.
3 Fostered by the jade of Sung   The family were natives of
        and Hua,   Hsin-yeh in Nan-yang.
4 Nurtured by the waves of the
        Ho and Lo,
5 We spent generations with our
        backs to the Lo,
6 Living at peace overlooking the Ho.

---

7 In the chaos of the Yung-chia   At the time of the fall of the
        period,   Western Chin,
8 When the Central Plain lost its
        ruler,

民枕倚於牆望
10　路交橫於射虎
值五馬之南奔
逢三星之東聚
彼凌江而建國
始播遷於吾祖
15　分南陽而賜田
裂東嶽而胙土
誅茅宋玉之宅
穿徑臨江之府
水木交運
20　山川崩竭
家有直道
人多全節
訓子見於純深
事君彰於義烈
25　新野有生祠之廟
河南有胡書之碣
況乃
少微真人
天山逸民
階庭空谷
30　門巷蒲輪

9 The people lay down against   with the North in ruins
   ruined walls;
10 Jackals and tigers prowled   and warring armies everywhere,
   the roads.
11 Then, when five horses fled   a member of the ruling Ssu-
   to the South,   ma family restored the Chin
12 And three stars joined in the   in the South, and the author's
   East,   ancestor Yü T'ao went to assist
13 A man crossed the Yangtze to   in the restoration.
   found a new state,
14 Thus uprooting my ancestors.
15 They were given lands like that   He was made Marquis of Sui-
   of Nan-yang,   ch'ang *hsien* in Chekiang.
16 Granted a fief like those on
   Mount T'ai.
17 They hoed the weeds at Sung   T'ao moved the family to a
   Yü's house   new home in Chiang-ling
18 And cleared a path at the Lin-   (in Hupeh).
   chiang palace.

---

19 As water and wood followed   The Eastern Chin was followed
   in sequence,   by the Sung and Ch'i,
20 Though mountains fell and rivers
   ran dry,
21 My family remained upright,   under both of which the family
22 Its members often loyal to the   continued its honorable
   death.   tradition.
23 The sons' upbringing was apparent
   in filial conduct;
24 Serving their lord they showed
   their devotion.
25 In Hsin-yeh was a shrine to a   The grateful people honored
   living man;   T'ao's son Hui and great-grandson
26 South of the Yellow River is a   Kao-yün.
   tablet in foreign script.

---

27 One was marked true man by the   The author's grandfather Yü Yi
   hermit star,   lived in retirement,
28 Named recluse by the hexagram.
29 Though his house lay in a   refusing all offers of official
   deserted valley,   posts.
30 His gate was visited by padded
   carriages.

移誃講樹
就簡書筍
降生世德
載誕貞臣
35 文詞高於甲觀
楷模盛於漳濱
嗟有道而無鳳
歎非時而有麟
既姦回之奰逆
40 終不悅於仁人
王子濱洛之歲
蘭成射策之年
始含香於建禮
仍矯翼於崇賢
45 遊洊雷之講肆
齒明離之胄筵
既傾蠡而酌海
遂測管以窺天
方塘水白
50 釣渚池圓
侍戎韜於武帳
聽雅曲於文絃
乃解懸而通籍
遂崇文而會武

31 Moved to speak, he talked of trees;	His life was one of rustic simplicity.
32 Wanting paper, he wrote on bamboo.	
33 Another, inheriting his ancestors' virtues,	The author's father Chien-wu, a famous poet, held office
34 Was born a loyal subject,	mainly under the Crown Prince
35 Writings admired in the Crown Prince's Palace,	Hsiao Kang (Emperor Chienwen) and Hsiao Yi (Emperor
36 Conduct a model on the bank of the Chang.	Yüan).
37 He grieved that possessing the Way, he met with no phoenix;	Chien-wu had been born in the wrong age,
38 Mourned that in an adverse time the unicorn should appear.	
39 After the traitor's raging rebellion,	and he died mourning Hou Ching's rebellion.
40 There was never any joy for this good man.	
41 As old as the Prince on the bank of the Lo	Yü Hsin took an official examination at 15 *sui*.
42 Was I when I took my examination.	
43 First I sweetened my breath by the Chien-li Gate;	He held such posts as secretary in an imperial ministry
44 Then I spread my wings in the Ch'ung-hsien Gate.	and scholar in the Crown Prince's household.
45 I attended the Heir Apparent's lectures,	Though he attended lectures by the Crown Prince,
46 Took my place in the Crown Prince's classes,	
47 Thus dipping up the sea in a draining gourd	he modestly announces his own inability to do them
48 And peering at the sky through a measuring tube.	justice.
49 Bright water in square ponds,	The author's life at court
50 Round pools within fishing banks,	
51 I attended war councils beneath martial canopies	
52 And heard classical music played on civil strings.	

---

53 Then, no longer on probation, I was inscribed in the lists,	
54 Did honor to letters and consorted with warriors,	

55 居笠轂而掌兵
出蘭池而典午
論兵於江漢之君
拭玉於兩河之主
於時
朝野歡娛
60 池臺鍾鼓
里為冠蓋
門成鄒魯
連茂苑於海陵
跨橫塘於江浦
65 東門則鞭石成橋
南極則鑄銅為柱
橘則園植萬株
竹則家封千戶
西賈浮玉
70 南琛沒羽
吳歈越吟
荊艷楚舞
草木之遇陽春
魚龍之逢風雨
75 五十年中
江表無事
王歈為和親之侯
班超為定遠之使
馬武無預於甲兵

55 Stood in a war chariot to direct
        troops,
56 Went out on a Lan-ch'ih horse to
        supervise cavalry.
57 I discussed war with the Lord of   He was made an adviser to
        Yangtze and Han   Hsiao Yi
58 And held jade insignia before   and sent on a diplomatic
        the ruler of Hsi ho.   mission to the North.
        In those days
59 Life was happy for court and   The Liang was then peaceful
        people,   and prosperous, filled with
60 Bells and drums amid   families of officials and
        lakes and towers,   scholars.
61 Caps and carriages in every quarter,
62 Tsou and Lu scholars in every ward.
63 It combined lush gardens with Hai-   The Liang capital at Chien-
        ling granaries,   k'ang.
64 Stretched from the Restraining Dike
        to the bank of the Yangtze,
65 Eastern portal where stones were   Its empire extended from
        whipped to make a bridge,   the east coast to the
66 Southern extremity where bronze   modern Vietnam.
        had been cast into pillars.
67 Of tangerines, myriads planted   The favorable climate ensured
        in gardens;   prosperity,
68 From bamboo, the income of a
        thousand households.
69 The West presented floating jade;   and the neighboring states
70 The South gave tribute of sinking   gave rich tribute.
        feathers.
71 Songs of Wu, chants of Yüeh,
72 Tunes of Ching, dances from Ch'u,
73 Spring warmth for plants and trees,
74 Wind and rain for fish and dragons.

---

75 For fifty years,   Diplomatic relations
76 The South had been without   with the North had largely
        incident.   eliminated the need for military
77 Wang Hsi was Marquis of Friendly   campaigns.
        Relations;
78 Pan Ch'ao was peace envoy to
        distant regions.
79 No need for Ma Wu to join in
        warfare,

80　馮唐不論於將帥

　豈知

　　山嶽闇然

　　江湖潛沸

　　漁陽有閭左戍卒

　　離石有將兵都尉

　天子方

85　　刪詩書

　　定禮樂

　　設重雲之講

　　開士林之學

　　談劫燼之灰飛

90　　辨常星之夜落

　　地平魚齒

　　城危獸角

　　臥刁斗於滎陽

　　絆龍媒於平樂

95　　宰衡以干戈為兒戲

　　縉紳以清談為廟略

　　乘漬水以膠船

　　馭奔駒以朽索

　　小人則將及水火

100　君子則方成猿鶴

　　敧箄不能救鹽池之鹹

80 Or for Feng T'ang to assess the
generals' merits.

Who could have told that
81 Mountains and peaks were blazing   Nothing suggested the possibility
inside,   of a rebellion.
82 Rivers and lakes were boiling in
their depths,
83 In Yü-yang there was a garrison
soldier from the left side of
town,
84 In Li-shih there was a military
governor commanding troops?

The Emperor was then   Emperor Wu of the Liang
85 Editing *Songs* and *Documents*,   was too busy with classical
86 Fixing rites and music,   and Buddhist questions to worry
87 Establishing the Ch'ung-yun   about the danger confronting
lectures,   the state.
88 Opening the Shih-lin Academy,
89 Discussing a burning world
scattering in ashes,
90 Explaining the fixed stars
falling in the night.
91 Ground flat as fishes' teeth,   The country was totally un-
92 Walls unstable as animal horns,   prepared for war,
93 Alarms put away in the Hsing-
yang storehouse,
94 War horses hobbled in the P'ing-
lo stable,
95 The Chief Minister thought of   and the situation was only made
weapons as children's toys;   worse by the folly of officials.
96 The officials considered word-
games state counsel.
97 We were sailing over leaking-in   Everything invited disaster,
water in a glued-together boat,   which they were powerless to
98 Driving runaway horses with rot-   prevent.
ten reins,
99 People headed for fire and water,
100 Gentlemen turning to apes and
cranes;
101 Trying with a wornout sieve to make
the salt lake less brackish,

阿膠不能止黃河之濁

既而

魴魚頳尾

四郊多壘

105 殷狎江鷗

宮鳴野雉

湛盧去國

艅艎火水

見被髮於伊川

110 知百年而為戎矣

彼姦逆之熾盛

久遊魂而放命

大則有鯨有鯢

小則為梟為獍

115 負其牛羊之力

凶其水草之性

非玉燭之能調

豈璿璣之可正

值天下之無為

120 尚有欲於羈縻

飲其琉璃之酒

賞其虎豹之皮

見胡柯於大夏

識鳥卵於條枝

125 射玕蜜勵

102 Or, with Tung-o glue, to make the
       Yellow River clear.

---

103 The bream's tail grew red;	Already there were omens
104 Outside the walls were many fortifications.	of war,
105 Seagulls sported in the halls;	death,
106 Pheasants cackled in the palaces.	
107 The Chan-lu sword left the state;	and the fall of a state.
108 The Yü-huang ship ran aground.	
109 Seeing a man with streaming hair at Yi-ch'uan,	
110 One knew within the century there would be barbarians there.	

---

111 That epitome of rebelliousness	Hou Ching had a history
112 Had long wandered like a ghost and scorned commands,	of rebellion; he was fully capable of destroying a state
113 At his worst, a whale or a shark,	or killing a benefactor.
114 At best, an owl or a *ching*.	
115 Drawing on his strength of ox or sheep,	Moreover, he was a barbarian.
116 Wild by his nomadic nature,	
117 Not to be moderated by the jade lamp;	Emperor Wu should have realized that he could not control him.
118 How could the *hsüan-chi* control him?	

---

119 Although the empire was ruled by inaction,	Emperor Wu, a relatively inactive ruler, decided to accept Hou
120 There still was a longing to bridle him.	Ching's offer of allegiance, sweetened as it was by the
121 He drank his gold-infused wine,	additional territory under Hou's
122 Rewarded him for his tiger and leopard pelts,	control.
123 Seeing in him the foreign stem from Ta-hsia,	
124 Recognizing the bird's egg from T'iao-chih.	
125 But the jackal was sharpening its teeth in secret;	The favor shown him could not change Hou's nature;

砒毒潛吹

輕九鼎而欲問

聞三川而遂窺

始則

王子召戎

130 姦臣介胄

既官政而離過

遂師言而泄漏

望廷尉之逋閃

反淮南之窮寇

135 出狄泉之蒼烏

起橫江之閒獸

地則石鼓精鳴山

天則金龍精動宿

北闕龍吟

140 東陵麟鬭

爾乃

桀黠構扇

馮陵畿甸

擁狼望於黃圖

填盧山於赤縣

145 青袍如草

白馬如練

天子履端廢朝

單于長圍高宴

兩觀當戟

150 千門受箭

126 The viper was blowing out its
       poison unnoticed.
127 Thinking the nine cauldrons   he was about to rebel.
       light, he was about to inquire;
128 Though cut off by three rivers,
       he would finally peer in.

_____

       To begin with,
129 A royal prince called in the   Hsiao Cheng-te, Emperor
       barbarian;   Wu's nephew, formed a secret
130 The treacherous subject donned   alliance with Hou Ching.
       armor and helmet.
131 Having grown estranged from   Because of Cheng-te's warning,
       the government,   Hou Ching rebelled against the
132 He leaked out the model words.   Liang, as he had earlier against
133 The fugitive criminal eyed the   the Eastern Wei.
       Minister of Justice;
134 The desperate bandit rebelled in
       Huai-nan.
135 A gray bird emerged at Ti-ch'üan;   There were baleful omens.
136 The cornered animal turned in
       Heng-chiang.
137 Stone drums rumbled in the moun-
       tains;
138 The Metal Star glittered in its
       mansion.
139 Dragons roared at the north
       gatetower;
140 Unicorns fought on the east tomb
       mound.

_____

141 He then stirred up the unruly   Hou Ching attacked the Liang
142 And invaded the royal domain,   capital at Chien-k'ang, turning
143 Thus putting down Lang-wang on   it into another Mongolia.
       the Yellow Map,
144 And adding Lu-shan to the Red
       Region.
145 His robes were green as grass;
146 His horse white as boiled silk.
147 The Emperor cancelled court on   Emperor Wu was too hard-pressed
       New Year's Day;   for ceremonies, but the barbarian
148 The Shan-yü made merry among   Hou found time to amuse himself.
       the besieging forces.   The palace was under attack,
149 Halberds hacked the twin towers;
150 Arrows struck the thousand gates.

白虹貫日

蒼鷹擊殿

竟遭夏臺之禍

終視堯城之變

155　官守無奔問之人

干戚非平戎之戰

陶侃空爭米船

顧榮虛搖羽扇

將軍死綏

160　路絕重圍

烽隨星落

書逐鳶飛

遂乃

韓分趙裂

鼓臥旗折

165　失群班馬

迷輪亂轍

猛士嬰城

謀臣卷舌

昆陽之戰象走林

170　常山之陣蛇奔穴

五郡則兄弟相悲

151 A white rainbow pierced the sun;   and Emperor Wu, destined to be
152 A gray hawk struck the palace.   killed in the end, now found
153 Finally it had come to the   himself under siege.
    disaster at Hsia-t'ai;
154 We were ultimately seeing the
    calamity of Yao-ch'eng.
155 No one went to report to the   Little help was forthcoming
    officers;   from the Liang princes away
156 Their weapons were not used to   from court, who were fighting
    put down the uprising.   one another.
157 Useless for T'ao K'an to fight   It was a hopeless struggle.
    with the rice ships;
158 Pointless for Ku Jung to wave
    his feather fan!

---

159 Though generals died rather   It was impossible to prevent
    than retreat,   circumvallation of
160 The way was cut off by walls   the city, which cut off com-
    within walls.   munications.
161 Signal fires fell in the wake
    of the stars;
162 Letters followed the flight
    of kites.

    Then,
163 Partitioned like Han, split up   After disastrous defeats, the
    like Chao,   Liang's bravest soldiers
164 Drums toppled, standards broken,   grew afraid to fight, and the
165 Riderless horses lost from the   wisest advisers could come
    troop,   up with no plan:
166 Confused tracks from fleeing
    chariots,
167 Brave warriors kept inside the
    walls;
168 Wise advisers held their tongues:
169 As if, at the battle of K'un-   as though fierce elephants
    yang, the elephants had run   were to run away,
    for the forest,
170 Or, in the Ch'ang-shan formation,   or ever-resourceful snakes
    the snake were to flee to its   were to flee.
    hole.
171 In five commanderies, brother   Families were broken up.
    mourned brother;

三州則父子離別
護軍慷慨
忠能死節
175　三世為將
終於此滅
濟陽忠壯
身參末將
兄弟三人
180　義聲俱嗚
主辱臣死
名存身喪
狄人歸元
三軍悽憺
185　尚書多方
守備是良
雲梯可拒
地道能防
有齊將之閉壁
190　無燕師之臥牆
大事去矣
人之云亡
申子奮發
勇氣總勃
195　寶身元戎
身先士卒
胄落魚門
兵填馬窟

172 In three provinces, father and
        son were parted.
173 The Protecting General was   Wei Ts'an, a third-generation
        spirited,   general, was killed with several
174 Loyal enough to die for his ruler: hundred of his family.
175 Generals for three generations,
176 It ended in this massacre.

---

177 Chi-yang was loyal and brave.   Chiang Tzu-yi and his brothers
178 Though he was among the lowest   were killed in a hopeless attack
        officers,   on Hou Ching.
179 His and the two younger brothers'
180 Loyal shouts rang out together.
181 When the ruler was shamed, the
        subject died;
182 His name survives, though his
        body perished.
183 The barbarian returned his head;
184 The three armies mourned him.

---

185 The Minister was an able strategist,   Yang K'an, Minister of Justice,
                                                        was the foremost
186 Skilled at defensive measures,   defender of the besieged city.
187 Able to repel scaling ladders,
188 Capable of blocking mines.
189 With a Ch'i general cutting off
        the city,
190 The Yen army's walls still could
        not be toppled;
191 But the great work failed;   His death ended all hope of
192 The man had died.   saving Chien-k'ang.

---

193 Shen-tzu was stirred to wrath;   Liu Chung-li, Commander-in-
194 His brave spirit raged.   Chief of the Liang army, led an
195 In overall command of the great   attack against Hou Ching, in
        army,   which he was defeated.
196 He himself led his troops into
        battle.
197 But he dropped his helmet by
        the Fish Gate,
198 And lost enough weapons to fill
        the horse-watering spring.

屢犯通中
頻遭刮骨
功業天枉
身名埋没
或以

隼翼鶪秋
虎威狐假
沾瀆鋒鏑
脂膏原野
兵駒虜強
城孤氛寡
閴鶴唳而心驚
聽胡笳而淚下
拒神亭而亡
臨橫江而棄之
崩于鉅鹿之
碎于長平之

於是
桂林顛覆
長洲麋鹿
潰潰沸騰
茫茫墋黷
天地離阻
神人慘酷

200
205
210
215
220

199 Although many times pierced by   After a long military career,
     weapons,   with many honorable wounds,
200 Often forced to have his bones   he now disgraced himself.
     scraped,
201 His distinguished service ended
     prematurely;
202 Body and name were buried
     together.

     Some,
203 Like the quail, put on falcon's   The other Liang generals were
     wings;   hopelessly outmatched.
204 Like the fox, borrowed the tiger's
     majesty,
205 Only to wet the enemy's spears and
     arrows with their blood
206 And fertilize the plain with their
     flesh.
207 Our troops were weak, the enemy
     strong;
208 The city stood alone, spirit was
     lacking.
209 Hearts alarmed when they heard the
     cranes cry,
210 Tears running down as they listened
     to the Hsiung-nu flute,
211 They lost their halberds fighting   After repeated defeats of its
     at Shen-t'ing,   armies,
212 Abandoned their horses on the way
     to Heng-chiang,
213 Crumbled like the sand of Chü-lu,   Chien-k'ang fell.
214 Broke up like the tiles at Ch'ang-
     p'ing.

---

215 Cassia Forest was laid waste,   The slaughter of the defenders.
216 Long Isle stripped of its deer,
217 Turbulent, boiling,
218 Disordered, chaotic,
219 Heaven and earth were cut off
     from us;
220 Spirits and men vented their
     wrath.

晉鄭靡依
魯衛不睦
兢動天關
爭迴地軸
225　探雀鷇而未飽
待熊蹯而詎熟
乃有
車側郭門
筋懸廟屋
鬼同曹社之謀
230　人有秦庭之哭
爾乃
假刻璽於關塞
稱使者之酬對
逢鄂坂之譏嫌
值耏門之徵稅
235　乘白馬而不前
策青騾而轉礙
吹落葉之扁舟
飄長風於上游
彼鋸牙而中鈎
240　又窺江而習流
排青龍之戰艦
鬥飛燕之船樓

221 Chin and Cheng refused to help;   The Liang princes, instead
222 Lu and Wei were not in harmony.   of uniting against the rebels,
223 They struggled to move the gate   fought one another for the
       of heaven,   throne.
224 Fought to turn the axis of the
       earth.
225 He hunted for young sparrows,   Hou Ching starved Emperor
       without satisfying his hunger;   Wu to death.
226 Waited for bear's paws, but no
       one would cook them.
227 Then chariots were buried by the
       outer gate;
228 One was hung by the tendons from
       the roof of the temple.
229 Ghosts planned as at the altar   The Liang dynasty was
       of Ts'ao;   threatened with destruction.
230 Men mourned as in the court of
       Ch'in.

---

231 At the passes I pretended of-   On the pretext of an official
       ficial business,   mission, the author left the
232 When challenged claimed to be   capital, but he found the over-
       an envoy.   land route impassable.
233 I was greeted with slander as
       at O-pan
234 And forced to pay taxes as at
       Erh's Gate.
235 Riding a white horse, I made no
       progress;
236 Whipping a black mule, I still
       was held back.

---

237 Blown in a little boat like a   The author then tried to
       fallen leaf,   sail up the Yangtze.
238 I was driven by the far-ranging
       wind toward the upper reaches.
239 Those saw-teeth and hook-claws   Hou Ching had launched a
240 Were patrolling the Yangtze pre-   campaign up the Yangtze
       paring for war.   against Hsiao Yi,
241 He marshalled his Green Dragon   who sent down his own forces
       warships,   to meet those of Hou.
242 Sent into battle his Flying
       Swallow towered craft.

張遼臨於赤壁
王濬下於巴丘
245 乍風驚而射火
或箭重而回舟
未辨聲於黃蓋
已先沈於杜侯
落帆黃鶴之浦
250 藏船鸚鵡之洲
路已分於湘漢
星猶看於斗牛

若乃

陰陵失路
釣臺斜趣
255 望赤岸而沾衣
艤烏江而不渡
雷池柵浦
鵲陵焚戍
旅舍無煙
260 巢禽火樹
謂荊衡之杞梓
庶江漢之可恃
淮海維揚
三千餘里
265 過漂渚而寄食
託蘆中而渡水
屆於七澤

243 Chang Liao came down to the Red
        Cliff;
244 Wang Chün sailed down to Pa-ch'iu.
245 Now, wind rising, they shot fire
        arrows;
246 Now, lopsided with arrows, the
        ships had to turn round.
247 Huang Kai's voice had not been   The Liang casualties.
        recognized;
248 Marquis Tu had already gone under.
249 I lowered my sail by the Yellow   The author stopped for a
        Crane bank   time in Chiang-hsia,
250 And hid my boat by Parrot Island.
251 Though I had reached the astro-   still concerned about events
        logical region of the Hsiang   in the capital.
        and Han,
252 Among the stars I still sought
        out the Dipper and Cowherd.

---

253 He lost his way at Yin-ling,   Hou Ching's flight down the
254 Took a detour at Tiao-t'ai;   Yangtze (?)
255 When he looked toward Ch'ih-an,
        tears wet his clothes;
256 With a boat waiting on the Wu-
        chiang, he did not cross.
257 He walled the bank at Lei-ch'ih,
258 Burned his camp at Ch'üeh-ling.
259 There was no smoke over the inn;
260 The birds had no trees left to
        nest in.

---

261 I thought him the best timber of   The author decided to join
        Ching and Heng;   Hsiao Yi in Chiang-ling.
262 Surely the Lord of Yangtze and
        Han could be trusted!
263 From Yang-chou, bounded by Huai The journey to Chiang-ling
        and ocean,
264 I traveled some three thousand *li*.
265 On the bank of the Li, I begged
        for my food,
266 Waited in the reeds to cross the
        river,
267 Traveled through all the seven
        marshes,

濱於十死
嗟天保之未定

270 見繁憂之方始
本不達於危行
又無情於祿仕
謬掌衛於中軍
濫尸丞於御史

信

275 生世等於龍門
辭親同於河洛
奉立身之遺訓
受成書之顧託
昔三世而無慙

280 今七葉而始落
泣風雨於梁山
惟枯魚之銜索
入欹斜之小徑
掩蓬藋之荒扉

285 就汀洲之杜若
待蘆葦之單衣

於是

268 Walked on the brink of a dozen
       deaths.
269 Grieved that the protection of   He soon realized that even
       heaven had not been secured,   greater disasters lay ahead for
270 I saw that our great sorrows had   the Liang.
       only begun.
271 Though incapable of lofty action,   Hsiao Yi made him General
272 And without all desire for   of the Right Guard and Vice
       salaried office,   Censor-in-Chief.
273 I was undeservedly put in charge
       of the guard in the central
       army
274 And negligently allowed to assist
       in the Board of Censors.

---

275 My birth had been similar to   Yü Hsin, like Ssu-ma Ch'ien,
       that at Lung-men;   was born in a *kuei-ssu* year;
276 My parting with my father was   Yü Chien-wu, like Ssu-ma T'an,
       like that at Loyang.   died in a *hsin-wei* year.
277 His last wish was that I make   Chien-wu's deathbed commands
       something of myself;   were also comparable to those of
278 Dying, he entrusted me with the   Ssu-ma T'an.
       completion of his book.
279 Before me, three generations had   The author, calling himself
       caused no shame;   the unworthy descendant of
280 Now I, in the seventh generation,   a distinguished family,
       was the first to decline.
281 I wept at the wind and rain on   grieved at the death of
       Liang-shan,   his father.
282 And thought of the dried fish
       hanging by a thread.

---

283 I went into a little winding   The author went into retirement
       pathway   for the period of mourning.
284 And closed my overgrown gate
       of straw.
285 I would go to the sweet pollia   He intended then to avoid
       on the little islet,   office for the rest of his life.
286 To await an unlined garment of
       rushes.

西楚霸王

劍及繁陽

鏖兵金匱

校戰玉堂

蒼鷹赤雀

鐵軸牙檣

沈白馬而誓衆

負黃龍而渡江

海潮迎艦

江萍送王

戎車屯於石城

戈船掩於淮泗

諸侯則鄭伯前驅

盟主則荀罃暮至

剗巢燻穴

奔魑走魅

埋長狄於駒門

斬蚩尤於中冀

然腹為燈

飲頸為器

直虹貫壘

長星屬地

昔之虎踞龍盤

加以黃旗紫氣

筧不

287 Then the Hegemon King of Western Ch'u   Hsiao Yi acted to save his dynasty.

288 Stretched out his sword as far as Fan-yang.

289 He directed his troops from among metal-bound caskets   He issued commands to his generals from the new capital at Chiang-ling.

290 And matched them in battle from marble halls:

291 Gray Eagles and Red Birds,   The ships of the navy

292 With iron prows and ivory masts.

293 Drowning a white horse, he addressed the army;   Offering a sacrifice to the gods of the Yangtze, he sent out his army. The gods responded favorably, as was shown by the omens accompanying Wang Seng-pien's navy as it sailed down the Yangtze.

294 Borne up by a yellow dragon, he crossed the river.

295 The tide from the ocean came to meet the warships;

296 The *p'ing* plants of the Yangtze escorted the King.

---

297 War chariots formed ranks at Shih-ch'eng;   The Liang army attacked Chien-k'ang, and the Northern Ch'i attacked Hou Ching from the north.

298 Spear-ships covered the Huai and the Ssu.

299 Among the feudal lords, the Earl of Cheng hurried ahead;

300 For the leader of the covenant, Hsün Ying arrived at dusk.

301 They cut up their nests, smoked them out of their lairs,   The rebels were driven out of the capital.

302 Drove away the *ch'ih*, chased out the *mei*.

303 The giant Ti was buried at the Chü Gate;   Hou Ching was killed; his corpse was eaten by the people of Chien-k'ang, and his skull was lacquered and placed in the arsenal.

304 Ch'ih-yu was beheaded at Chung-chi.

305 They burned his stomach for a lamp

306 And used his skull as a drinking vessel.

307 A straight rainbow pierced the ramparts;   The capital had been retaken,

308 A comet struck the ground.

309 The old crouching tigers and coiling dragons,   but it lay in ruins.

310 The yellow banners and purple clouds,

隨狐兔而窟穴

與風塵而殄瘁

西瞻博望

北臨玄圃

315 　月榭風臺

池平樹古

倚弓於玉女窗扉

繫馬於鳳凰樓柱

仁壽之鏡徒懸

320 　茂陵之書空聚

若夫

立德立言

謨明寅亮

聲超於繫表

道高於河上

325 　更不遇於浮丘

遂無言於師曠

以愛子而託人

知兩陵而誰望

非無北闕之兵

330 　猶有雲臺之仗

311 Had been riddled with burrows of
       foxes and hares,
312 And swept away by the wind-blown
       dust.

---

313 Toward the west in the Broadview   The rebels had quartered their
       Park,   troops in the palaces of Hsiao
314 To the north in the Hanging Gar-   Kang (Emperor Chien-wen).
       dens,
315 Moon-viewing towers and breeze-
       swept terraces,
316 Lakes now stagnant, trees grown
       old.
317 They had propped bows against
       Jade-girl windows
318 And tied horses to columns of the
       Phoenix Hall.
319 Useless to have hung the mirror   Hsiao Kang had been murdered.
       of longevity;
320 Pointless to have gathered the
       books of Mao-ling!

       Emperor Chien-wen   Hsiao Kang had been a worthy
321 Is remembered for his virtues as   assistant to his father, Emperor
       for his words;   Wu
322 He was wise in counsel, reverent
       in service.
323 His speech went beyond the con-   Despite his interest in Taoism,
       tingent;
324 His Tao was loftier than that of
       Ho-shang,
325 But he neither met Fu-ch'iu Kung   he had failed to achieve
326 Nor spoke to Music-Master K'uang.   immortality.
327 He had entrusted his beloved sons   Most of his sons had also been
       to others;   killed, leaving almost no one
328 Though knowing of the western   to mourn him.
       mound, who was there to look
       toward it?
329 However, we were not without   Despite this disaster, there still
       weapons in the north gate-   were loyal troops capable of
       tower;   avenging him and restoring the
330 There still were the arms of   dynasty.
       Cloud Terrace

司徒之表裏經綸

狐偃之惟王寶勤

橫琱戈而對霸主

執金鼓而問賊臣

335　平吳之功　壯於杜元凱

王室是賴　深於溫太真

始則地名全節

終則山稱枉人

南陽校書　去之已遠

340　上蔡逐獵　知之何晚

鎮北之

　負譽矜前

　風飇凜然

　水神遄箭

　山靈見鞭

是以

345　蟄熊傷馬

　浮蛟沒船

　才子拚命

　俱非百年

中宗之

　夷凶靖亂

350　大雪冤恥

331 The Premier restored order within   They were led by Wang
     and without;   Seng-pien,
332 Like Hu Yen, he strove for the
     King.
333 Grasping an engraved axe, he   who recaptured the lost
     confronted the hegemon;   territory
334 Holding a bronze drum, he   and put down Hou Ching's
     questioned the rebel.   rebellion.
335 His accomplishment in pacifying   He thus performed an un-
     Wu was more heroic than Tu   paralleled service for the
     Yü's;   Liang.
336 His service to the royal house
     was greater than Wen Ch'iao's.
337 Where earlier the place name Total   Despite this, he was murdered
     Devotion would describe him,   in a coup by Ch'en Pa-hsien.
338 In the end the mountain Innocent
     Victim might apply.

-----

339 His collating texts at Nan-yang
     had ended long ago;
340 The hunting at Shang-ts'ai, he
     appreciated only too late.

     The Defender of the North   Hsiao Lun, Emperor Wu's
341 Was confident of praise, proud   sixth son,
     of his origins,
342 Fierce and forbidding.
343 The gods of the water had en-   by his conduct had offended
     countered his arrows;   the gods,
344 The spirits of the mountains had
     suffered from his whip.
     And therefore
345 A hibernating bear injured his   who avenged themselves on
     horse;   him:
346 Roving dragons sank his ships.
347 His able sons shared his fate: he and his sons all died
348 None of them died a natural death. violently.

     The Restoring Ancestor,   Hsiao Yi (Emperor Yüan),
349 Having wiped out the evil and   after putting down Hou Ching's
     put down the rebellion,   rebellion,
350 Largely blotting out our shame,

去代邱而承基
遷唐郊而纂祀
久舊章於司隸
歸餘風於正始
355　沈猜則方逞其欲
藏疾則自矜於己
天下之事沒焉
諸侯之心搖矣

既而

齊交北絕
360　秦患西起
況背關而懷楚
異端委而開吳
驅綠林之散卒
拒驪山之叛徒

365　營單梁滋
蒐乘巴渝
問諸淫昏之鬼
求諸厭劾之巫
荊門遭廩延之戮
370　夏口濫逯泉之誅
篾因親以教愛
忍和樂於彎弧

351 Left the Palace of Tai to suc-   took the throne.
      ceed to the throne;
352 Went from the outskirts of T'ang
      to continue the sacrifices.
353 Though he restored the ancient   He had restored the dynasty,
      institutions of the Governor
      of the Capital
354 And brought back the customs of
      the Cheng-shih period,
355 Sunk in suspicion, he followed   but his own nature made
      only his own desires;   his fall inevitable.
356 Concealing his faults, he prided
      himself on his accomplishments.
357 The business of the empire came   He found himself at war with
      to nought;   enemies in his own state
358 The hearts of the feudal lords
      were shaken.
      And in the end
359 The relations with Ch'i were   and with the Northern Ch'i
      broken off in the North,
360 And the enmity of Ch'in developed   and Western Wei.
      in the West.

---

361 Worse, since he turned his back   He made Chiang-ling his
      on the Pass and longed for   capital,
      Ch'u;
362 He differed from T'ai-po, who   instead of returning to the
      founded Wu.   better-defended Chien-k'ang.
363 He sent out the scattering   He defended himself with
      soldiers of Green Wood   weak armies against numerous
364 To hold off the rebel conscripts   rebels,
      of Black Mountain,
365 Camped his army by the bridge on   such as his nephew Hsiao Ch'a
      the Cha,   in Hupeh
366 Inspected his chariots in Pa and   and his brother Chi in
      Yü;   Szechwan.
367 Questioned a dark, unclean spirit,   He even resorted to sorcery
368 Sought out an exorcising shaman,   against Chi.
369 Killed one at Ching-men as at   His forces killed Chi and
      Lin-yen,
370 Executed another at Hsia-k'ou as   drove Hsiao Lun to his death
      at K'uei-ch'üan.   at Western Wei hands.
371 He scorned teaching love by means   Hsiao Yi was thus guilty of
      of his relatives,   fratricide.
372 Cast out fraternal feeling in
      drawing back his bow.

既無謀於肉食

非所望於論都

375 未深思於五難

先自擅於二端

登陽城而避險

臥砥柱而求安

既言多於忌刻

380 賣志勇於刑殘

但坐觀於時變

本無情於急難

地惟黑子

城猶彈丸

385 其怨則黷

其盟則寒

豈寇禽之能塞海

非愚叟之可移山

況以

沴氣霄浮

390 妖精夜隕

赤鳥則三朝夾日

蒼雲則七重圍軫

亡吳之歲既窮

373 Since the meat-eaters were in-   Despite the proven weakness
      capable of planning,   of Chiang-ling, he still refused
374 The choice of capital was not   to return to Chien-k'ang.
      what one would have wished.

---

375 Before thinking deeply about the   His very decision to seek
      five difficulties,   the throne had been unwise,
376 He had decided on treachery,   and he had obtained it through
377 Thus avoiding the heights by   treason.
      climbing Yang-ch'eng,
378 Seeking security by lying on
      Ti-chu.
379 His words full of envy and am-   He had been too busy killing
      bition,   his relatives to offer any
380 His will bent on killing and   significant help to the besieged
      destruction.   capital at Chien-k'ang.
381 He had sat back and watched the
      course of events,
382 Not wanting to help in diffi-
      culties.
383 Now, territory reduced to a wart,   Now, the Liang much weakened,
384 With a fortress like a crossbow
      pellet,
385 His enemies bitter,   with enemies everywhere,
386 His alliances cold,
387 This vengeful bird could fill up   he was in a hopeless
      no sea;   situation.
388 This simple old man could move
      no mountains.

---

389 Baleful vapors rose up in dark-   Emperor Yüan was doomed to
      ness;   destruction,
390 Ominous stars fell in the night.
391 Red birds for three days sur-
      rounded the sun;
392 Dark clouds formed seven circles
      around the constellation Chen.
393 The time for the destruction of   and now the time had come.
      Wu had run out;
394 The year of the entry into Ying
      had come.

入郢之年斯盡
395　周含鄭怒
楚結秦冤
有南風之不競
值西鄰之責言
　俄而
梯衝亂舞
400　冀馬雲屯
儵秦車於暢轂
戛漢鼓於雷門
下陳倉而連弩
渡臨晉而橫船
　雖復
405　楚有七澤
人稱三戶
箭不麗於六麋
雷無驚於九虎
辭洞庭兮落木
410　去涔陽兮極浦
熾火兮焚旗
貞風兮害蠱
　乃使
玉軸揚灰
龍文折柱
415　下江餘城
長林故營

395 Chou had incurred the wrath of
        Cheng;
396 Ch'u had invited the vengeance
        of Ch'in.
397 Just when our weakness was be-
        trayed by the airs of the South,
398 We met with the reproaches of the
        neighbor to the west.
399 Scaling ladders danced crazily;
400 Horses of Chi gathered like clouds.
401 They built shallow Ch'in chariots,
        with protruding wheel-naves,
402 Beat the Han drum at the Gate of
        Thunder,
403 Lined up crossbowmen below Ch'en-
        ts'ang,
404 Spread out ships as though cross-
        ing at Lin-chin.

Hsiao Yi was confronted by
the combined forces of Hsiao
Ch'a and the Western Wei,
much superior to his own.

---

405 Although Ch'u had seven marshes,
406 And its people had been praised
        in terms of three households,
407 Our arrows could not hit the six
        deer;
408 Our thunder could not frighten
        the nine tigers.
409 I bade farewell to Lake Tung-
        t'ing amid falling leaves,
410 And set out from Ts'en-yang
        for the far shore.
411 Fierce flames burning our
        banners,
412 Wind below — the baleful *Ku*,
413 Would cause scrolls on jade roll-
        ers to be scattered in ashes,
414 And Dragon-Pattern swords to
        hack the pillars.

The Liang had once been a
a mighty nation,

but it was now no match
for the Western Wei.

Realizing this, Emperor
Yüan sent Yü Hsin to seek peace
with the Western Wei. The mission
was doomed to failure; Emperor
Yüan would be defeated.

his great library burned,

and his palace destroyed (?).

---

415 In the old fortress of the troops
        from the lower Yangtze,
416 In the former camp of the men of
        Ch'ang-lin,

Chiang-ling was unable to with-
stand the siege.

秣兵走行渡嗚坼地敖帥哭淚

之之穀簇馬雛骨槃祭遊於於拉攢零沸之之涇陘里亭燕

馬什以以而而望偽蘊囚摺批夏秋杙湘秦趙五短槊

拊燒枝之無末臣子蕈夢谷父穽鸇霜泉崩梁毒高里亭隨

思見曼宮河關忠君章雲荒冶硎鷹寃憤城竹水山十長饑

徒未章

420

425

430

435

417 It was useless to think of gag-
     ging their horses before
     feeding them;
418 They had never seen the strata-
     gem of the burning oxen.
419 Ch'ih-chang Man-chih fled with   Some fled, foreseeing the outcome.
     wheel-naves cut down;
420 Kung Chih-ch'i went away with
     all his family.
421 Their horses crossed over, with
     no ice on the river;
422 Cocks crowed before dawn at the
     pass.
423 But loyal subjects scattered   Others remained, hoping
     their bones;   to save the dynasty.
424 Superior men choked back their
     sobs.

---

425 The Chang-hua Tower became the   They were slaughtered by
     scene of sacrifices;   the attackers.
426 The Yün-meng Park was the site
     of a mock hunt.
427 At Huang-ku was strangled the   The officials were either
     Mo-ao;   killed or taken prisoner.
428 At Yeh-fu were imprisoned the
     generals.
429 They broke and smashed like . . .
430 Attacked and struck down like
     hawks and falcons.
431 A vengeful frost fell in summer;   Nature herself joined in
432 Angry springs boiled up in   the grief of the survivors.
     autumn.
433 Ch'i's wife brought down a wall
     by her sobs;
434 The Ladies of the Hsiang stained
     bamboo with their tears.

---

435 Rivers poisonous as the Ching   Those not killed were
     in Ch'in,   carried off into slavery
436 Mountains high as Ching-hsing   in the North.
     in Chao,
437 Ten *li*, five *li*,
438 Long halts, short halts,
439 Driven by hunger after hiber-
     nating swallows,

440　暗逐流螢
　　　秦中水黑
　　　關上泥青
於時
　　　瓦解冰泮
　　　風飛電散
445　渾然千里
　　　淄澠一亂
　　　雪暗如沙
　　　冰橫似岸
　　　逴赴洛之陸機
450　見離家之王粲
莫不
　　　聞隴水而掩泣
　　　向關山而長歎
況復
　　　君在交河
　　　妾在青波
455　石望夫而逾遠
　　　山望子而逾多
　　　才人之憶代郡
　　　公主之去清河
　　　栩陽亭有離別之賦
460　臨江王有愁思之歌
別有
　　　飄颻武威
　　　羈旅金微

440 Chasing in darkness the darting
        firefly.
441 The water is black in Ch'in;
442 The mud is green on the pass.

_____

    At that time
443 Scattering like tiles, breaking   The misery of the captives
        up like ice   in the desolate North.
444 Wind-whipped, lightning-scattered,
445 Chaos for a thousand _li_:
446 The Tzu and the Sheng were swirl-
        ing together.
447 Snow dark as sand,
448 Ice thrusting out like cliffs.
449 When one met a Lu Chi hurrying   Their longing to return
        to Loyang   home.
450 Or saw a Wang Ts'an parted from
        his family,
451 None of them but wiped his tears
        on hearing the Lung River
452 And heaved long sighs gazing
        toward the passes.

_____

    Even worse with
453 Husband in Chiao-ho,   The situation was even more
454 Wife in Ch'ing-po,   tragic when families had been
455 Turned to stone watching for   broken up.
        husbands now more distant,
456 Climbing mountains to look for
        sons far more numerous.
457 The Palace Woman remembering
        Tai-chün,
458 The Princess now gone from
        Ch'ing-ho,
459 There were _fu_ on parting at the
        Hsü-yang Pavilion,
460 Songs of sorrow by the King of
        Lin-chiang.

_____

    Another,   The author himself, a captive
461 An exile in Wu-wei,   in the North,
462 A wanderer on Chin-wei,

班超生而望返

温序死而思歸

465　李陵之雙鳧永去

蘇武之一雁空飛

若江陵之中否

乃金陵之禍始

雖借人之外力

470　實蕭牆之內起

撥亂之主忽焉

中興之宗不祀

伯兮叔兮

同見戮於猶子

475　荆山鵲飛而玉碎

隨岸蛇生而珠死

鬼火亂於平林

殤魂遊於新市

梁故豐徙

480　楚實秦亡

不有所廢

其何以昌

有媯之後

遂育於姜

485　輸我神器

居為讓王

463   Like Pan Ch'ao, hoped to return   longed to go home alive or
       alive,   even dead,
464   Like Wen Hsü, longed to go home
       even dead.
465   But both Li Ling's ducks were   but could not.
       gone forever;
466   Su Wu's one goose had flown in vain.

---

467   When Chiang-ling was cut off   Emperor Yüan's destruction
       midway,   led to the fall of his dynasty.
468   That began the disaster at Chin-   The Western Wei invasion had
       ling.   only been possible because of
469   Though forces had been brought in   his wars with relatives,
       from outside,   particularly Hsiao Ch'a.
470   It actually originated within the
       enclosure.
471   The order-imposing ruler was cut   Emperor Yüan was killed,
       off suddenly;   and his line was cut off;
472   The restoring monarch received no   at least two of his sons were
       sacrifices: murdered by his nephew
473   Elder and younger   Hsiao Ch'a.
474   Alike were killed by one like a
       son.
475   The magpie flew away on Mount   In this series of wars, Yüan
       Ching, but the jade was   had thrown away the lives
       smashed;   of everyone who might now
476   The snake survived on the bank in   have saved the Liang.
       Sui, but the pearl died.
477   Ghost fires ran wild at P'ing-lin;
478   The spirits of the slain wandered
       at Hsin-shih.

---

479   Feng was now transferred to Liang;   Now, the capital back at
480   Ch'u was in fact wiped out by   Chien-k'ang, and Yüan himself
       Ch'in: dead, the way was cleared for
481   If others had not been removed,   Ch'en Pa-hsien,
482   How could he have risen?
483   This descendant of the Kuei   a trusted official of the Liang,
484   Was indeed nurtured by the Chiang;
485   He took away their sacred vessel   to force a puppet's abdication
486   And left them abdicated rulers.   and found the Ch'en dynasty.

天地之大德曰生
聖人之大寶曰位
用無賴之子弟
490　舉江東而全棄之
惜天下之一家
遭東南之反氣
以鶉首而賜秦
天何為而此醉
　　且夫
495　天道迴旋
生民預焉
余烈祖於西晉
始流播於東川
500　洎余身而七葉
又遭時而北徙
提挈老幼
關河累年
死生契闊
不可問天
　　況復
505　零落將盡
靈光巋然
日窮於紀
歲將復始
510　逼切危慮
端憂暮齒

487 As the greatest gift of heaven
    and earth is life,   The Liang was largely
488 So the greatest treasure of the   responsible for its own fall,
    sage is the throne.
489 By employing worthless upstarts,
490 They took the whole South and
    threw it away.
491 One grieves that the empire,   but the author cannot help
    united in one household,   grieving at the whole course
492 Should have met with rebellion   of events, from Hou Ching's
    in the Southeast,   rebellion through the fall
493 And to have given the Quail's   of Chiang-ling (this grief
    Head to Ch'in —   being the first of his reasons
494 How could God have been so   for writing the 'Lament').
    drunk!

---

495 The heavens move in circles,   Human life moves in cycles.
496 And man joins in them.
497 My illustrious ancestor in the   Yü T'ao had moved south
    Western Chin   at the end of the Western
498 First was driven away to the   Chin (early 4th. century).
    Eastern River.
499 Now with me, in the seventh   The author has now returned
    generation,   to the North.
500 The time had come to return to
    the North.
501 Supporting old and young, I went   The author, in exile in the
502 To spend year after year beyond   North, has in his own sorrow
    passes and rivers;   and homesickness a second
503 Though far away in life and death, reason for writing the
504 One may not question heaven.   'Lament'. The writing is given
    Not even though   particular urgency now by the
505 The rest have almost all withered   fact that most of his friends
    and fallen,   have died and he obviously
506 And, another Ling-kuang, I alone   cannot live much longer.
    remain.

---

507 The sun is entering its last   Writing in the last month
    conjunction;   of the year,
508 The year is about to begin again.
509 Constantly driven by fear and   The author can find no comfort in
    anxiety,   the ancient capital at Ch'ang-an,
510 Grieving in my twilight years,   where even the place-names
                                        mock him.

践長樂之神皋

望宣平之貴里

渭水貫於天門

驪山迴於地市

515 幕府大將軍之愛客

丞相平津侯之待士

見鍾鼎於金張

聞絃歌於許史

豈知

灞陵夜獵   猶是故時將軍

520 咸陽布衣   非獨思歸王子

511　I walk in the sacred precinct
　　　　of Everlasting Joy
512　And gaze toward the noble quarter
　　　　of Universal Peace,
513　Where the Wei River pierces the
　　　　Heavenly Gates,
514　And Mount Li encircles the under-
　　　　ground market.
515　As an honored guest of the Com-
　　　　mandant, the Grand General,
516　Treated with kindness by the Prime
　　　　Minister, the Marquis of P'ing-
　　　　chin,
517　I see bells and cauldrons with
　　　　the Chin and the Chang,
518　And hear strings and song with
　　　　the Hsü and the Shih,
　　　　But how can they know that
519　The one hunting at night below
　　　　Pa-ling still is the General
　　　　of past times,
520　Among the commoners of Hsien-
　　　　yang, not only the Prince
　　　　longs for home?

He is treated with honor
by the highest officials.

and befriended by the
greatest families of the
Northern Chou,

but no one can possibly
understand the extent
of his grief and
homesickness.

4

COMMENTARY

The title of 'The Lament for the South' is taken from the last line of 'The Summons of the Soul' ('Chao hun'): 'O soul, come back! Alas for the Southern Land!'[1] Both the authorship and the purpose of the original 'Summons' were disputed. For our purposes the most appropriate theory is that of the *Ch'u tz'u* compiler Wang Yi (second century A.D.), that 'the Ch'u poet Sung Yü wrote *Chao Hun* in order to summon back the wandering soul of Ch'ü Yüan after he had been banished and was suffering from shock'.[2] By this choice of title, Yü Hsin, a native of Chiang-ling (the ancient capital of Ch'u), can thus suggest the twin themes of his work: his own exile and the fall of a state. With this title he also locates his work firmly in the *sao* tradition.[3]

The year *wu-ch'en* was 548. It was traditionally believed that the direction indicated by the handle of the Dipper (*Ursa Major*) at a fixed time at the beginning of each lunation served as a natural calendar. The twelve directions, each an arc of thirty degrees, were named for the terrestrial branches. In the supposed calendar of the Hsia dynasty, which was prescribed by Confucius[4] and used by the Han and most later dynasties, the year began when the Dipper pointed to *yin* (045°–075°). Therefore, in line 2, *hai* (315°–345°) indicates the tenth month; northwest is an approximation.[5]

Line 3 is quoted from the historian's comment appended to the 'Annals of Emperor Kuang-wu', *Hou-Han shu* IB.33a (Wu). Originally referring to Wang Mang, it had become the classic description of any rebel or usurper. Chin-ling in line 4 was an ancient name of Chien-k'ang, also called Chien-yeh (the modern Nanking). I have supplied the defenders, since scattering like tiles was by Yü Hsin's time a stock metaphor for the collapse of an army; see commentary on lines 213–14 of the *fu* proper.

Huang-ku in line 5 serves as a literary name of Chiang-ling; see line 427 below. The last half of the line says literally, 'Officials and people were in mud and coals', a traditional figure for the suffering caused by bad government. The phrase originates in the *Classic of Documents* (Legge (1), III, 178); the pseudo-K'ung An-kuo, thinking of the more common phrase 'water and fire', takes the coals as live ones and paraphrases as 'fire', *Shang shu* 4.2b.

The Chinese have always found a reference to the 'Tribute of Yü' a convenient and elegant way of dealing with large tracts of geography; line 6 is the first of many in the 'Lament'. Hua-yang ('the south side of Mount Hua') was one of the canonical landmarks of Liang-chou; see Legge (I), III, 119; and Herrmann, p. 4 I BC3. The line tells us nothing of Yü's destination at Ch'ang-an, and almost nothing about his route; he probably followed the traditional one, north from Chiang-ling, along the Han River, and then between the Chin-ling Range and Mount Hua.[6]

In line 8, the Chinese year *chia-hsü* corresponds in the main to 554; Emperor Yüan was killed on January 27, 555, at the end of that year. Since this was the effective end of the Liang (though a puppet lingered on for two years more), the author might appropriately imitate Lo Hsien, who on learning of the abdication of the last ruler of the Three-Kingdoms state of Shu 'wailed for three days in the city hostel'; see P'ei Sung-chih's commentary, *San-kuo chih* 53.3a (Wang).

Line 10 is, as Wu Chao-yi suggested, almost certainly a reference to Shu-sun Ch'o, an ambassador from Lu, who was detained in Chin. The 'three years' is a problem; Yü's normal practice is to be specific about his allusions, but general about their current reference. In other words, the details almost invariably are taken from the allusion sources. That apparently is not true in this case, but it need not concern us here, since Yü clearly means that he, another ambassador, was also detained in a foreign country, though now for the rest of his life.[7]

Line 11 refers to cyclical movements in the heavens, but it is not clear whether the reference is merely to the heavenly bodies in general or specifically to the twelve-year cycle of the Year Star, Jupiter. In the latter case, we would have here a date for the composition of the 'Lament'; I prefer to take the line more generally, for reasons explained in Appendix IV.

Lines 13–14 are the first of several statements of the author's twofold reason for writing the 'Lament': grief at his own misfortunes and at the fall of the Liang. Fu Hsieh was killed in 187 A.D. defending a city against rebels. He had refused an offer of safe-conduct, saying, 'Where should I go? I must die here' (*Hou-Han shu* 58.16a; Wang). Yüan An (d. 92 A.D.) is supposed to have wept every time he went to court out of concern at the plight of the dynasty, *Hou-Han shu* 45.7a (Wang).

Lines 15–20 give precedents for the sort of work Yü has in mind. Unfortunately I have been unable to fit into the translation the critical phrase *tzu hsü* in line 18, which here has its basic sense of autobiography rather than the derived one of author's preface/postface.[8] The autobiographies of Huan T'an (T. Chün-shan) and Tu Yü (T. Yüan-k'ai) have been lost except for fragments quoted in the encyclopedias.[9] P'an Yüeh's poem 'My Family's

Acts' (or 'Mores', 'Chia feng shih') survives, as do two *fu* by Lu Chi on his own family.[10]

In line 21, the phrase 'two hairs' (*erh mao*) gets its meaning of hair turning gray from the *Tso chuan*.[11] P'an Yüeh had applied the phrase to himself at 32 *sui* (*WH* 13.4a); Yü, born in 513, would have been 35 at the outbreak of Hou Ching's rebellion in 548.

Line 23 refers to the song sung by Ching K'o when setting out on his suicidal mission to assassinate the First Emperor (Ch'in Shih-huang); compare *Works* 9.13b: 'Ching K'o set out from the marketplace of Yen, his grief unbearable' (*pei pu tzu sheng*, identical to line 23).[12] The *Yi-wen lei-chü* variant 'river' (*ho*) for 'song' (*ko*) would make the allusion even clearer; I have left the song in, partly because of Yü's constant references to Ching K'o's song (e.g , line 38 of the Preface), and partly because of a line in a farewell poem by Li Po: 'A song of Yen on the bank of the Yi River' (*Yen ko Yi-shui pin*), where Li Po's commentator Wang Ch'i points out the unmistakable allusion to Ching K'o.[13] It is almost certain, but here irrelevant, that Yü Hsin would himself have written farewell poems on his departure for the North.[14]

Similarly, in line 24, the old man from Ch'u was not simply an old friend from home; the reference may seem vague, but this was a famous historical figure. Kung Sheng, a native of Ch'u and an official under the Former Han, was forced to starve himself to death at his home, this being the only way to avoid service under the usurper Wang Wang. 'An old man came to condole. Having wailed with extreme sorrow, he said, "Alas! The fragrant plant gets itself burnt for its fragrance; tallow gets itself burnt for its brightness. Master Kung ended up dying prematurely: he is no follower of mine!" He then hurried out; no one knew who he was', *Han shu* 72.23b (Yeh Shu-ch'ung). In the circumstances, we must infer that the elderly mourner was from Ch'u, but others have already done so. Read in isolation, a Hsieh Ling-yün line could mean either 'The old man from Ch'u grieves at his orchid fragrance' or 'One grieves at the orchid fragrance of the old man from Ch'u.'[15] Another mourning poem, this one by Li Po, removes the ambiguity: 'Like the old man from the state of Ch'u, I come to mourn a Kung Sheng's death.'[16] Line 24, then, means that Yü Hsin, unlike Kung Sheng, had consented to serve two houses, and that the old mourner would shed no tears for him.

In line 25, to fear the rain of South Mountain is to seek to avoid official posts by living in retirement. The reference is to a parable told by a woman who feared that harm would come to her husband, a greedy official:[17]

I have heard that there was a black panther on South Mountain, which during a period of seven days of fog and rain would not go down

to eat. Why? [He was afraid that] his fur would get wet and turn
spotted, so he hid and avoided harm.

Compare a poem by Hsieh T'iao: 'Though of different form from the black
panther, finally I am hiding in the mist of South Mountain.'[18]

Line 26 refers to a group of recluses at the end of the Shang dynasty,
by way of an allusion to Mencius:[19] 'Po Yi fled from Tchou [last king of the
Shang] and settled on the edge of the North Sea . . . T'ai Kung fled from
Tchou and settled on the edge of the East Sea' (*tung hai chih pin*, as in line
26). T'ai-kung went on to become one of the most important ministers of
King Wu of the Chou dynasty, but Po-yi 'loyally refused to eat the grain of
Chou', which had overthrown his own dynasty, and finally starved to death
(*Shih chi* 61.9−10). Yü Hsin, in eating the grain of Chou, contrasts himself
with Po-yi; his reference to the eastern sea, rather than the northern, takes
some of the curse off the allusion. T'ai-kung did after all end up serving the
quite admirable Chou dynasty. The fact that the author wound up in the
service of the Northern Chou is merely a bonus; the allusion would apply
equally well to service under the Western Wei, and he did in fact hold titles
before the forced abdication of that dynasty.[20]

It is possible that the allusions in lines 27−8 have not been correctly
identified, or that the place names are used only for the contrasting *low/high*
(*hsia/kao*). K'ung Sung, stopping over at Hsia-t'ing (not certainly a place name)
on his way to the capital, had his horse stolen; it was later returned (*Hou-
Han shu* 81.16b; Wu). Liang Hung, who is remembered for his plain but
virtuous wife, would appear to have worked as a hired hand at Kao-ch'iao
(*Hou-Han shu* 83.13b−14a). The location of the two places is not significant
in itself; context puts Kao-ch'iao in Wu, and Hsia-t'ing was apparently near
the Latter Han capital of Loyang.

Wine and song would be natural ways to dispel cares; T'ao Ch'ien calls
wine 'this Care Dispelling Thing'.[21] By specifying the places of origin, Yü
eliminates any possible efficacy. Ch'u songs, impromptu compositions like
the Ching K'o song mentioned above in line 23, were notoriously sad. Lu
wine had a bad reputation because of *Chuang tzu* 24/10/14: 'Because the
wine of Lu was thin, Han-tan was besieged.'[22]

In line 32 the *fu* is literally to 'record words', referring to the old tradition
about the ruler's two recorders, one for events, the other for statements
(e.g., *Han shu* 30.8a). Here one would expect 'to record events' (*chi shih*),[23]
since the 'Lament' contains no speeches whatever. Perhaps, as Wang Li suggests,
'words' (*yen*) is used instead for the sake of tonal contrast.

The phrases *wei k'u* and *pei ai* had been paired in Hsi K'ang's 'Rhapsody
on the Lute' ('Ch'in fu', *WH* 18.12b; Wang). In the original they seem

synonymous; von Zach there translates them respectively as 'der melancholische' and 'die traurigen' (p. 250). In lines 33—4, however, they are clearly contrasted; I have followed Wang Li's interpretation.[24]

There is a useful gloss on line 35 in a letter by Yü Hsin's contemporary Wang Pao (Ch'üan Hou-Chou wen 7.1b—2a): 'The sun is setting, my road is long (jih mu t'u yüan): this was why past worthies announced their resignations.'[25] In view of this, and Yü Hsin's constant references to his old age, we are prepared to deal with the extraordinary line 36. It is, first of all, a play on the Chuang tzu chapter title 'The World of Men' ('Jen-chien shih'), but beyond that it can be seen as Yü Hsin's remarkable reworking of the common statement in Chinese prefaces that the author, growing old, cannot postpone the writing of his work. Here, too, we have a contemporary gloss, Hsiao Yi's preface to his Chin lou tzu: 'The world of men is fleeting and brief.'[26]

Line 37 involves a totally reworked allusion. Whenever the other generals were boasting of their victories, Feng Yi would go away and sit alone under a tree; he thus acquired the nickname of 'big tree general' (Hou-Han shu 17.3b; Wu). There is no doubt that this is the reference here; the problem, once again, is one of interpretation. Feng Yi did not 'go away', nor did his trees wither. He had a long, successful career, and was instrumental in establishing the Latter Han. Line 37 becomes much clearer if we compare it with line 409 of the fu itself: 'I bade farewell to Lake Tung-t'ing amid falling leaves.' The latter line is a reference to the author's departure from Chiang-ling on his mission to the Western Wei. Since he left in May, the falling leaves cannot be real ones, but only a metaphor for the great winter ahead for the Liang; the withered tree of line 37 is therefore almost certainly a symbol of the fallen state.

Line 38 is based on Ching K'o's song, already mentioned in line 23: 'The wind's sound is plaintive, the waters of the Yi are cold. Once the hero leaves, he will never return.'[27] The assassin knew that he would be killed; Yü Hsin cannot return because he is not allowed to leave the North.

Lin Hsiang-ju was sent by Chao to carry a jade disc to Ch'in, which had offered fifteen cities in exchange. Realizing that the King of Ch'in had no intention of giving up the cities, he threatened to smash both the disc and his head against a pillar, and thus was able at least to return the disc intact to Chao (Shih chi 81.2—7; Wu).

Mao Sui, an attendant of another Chao emissary, finding a King of Ch'u reluctant to conclude a treaty, climbed the steps of the platform with sword in hand; the frightened King agreed (Shih chi 76.5—7; Wang). The participants in such covenants sealed their oath by smearing their lips with the blood of a sacrificial animal, held in a pearl-ornamented basin.

Chung Yi, from Ch'u, continued to wear his southern cap in confinement in Chin; he is called a gentleman (*chün-tzu*) in the original *Tso chuan* account; Legge (1), V, 371 (Wang). Chi-sun Yi-ju, from Lu, was taken prisoner by Chin. His captors later found his presence inconvenient, but he refused to go back without an official apology. They then threatened to move him to the area west of the Yellow River bend (Hsi ho), even farther from Lu; he returned home without more ado, Legge (1), V, 652, 653 (Wang).

Shen Pao-hsü went to Ch'in to get military help desperately needed by Ch'u; he struck his head on the ground nine times in gratitude when the ruler of Ch'in consented, Legge (1), V, 757 (Kuei Chuang). It is commonly noted that the grammar of line 43 is odd, and that Shen Pao-hsü did not break his head against the ground anyway, though this is obviously what Yü means by the line. He is simply overstating things a little. Wei-kung of Lower (Hsia) Ts'ai once wept for three days and nights, weeping blood after his tears ran dry. Asked why, he replied, 'My state is about to fall.'[28]

Lines 45—6 clearly mean that the author cannot go home again, so it does not matter much that the allusion in line 45 has not been satisfactorily identified; no one has found a source combining the willows, fishing terrace, and Jade Pass. Lu Chi, about to be executed after his defeat at Ho-ch'iao, lamented that he could not again hear the cranes crying at Hua-t'ing ('Flower Pavilion'), where he had lived in his youth.[29]

Sun Ts'e, brother of Sun Ch'üan, starting with an army described as less than a battalion, was able to lay the foundations of the Three Kingdoms state of Wu (*San-kuo chih* 58.9a, 46.17a; Wu, Wang). Hsiang Chi, better known by his *tzu* Yü, the great rival of the founder of the Han, said shortly before his death that he had originally crossed the Yangtze and gone west with eight thousand young men from Chiang-tung (here roughly equivalent to Chiang-nan, 'the South'; *Shih chi* 7.72; Wang).

Lines 55—6 are reminiscent of several earlier passages, particularly Lu Chi's discussion of the fall of Wu (*WH* 53.24b), which Emile Gaspardone translates (p. 207): 'Les forteresses n'eurent plus même la solidité des haies, la montagne et les fleuves n'eurent pas la force de fossés et de tertres.'

Lines 57—8 are quite obscure; I can offer only a tentative interpretation, based on what the context seems to require. All the references are to the fall of Ch'in. The first part of line 57 referred originally to the oppressive taxation under that state, first mentioned by someone urging a rebellion against it (*Shih chi* 89.6; Wang). Later it became a common feature of the denunciation of a state about to be attacked, used by the Sui against the Ch'en (*Ch'üan Sui wen* 16.3b) and later against the Sui itself (*T'ang shu* 53.5a). In other words, the taxes are a cause of rebellion, not a means of raising funds to support one. On the other hand, the second part of line 57 referred originally to the 'vertical alliances' against the Ch'in (Chia Yi's 'Mistakes of Ch'in', quoted in *Shih chi* 6.92; trans. Chavannes, II, 226; Wu). In line 58 we have the opposite sequence, the first half referring to the makeshift weapons used by the rebels against the Ch'in, who had been deprived of arms ('Mistakes of Ch'in', *WH* 51.5a; Chavannes, II, 230; Wu), and the second part to the opportunism of the conquering Ch'in ('Mistakes of Ch'in', *WH* 51.3a; Chavannes, II, 228; Wu). There are two solid points in lines 57–8: the head taxes and the improvised weapons, the former the causes of a rebellion, and the latter the means to carry it out. Lines 55–8 thus seem to mean that however large the armies may have been, the Liang was insufficiently prepared for war, and that through bad government in general (rather than mere taxation) it had lost the hearts of the people.

Fate was also against the Liang. Kuo P'u (276–324) was supposed to have predicted that the splinter states of the South (known later as the Six Dynasties) would be reunited with the North after three hundred years. There is little point in trying to fix an end to this period; we in fact now know of the supposed prediction only because it was quoted in 588 as a guarantee of success on the Sui campaign against the Ch'en, *Sui shu* 57.10b–11a (Wu).

Despite the Ch'in unification of the Empire, described here in terms perhaps borrowed from the 'Mistakes of Ch'in' (*WH* 51.1b, 3b; Wu, Ni), its last ruler was forced to abdicate at Chih-tao (*Shih chi* 6.8b; Wu). The Western Chin was able to unite China by conquering Wu but fell a few years later, two of its emperors being murdered in captivity at P'ing-yang (in 313 and 317; *Chin shu* 5.5a–6b, 5.9b, Wu). Standardized axles and script are established as symbols of a unified empire by the 'Chung yung' (Legge (1), I, 424; Wu); Kan Pao had so described the period following the conquest of Wu (*WH* 49.7a; Hsü).

Falling mountains are a traditional omen (*Kuo yü* 1.10b; Wang) and here a symbol for the fall of a state; the same *Kuo yü* passage provides the additional omen of rivers running dry, used in line 20 of the 'Lament' proper. Line 64 is given additional point by the author's statement in lines 507–8 that he is writing at the end of a year. *Ch'ü ku* is his regular expression for the fall of a dynasty. In line 65 he is almost certainly thinking of Kan Pao's discussion of whether it is the will of heaven (*t'ien yi*) or man's deeds (*jen shih*) that cause the rise and fall of dynasties (*WH* 49.3b; Yang Fu-chi). Yü is fully aware that the Liang did much to bring about its own fall, but whatever the cause may have been, he cannot help mourning the fallen dynasty.

Lines 67–8 indicate in hyperbole the impossibility of returning home. Someone was reported to have succeeded in sailing up the Milky Way (*Po-wu chih* 10.3a–b; Ni), but the winds prevented anyone from reaching P'eng-lai, one of the Islands of the Immortals (*Shih chi* 28.24–5; Kao).

Wang Yin once said, 'When the ancients were born in the right time, they communicated their Tao in their accomplishments; if not, they showed their ability through words' (*yi yen ta ch'i ts'ai, Chin shu* 82.4a; Wang). Yü was perhaps thinking of this remark, but line 69 does not require it. Line 70 seems to have been a popular saying; it appears, for example, in the commentary on the *Kung-yang chuan* by Ho Hsiu (129–182, *Ch'un-ch'iu Kung-yang ching-chuan chieh-ku* 7.15b).

Lu Chi is reported to have clapped his hands and laughed on hearing that Tso Ssu, a Northerner, was presuming to write a rhapsody on the three metropolises (*Chin shu* 92.5a–b; Wang). Chang Heng is said to have found Pan Ku's 'Rhapsody on the Two Capitals' crude (*Yi-wen lei chü* 61.3b–4a; Wu). As a modest author, Yü Hsin can expect no more favorable reaction from his readers.

Ch'ü Yüan began the 'Li sao' with the briefest of genealogies: 'Scion of the High Lord Kao Yang, Po Yung was my father's name' (Hawkes (1), p. 22). The passage, not very noticeable in itself, was made conspicuous by its placement, and later *fu*-writers have commonly marked their indebtedness to the Ch'ü Yüan tradition by opening their works with an account of their own family history. Such things are generally a good deal longer than their model; the corresponding section of the 'Lament' is lines 1–40. The reader may find the genealogy in Appendix VII useful in reading this part.

Line 1 explains the origin of the clan-name Yü ('granary') as a reward for generations of service in the same official post, as prescribed in the *Tso chuan*; see Legge (1), V, 25, 26b. Line 2 is apparently a reference to Yü Meng, the earliest known ancestor, who was an Imperial Secretary, one of the Three Lords (*san kung*); the line is based on the 'Officials of the Chou' chapter of the *Classic of Documents*: 'These are the Three Lords; by discussing the Way they govern the state' (cf. Legge (1), III, 527). To 'discuss the Way' is thus, by definition, to be one of the Three Lords. Lines 1–2 are prosodically interesting. Each is a double line, with a four-word topic and a six-word comment. Such double lines were standard features of sixth-century parallel prose, such as the Preface to the 'Lament', but rather uncommon in a *fu* itself.[30]

The geography of lines 3–6 should not be taken too literally; the place names serve only to locate the original family home in the 'Tribute of Yü' province of Yü-chou, the most 'central' of the nine provinces.[31] Hsin-yeh was a long way from all the places mentioned. The family were fostered by jade, and so on, because of the geomantic influence of a region on its inhabitants.

After the fall of the Western Chin to barbarians in the Yung-chia period (307–13), five princes of the imperial family managed to survive in the South, and one of them, known posthumously as Emperor Yüan, restored the dynasty in a new capital at Chien-k'ang. This was supposed to have been predicted in a 'boys' song': 'Five horses [*ma*] will swim across the Yangtze, one horse will turn into a dragon' (*Chin shu* 6.8b; Wu). The horses are a play on the imperial surname Ssu-ma, and the dragon is, of course, an Emperor. Also, in 312, Mars, Jupiter, and Venus were said to have gathered together between the Cowherd and the Weaving Girl, auguring the rise of an Emperor in the Wu-Yüeh region (*Chin shu* 6.8b, Wu; trans. in Ho Peng Yoke, p. 177).

The seemingly concrete statement in lines 15–16 is only metaphorical. Yü T'ao, who fled south to join Emperor Yüan, was moving *away* from Hsin-yeh, so this cannot be the Nan-yang *chün* in which Hsin-yeh was located. The reference is to the Chou grant of the lands of Nan-yang to Chin (Legge (1), V, 196a, 660a; Wang); that Nan-yang was along the Yellow River, far away from Yü T'ao's fief in Chekiang. According to the *Kung-yang Commentary*, the feudal lords all had bathing and hair-washing fiefs at the foot of Mount T'ai, for use when accompanying the King there.[32]

Chiang-ling, the ancient capital of Ch'u, would have been a plausible site for the home of Sung Yü; he is, however, one of the most shadowy of all Chinese authors, and I know of no surviving source earlier than this passage that specifically states the fact.[33] It seems likely, in view of Yü Hsin's normal practice, that he means only that Yü T'ao moved to Chiang-ling, not that the new home was on the actual site of a third-century B.C. residence of Sung Yü, or on that of the palace of the third- and second-century B.C. Kings of Lin-chiang, who had their capital at Chiang-ling.[34]

According to Five Element theory, the Sung (420–79) and Ch'i (479–502) dynasties were governed by water and wood respectively (*Nan shih* 4.18a, 76.7b; Wu). Water and wood thus symbolize the two dynasties, and in line 20, mountains falling and rivers running dry symbolize their fall; see commentary on line 63 of the Preface.

Lines 25–6 refer to a branch of the family which remained in the North after T'ao's flight south; Yü Hsin was not directly descended from them but could still claim them as distinguished relatives. T'ao's oldest son Hui was said to have been honored with a shrine erected during his lifetime by the grateful people of Hsin-yeh, the old Yü family home, where he was Prefect (*t'ai-shou*; see *Yüan-ho hsing tsuan* 6.20a). Kao-yün, a grandson of Yü Hui, was Military Governor (*tz'u-shih*) of Ch'ing-chou, in modern Shantung; the Ch'iang erected a monument to him (*Yüan-ho hsing-tsuan* 6.20a). There had been a large displacement of Ti and Ch'iang, the latter proto-Tibetans, into Hopeh, Shantung, etc., during the fourth century A.D. (Michael C. Rogers, pp. 24, 90 n. 140); Kao-yün, a great grandson of Yü T'ao, can hardly have lived earlier than the end of that century.

Lines 27–32 deal with the author's grandfather Yü Yi (d. after 499), a

recluse. *Shao-wei* in line 27, also called the Recluse (*Ch'u shih*), is a group of
four stars supposed to govern the destiny of the scholar; cf. Ho Peng Yoke,
p. 94. 'True man' is a common term for the Taoist adept. Line 28, for 'hexagram', says literally 'heaven and mountain'; the recluse hexagram in the *Yi
ching* is composed of two trigrams, one symbolizing heaven, the other,
mountains (*Chou yi yin te* 21/33). The phrase 'heaven and mountain' became
a cliché for the recluse (e.g. *Ch'üan Liang wen* 13.11a10).

Lines 29–30 are equally conventional. The deserted valley is not merely
rustic, it is a suitable setting for a recluse, because of an occurrence in *Songs*
186, which was believed by the commentators Mao and Cheng Hsüan to refer
to the ruler's failure to bring good men into official service (*Mao Shih Cheng
chien* 11.5a; Wu). The traditional way to do that was to send out a padded
(i.e. comfortable) carriage to convey them to the capital; someone actually
proposed using one to fetch Yü Yi, according to *Nan shih* 50.13b (Ni).

Line 31 is not about a conversation beneath a tree ('he moved beneath
a tree to talk');[35] the syntax rules that out, as does the parallel with line 32.
Literally, the two lines say, 'Coming to speak, he talked of trees; Turning
to writing materials, he wrote on bamboo.' This being the case, all we need is
a conversation about a tree which would be appropriate for a Taoist recluse.
The most obvious would be one of the many *Chuang tzu* parables about
trees so useless that there was no point in cutting them down (for example,
Watson (3), pp. 63–6, 209). These are probably the most famous trees in
Chinese literature, and they are also perfect symbols for the life of the
recluse.

Lines 33–40 deal with the author's father Chien-wu; oddly enough,
there is no rhyme-change either before or after them. One would ordinarily
expect a change of rhyme with a new subject in a *fu*. Yü Hsin singles out his
father's years of service of Hsiao Kang, Crown Prince from 531 to 549
(line 35),[36] and also, apparently, the two much shorter periods under Hsiao
Yi (line 36). Wu Chao-yi takes the 'bank of the Chang' as a reference to the
city of Yeh, capital of the Three Kingdoms Wei and later of the Eastern Wei;
in that case, line 36 would mean that Chien-wu found in the Hsiao a family
of imperial patrons of literature comparable to the Ts'ao of the Three Kingdoms Wei. This would make sense, and it is true that the phrase 'bank of the
Chang' does generally refer to Yeh (for example, in *Works* 11.12a), but in
that case lines 35 and 36 would be rather redundant. I am inclined to suspect
that Yü is here reworking the cliché, and that this Chang is not the one that
flows past Yeh but one of the four great rivers of Ch'u (two others being
the Yangtze and Han) mentioned in a famous passage of the *Tso chuan*, Legge
(1), V, 810b. Hsiao Yi appears in the 'Lament' most often as ruler of Ch'u, and
commonly in connection with the Yangtze and Han, as in lines 57 and 262.[37]

Confucius is said to have found omens of his own misfortune in the failure of phoenixes to appear, and in the injury done to a unicorn; the latter event was the reason for his abandoning work on the *Spring and Autumn Annals*, according to the *Kung-yang Commentary* (Legge (1), I, 219; V, 833–5).

With line 41, the author turns to his own life, the first section of which is given largely in terms of a series of official posts; these are discussed in more detail in Appendix II. Line 41, perhaps taken from a grave inscription by Shen Yüeh (*WH* 59.16a; Wu Chao-ch'ien), is based ultimately on Juan Chi's statement that the Prince, or *Wang-tzu*, Ch'iao at 15 *sui* wandered on the banks of the Yi and Lo Rivers, in the area of Loyang.[38] There has been a long controversy over lines 41 and 42, centered on the question whether Lan-ch'eng in the latter was in fact a nickname for Yü Hsin. If not, one would have to take both lines as merely introductory: 'At the age when . . . And when Lan-ch'eng . . . I first . . .' The evidence for the nickname is shaky, but that for Yü Hsin's holding an official position at 15 *sui* (as this would require) nonexistent. On the other hand, there were government examinations under the Liang, and Yü is recorded as having taken one; hence my translation.[39]

A Han emperor is said to have given an elderly attendant cloves to hold in his mouth as a remedy for bad breath; the unfortunate man thought he was being poisoned, *Ch'üan Hou-Han wen* 34.13a (Kao). Later it became the custom for Secretaries in the Imperial Secretariat (*shang-shu lang*) to sweeten their breath and report for duty inside the Chien-li Gate, *Pei-t'ang shu-ch'ao* 60.10b (Ni). Line 43 apparently refers to the author's post as Senior Secretary of the Bureau of Public Revenue in the Imperial Secretariat (*shang-shu tu-chih lang-chung*), though this is by no means the first office he held. The Ch'ung-hsien Gate, depending on which commentator one follows, was either an east gate of the imperial palace or a gate of the Crown Prince's palace (*WH* 26.20b, Ni). The latter seems more likely; in that case, line 44 would indicate the author's service as a Scholar under Hsiao Kang. For *jeng* in the sense of 'then', compare *Works* 13.38b9, where a Chinese is first given a title and then (*jeng*) a foreign surname.

In lines 45 and 46 I have paraphrased two tags from the *Yi ching*, both descriptions of the structure of hexagrams. Hexagram 51 is composed of two identical trigrams, each symbolizing thunder, the hexagram is thus described as 'doubled thunder' (*chien lei, Chou yi yin-te* 31/51). Hexagram 30 is likewise composed of two identical trigrams, in this case symbols of brightness; the *Yi ching* therefore says, 'Brightness repeated forms [the hexagram] Li' (*ming liang tso li, Chou yi yin-te* 19/30; Wu). Both tags were firmly associated with the Crown Prince.[40] Beginning with line 45, the author turns from specific posts to his general activities at the capital. Like most of the Liang

ruling family, the first Crown Prince, Hsiao T'ung (501–31), and his successor
Kang were fond of lecturing; the latter is probably intended here. Lines 47–8
are the obligatory modest disclaimers, two clichés also combined in *Han shu*
65.18a (Wang). Here, as usual when confronted with the commonplace, Yü
rejuvenates it, in this case with the extraordinary word-order, which is ap-
proximated in the translation. It would be more natural to transpose the
second and fifth words of each line, and most natural of all simply to say
'dipping out the sea with a gourd/And peering at the sky through a tube'
(as in *Works* 1.7a, where the order of the lines is reversed).

Lines 49 and 50 probably contain unidentified allusions.[41] The lines are
perfectly parallel as they stand, but a lesser writer would surely have paired
the 'square' and 'round'.

Lines 51 and 52 may refer to specific posts, but it is simpler to take them
as a general reference to civil and military positions, announcing the subject
of the new rhyme to follow. Such use of the last couplet before a rhyme-
change is characteristic of Yü; compare lines 319–20, 329–30, and 423–4.

Line 53 is self-deprecatory; it means, in effect, 'The Emperor forgave me
my crimes and allowed me entrance to the palace.' The phrasing is derived
from a defense of a man faced with possible punishment, *Han shu* 70.14b
(Wu). Writing about someone else, with no need for modesty, Yü simply
says, 'He was inscribed in the lists of the two palaces [those of the Emperor
and Crown Prince]', *Works* 15.49b.

In line 56, *tien wu* is an old play on the surname Ssu-ma, *San-kuo chih*
42.16b (Wu); *tien* and *Ssu* are synonymous, and the horse (*ma*) corresponds
to the terrestrial branch *wu*. The word 'horse' is added; Lan-ch'ih could be
the name of a palace (Wu), but *Shih tzu* B.18a mentions a Lan-ch'ih horse.
That would fit the context better and make a better parallel with the war
chariot of line 55.

The Lord of Yangtze and Han was Hsiao Yi, or Emperor Yüan, who
appears here in his normal guise of ruler of Ch'u. The Yangtze and Han are
'Tribute of Yü' landmarks of Ching-chou (Legge (1), III, 113), which was
more or less synonymous with Ch'u. Yü Hsin was reportedly sent to discuss
naval warfare with him during a rebellion, apparently the minor one in 542
(see Yü-wen Yu's Preface 7a).

Line 58 says literally 'to wipe jade', a ritual prescribed for ambassadors
(*Yi-li* 49b, Wu). By Yü's time, the phrase had become a standard expression
for an embassy (*Works* 11.3b1 and *Ch'üan Ch'en wen* 9.8a3). This line,
despite the general agreement among commentators, cannot refer to Yü's
embassy to the Eastern Wei. Hsi ho ('West River', the section of the Yellow
River where it flows south, before turning to the east near the Han-ku Pass)
was the eastern boundary of Yung-chou in the 'Tribute of Yü', Legge (1),

III, 123. As Yangtze and Han in line 57 stood for Ching-chou, so Hsi ho here stands for Yung-chou, roughly equivalent to Shensi and Kansu. The Eastern Wei never held any of Yung-chou,[42] and their arch enemies of the Western Wei/Northern Chou would not have forgiven Yü Hsin for such an implication. Yü-wen Yu, the Northern Chou Prince of T'eng, mentions Yü's trip to the Eastern Wei only grudgingly, as a mission to 'Wei territory' (Preface 7b4). Later in the same preface (13b1–2), Yü-wen Yu accidentally provides the key to line 58: Yü Hsin was particularly well known to Yü-wen T'ai, dictator of the Western Wei, having 'repeatedly come on embassies' (*lü p'in*) to that state. Line 58 obviously refers to these embassies, which must have been diplomatic feelers of some sort. It is not surprising that they are not mentioned in Yü's biographies, since this double-dealing would certainly have been kept a secret from Emperor Wu's long-term allies of the Eastern Wei.[43]

Caps and carriages are symbols of officials, and Tsou and Lu in line 62 were the birthplaces of Mencius and Confucius respectively.

With line 63, compare Tso Ssu's 'Rhapsody on the Wu Capital', which mentions almost in the same breath the 'lush garden of Long Isle' (Ch'ang-chou) and the 'red grain of Hai-ling', the latter so abundant that it had been allowed to rot (*WH* 5.12b; von Zach, p. 62). The lush garden would be self-explanatory, but Yü is probably thinking specifically of Long Isle, which appears below in line 216 as a symbol of Chien-k'ang. Line 64 says, in effect, 'Manhattan stretches from the East River to the Hudson.' The Restraining Dike, originally built by the Three Kingdoms Wu, ran along the Ch'in-huai south of Chien-k'ang; it was rebuilt by the Liang in 510 (*Liang shu* 2.11b, 2.20a; Wu). The Yangtze, of course, passes to the north of Nanking, or Chien-k'ang.

Lines 65–6, of more extended scope, still avoid the awkward question of the northern boundary of the Liang. The First Emperor (Ch'in Shih-huang) is said to have hoped to build a bridge across the ocean in order to go to see where the sun rose; he was assisted by a god who could drive the stones down to the sea, whipping them to make them go faster.[44] The Latter Han general Ma Yüan in 43 A.D. set up two bronze pillars in the present Vietnam, to mark the southern boundary of the Han (*Shui ching chu* 36.30b, Wang).

Ssu-ma Ch'ien says that the possessor of a thousand tangerine trees in one area, or of a thousand *mou* of bamboos in another, is the equivalent of a marquis over a thousand households (*Shih chi* 129.31–2, Wu). There was supposed to be a floating jade mountain west of the Western Ocean (*Shih-yi chi* 1.9a, Wang), and 'sinking feathers' were said to have been presented as tribute in the time of Yao.[45] The latter were probably arrows that would pierce as far as the stabilizing feathers, but the exact meaning is irrelevant. No one in the Liang ever saw either floating jade or sinking feathers; Yü

has chosen them simply because these two names suggest the most exotic
of tribute, and do so more economically than the long catalogue an earlier
fu-writer would have provided.[46] The same thing is true of the bamboos and
tangerines. Ssu-ma Hsiang-ju had been criticized for crediting his Shang-lin
Park with plants that could never have survived in the northern climate.[47]
Almost anything would thrive somewhere in the Liang territory, but Yü,
with great restraint, limits himself to two plants.

Lines 71–2 are taken in reversed order from Tso Ssu's 'Rhapsody on the
Wu Capital' (*WH* 5.24a, Wu).

Emperor Wu founded the Liang in 502, and Hou Ching rebelled in 548.
The fifty years is a round number, and lines 75–6 involve a little exaggeration.
There had been war with the Northern Wei in the first two decades, and some
rebellions after that, but in retrospect the period must have seemed idyllic.

Wang Hsi, Wang Mang's envoy to the Hsiung-nu, was made Marquis of
Friendly Relations (*Ho-ch'in hou*; *Han shu* 94B.15a, Wang). Pan Ch'ao, the
great Latter Han general, was made Marquis Who Pacified Distant Regions
(*Ting-yüan hou*) in 51 A.D. (*Hou-Han shu* 47.15a, Wu). In some texts, the
lines read, 'Pan Ch'ao was Marquis Who Pacified Distant Regions; Wang Hsi
was envoy of friendly relations.'[48] I have followed Ni's text, which moderates
the martial ring of *ting-yüan* and removes it from the context of a famous
general; the whole point of the passage is that the Liang did not make war.

Ma Wu urged Emperor Kuang-wu of the Latter Han to attack the Hsiung-
nu; the Emperor, uncertain of the outcome, refused consent (*Hou-Han shu*
18.23a–24b, Wang). Emperor Wen of the Former Han, however, was delighted
at Feng T'ang's frank assessment of contemporary generals (*Shih chi* 102.12–
17, Wu).

In line 81, the parallel requires taking *jan* as a full word 'burn' rather than
a particle; *an-jan* 'dark' would not make much sense. Lines 83–4 are metaphors
for Hou Ching. Ch'en She, originator of the rebellion which destroyed the
Ch'in, had begun as the leader of conscripts chosen from 'the left side of
town' to garrison Yü-yang (*Shih chi* 6.74, 48.3; Wang). Line 84 is taken from
Kan Pao's description of Liu Yüan (*WH* 49.9a, Wu), a Hsiung-nu who held
important military positions under the Western Chin but rebelled and founded
his own dynasty (*Chin shu* 101.1a–6a). As Ch'ü Shui-yüan says, Liu Yüan
is particularly like Hou Ching, even in his non-Chinese origins.

Lines 85–90 deal with Emperor Wu's scholarly activities. Such things were
considered a proper pursuit for an Emperor, though Confucians would object
to the attention Wu gave to Buddhist questions. The passage is especially
interesting for lines 89–90, where two favorite Buddhist subjects are manipulated
to suggest imminent doom. Line 85 is a common phrase referring to Confucius's
supposed selection of some three hundred songs out of three thousand to

make up the *Classic of Songs*, and similar editing of the *Classic of Documents*. Line 86 was equally traditional; the preface to the 'Li sao' has a passage identical to lines 85–6, except for *cheng*[a] instead of *ting* in the second line (*Ch'u tz'u* 1.49b). Emperor Wu lectured on Buddhist subjects in the Ch'ung-yün Hall (*tien*); he established the Shih-lin Academy (*kuan*) in 542 (*Liang shu* 3.37b, *Nan shih* 7.10b; Wu).

Line 89 refers to a popular Buddhist story, found, for example, in *Sou-shen chi* (1), p. 98 (Kao). The excavators of the Han Emperor Wu's K'un-ming Lake, having reached a great depth, came upon ashes and burnt earth. This curious fact was later explained by Buddhists in the time of Emperor Ming of the Latter Han as a result of one of the periodic destructions of the world at the end of each *kalpa* (Chin. *chieh*). There was a good deal of controversy about the date of the Buddha's birth, but some feeling that it must have a connection with the extraordinary events of the seventh year of Duke Chuang of Lu (686 B.C.) According to the *Tso chuan* account, 'The fixed stars were not visible, because the night was so bright.' Later, 'the stars fell like rain' (cf. Legge (1), V, 79, 80; Wu).

The context, which indicates that lines 91–2 must deal with the military weakness of the Liang, is particularly helpful in line 92. 'Fishes' Teeth' appears in the *Tso chuan* as the name of a mountain, Legge (1), V, 479b (Wang); *Lü-shih ch'un-ch'iu* 20.14b mentions the appropriateness of animal horns as walls. The two objects make an ideal pair, and Yü has turned his sources upside down in order to avoid using more conventional metaphors. In line 91 he may not have had the oddly-named mountain in mind, but in line 92 he was almost certainly thinking of the *Lü-shih ch'un-ch'iu* passage, and reasoning that animal horns, however admirable for defense, are sometimes shed. Compare the *Classic of Documents*: 'His people stand in trembling awe of him, as if the horns were falling from their heads.'[49]

The alarm gongs in line 93 were used as cooking pots by soldiers during the daytime, and at night by the watch; the line seems based on the third-century commentator Meng K'ang's statement that 'the *tiao-tou* are now in the Hsing-yang storehouse', *Han shu* 54.2b (Wu). In line 94 the horses are literally dragons' go-betweens, an old name for the celestial horses of the Han, so called because, as the next thing to dragons, they heralded the coming of the latter, *Han shu* 22.21a (Wang). The P'ing-lo stable appears in *Han shu* 17.8a (Kao).

The Chief Minister in line 95 is Chu Yi, cast by the historians as the bad minister who destroys a dynasty, but mentioned in the 'Lament' only in passing. The word-games of line 96 are literally pure conversation, an art much cultivated in the Six Dynasties.

King Chao of the Chou was supposed to have drowned after the breakup of a boat held together only by glue, which had been supplied to him by a vengeful boatman.[50] Line 98 is based on the 'Songs of the Five Sons': 'I should feel as much anxiety as if I were driving six horses with rotten reins', Legge (1), III, 158 (Wu). Both 'leaking-in' and 'runaway' are what one might call anticipatory verbs, announcing the results to be expected from a glued-together boat or rotten reins. Such usage is unusual; most if not all of the many variants for 'leaking-in' in line 97 are probably emendations by editors less imaginative than Yü Hsin himself.[51]

Fire and water is a common metaphor for the suffering of the people, for example Legge (1), II, 274 (Wang); compare line 5 of the Preface. According to legend, during a southern campaign of King Mu of the Chou, 'the whole army were transformed. The gentlemen became apes and cranes; the commoners (*hsiao jen*) became insects and sand.'[52]

Lines 101—2, suggesting the ultimate futility, are taken with slight modifications from a work by K'ung Jung, *Ch'üan Hou-Han wen* 83.11b (Wang). Glue from Tung-o actually was used to clarify water (Morohashi, 41599/40), though it could not cope with the Yellow River.

In lines 103—10 the author has collected traditional omens of disaster for a state. Line 103 is taken from *Shih ching* 10: 'The bream has a red tail; the Royal House is as if burning.' Karlgren (2), p. 7, explains: 'The bream in danger lashes its tail until it becomes bloody — symbolical of great danger and distress.' Line 104, referring to enemy camps, comes from the *Record of Rites*, where it is followed by 'This is the fault of the ministers and great officers' (*Li chi cheng-yi* 3.7a, Wu).

Wild birds in human habitations have been ominous at least since Chia Yi's 'Owl'; seagulls and pheasants appear as omens in *Sung shu* 68.6a (Wang). The departure of the magic sword Chan-lu for Ch'u was a sign of the imminent fall of Wu (*Wu-Yüeh ch'un-ch'iu* A.34b—35a, Wu). Wu also lost its ship Yü-huang in battle with the Ch'u forces, who drained away the surrounding water to leave it aground, Legge (1), V, 668b (Wang). Someone had made the prophecy in line 110 on seeing a man with unbound hair sacrificing in the countryside, since 'the rites are already lost', Legge (1), V, 182 (Wang). The above section is not historical narrative, of course; the author is simply indicating the approaching disaster.

Line 111 begins the account of the rebel Hou Ching. As Hu Wei-sheng points out, Hou Ching had betrayed the Eastern Wei and been rebuffed by the Western Wei before offering allegiance to the Liang; he hardly inspired confidence. Line 112 quotes a tag from the *Yi ching* (*Chou yi yin-te* 40/ *Hsi shang*/4, Ni). Like much in that book, the original line is ambiguous, but it could be taken to mean 'the wandering ghost rebels'. 'Wandering ghost' thus became, in the right context, a stock phrase for a rebel, applied again and again to Hou Ching, for example in *Ch'üan Liang wen* 22.3b2.

The creatures in line 113 are glossed as male and female whales; I have supplied the shark to balance line 114. Tu Yü explains a *Tso chuan* reference to whales (Hsüan, 12) as 'metaphors for unrighteous men, who gobble up small states'.[53] The owl and the *ching* were said to eat their parents; the idea here is that of killing an emperor, by convention the father of his subjects. Whales were stock figures for Hou Ching, as in *Ch'üan Liang wen* 22.3b1 and *Ch'üan Ch'en wen* 8.1b3; so were the owl and *ching*, for example in *Ch'üan Ch'en wen* 7.1b1.

As the reader will have gathered by now, the 'Lament' is marked by constant use of metaphors. Some of them, such as those in lines 112–14, were by Yü Hsin's time almost the inevitable ones; others, for example lines 169–70 and 223–4, are original enough to require a good deal of thought. Lines 117–18 would fall somewhere in between. They are by no means obvious, but the context, and the ancient idea that the Son of Heaven had magical power over the cosmos, enable us to recognize a reference to the activities of the emperor. According to *Erh-ya* B.6a (Wang), 'When the ethers of the four seasons are in harmony, it is called the jade lamp.' The phrase quite early became a metaphor for the ruler; Li Hsün, of the Latter Han, says, 'The virtue of the ruler is as beautiful as jade and as bright as a lamp.'[54] Having accepted the abdication of Yao, Shun is supposed to have used the *hsüan-chi* to control the movement of the celestial bodies.[55] Both the jade lamp and the *hsüan-chi* here are symbols of rule; compare lines 223–4, which have similar references to the emperor's power to control the heavens.

In lines 119–20 the author continues his tactful treatment of Emperor Wu; he is certainly the subject of the lines, but it is not stated in so many words. Line 120 refers to the traditional 'loose reins' policy of the Chinese toward neighboring states, the classic example being the Hsiung-nu.

Line 121 is problematic; let us postpone discussion of it temporarily. Line 122 is a clear reference to a *Tso chuan* passage where the Jung presented tiger and leopard pelts (*hu pao chih p'i*) to Chin and asked for peace, Legge (1), V, 424a (Wang).[56] Wu Chao-yi suggests a similar allusion for line 121, the *Han shu* 94B.5b–6b account of an oath to seal a treaty between the Shan-yü, ruler of the Hsiung-nu, and Han envoys. The critical section of the text is probably corrupt; as explained by Ying Shao, it says that, having killed a white horse, the Shan-yü 'with a *ching-lu* knife cut up a golden rice-scoop [*liu-li*[a]] and stirred it into the wine . . .' and he and the envoys 'drank a blood-draught oath together'.[57] Yü Hsin knew this story (*Works* 13.30a), and it would do nicely as a reference for line 121; Emperor Wu would then

be agreeing to a treaty with the barbarian Hou Ching. The only problem is
one of orthography, the *liu-li*[b] of line 121 normally means glass, a common
tribute article under the Liang (*Liang shu* 54.21a1), and Yü Hsin elsewhere
uses the phrase in the sense of glass (*Works* 5.18a, 8.2a). However, what is
in question here is the wine itself, not the vessel containing it. I prefer therefore to take the *liu-li*[b] in line 121, for which there is apparently no variant,
as a phonetic borrowing for the at least nearly homophonous *liu-li*[a] of the
Han shu, possibly a corruption replacing a very obscure word with a common
one.

Lines 123–4 mean that Hou Ching, and the additional territory he offered,
were treated as valuable foreign commodities, like the bamboo canes from
Szechwan that Chang Ch'ien noted with interest in Ta-hsia (*Shih chi* 123.16
Wu) or the ostrich eggs from T'iao-chih (*Shih chi* 123.12, Wu), admired as
much in China then as they later would be in Europe.[58]

A ruler of Ch'u is supposed to have asked the weight of the nine cauldrons,
the symbols of Chou rule. He was told that his question was premature, and
that the Chou was not destined to fall just yet, Legge (1), V, 293 (Wu). To
'ask about the cauldrons' became a standard figure for rebellion. A ruler of
Ch'in with similar designs on the Chou once said that he would like to have
a road wide enough for a chariot reaching to the three rivers (around the
Chou capital at Loyang), so that he might peer in at the Chou house (*Shih
chi* 71.9; cf. *Chan-kuo ts'e* 1.30–31; Wu). The object of his proposed peering
is made clear in Chia Yi's 'Mistakes of Ch'in', which opens with a similar
phrase.[59]

Lines 129–32 refer to Hsiao Cheng-te, Emperor Wu's nephew (biography
in *Liang shu* 55.7b–9a). The future emperor, lacking male offspring, had
adopted Cheng-te as his heir but later made an actual son crown prince.
Cheng-te's resultant bitterness eventually led him to make a secret alliance
with Hou Ching, who was then plotting to rebel. Hou set up Cheng-te as a
rival emperor temporarily during the attack on the capital, but later deposed
and killed him. Line 129 presents Cheng-te in the guise of a prince who had
in 648 B.C. called in the Jung to attack the Chou capital, Legge (1), V, 158
(Wang). Line 130 would apply to Hou Ching, but it probably means Cheng-
te, who remains the subject of lines 131–2; Cheng-te joined his army to Hou's
during the attack on Chien-k'ang.

The nature of the leak in line 132 is a problem. The phrase 'model words',
taken from the *Shu ching* (Legge (1), III, 572), indicates the words of the
ruler or high government officials – official secrets, in short.[60] Hu Wei-
sheng is probably right in taking the leaked secret to be the news of a peace
treaty between the Eastern Wei and the Liang, ending the war over Hou
Ching's territory and presumably also sealing his fate. Hou himself complained

in a denunciation of the Liang that the Emperor had 'believed the lying letter' proposing the treaty and agreed to peace (*Ch'üan Liang wen* 70.3a1). According to one anecdote, Hou learned of the treaty as a result of interrogation of an envoy foolish enough to pass through the city Hou controlled. The anecdote sounds suspect, whatever the truth of the matter, Yü himself, unable to read seventh-century histories of the Liang, might reasonably believe that Cheng-te, suddenly revealed as a traitor, had all along been providing information to Hou Ching.

Lines 133–4, once the allusions are identified, would be perfectly intelligible as they stand: Hou Ching was frightened into rebelling. However, the lines are enriched considerably if one realizes that they are almost certainly deliberate echoes of an earlier writer's predictions about Hou Ching. When Hou first went over to the Liang, the Eastern Wei had warned his new rulers not to trust a recent convert like him; he might very easily rebel against the Liang too:

> He is sure,
> Eyeing the Minister of Justice in the distance, not to be
>   willing to remain a subject;
> Possessed of Huai-nan, likewise to want to style himself Emperor.

The above, part of a much longer piece, is quoted in the *Tzu-chih t'ung-chien*, p. 4966 (Wu), and Hu San-hsing identifies the allusions. The first line refers to Su Chün, who set himself up as a local warlord in the North after the fall of the Western Chin and finally fled south to the Eastern Chin, where he was made a general. Once again growing fearful of his new masters' intentions, he refused to obey summonses to court. Criticized by an imperial envoy, he replied, 'Your Excellency has said that I want to rebel. [Now that I am under such suspicion,] how can I survive? Better for me to watch the Minister of Justice from the mountain top than to look toward the mountain top from [the custody of] the Minister of Justice' (*Chin shu* 100.14b).

The second line, Yü's line 134, refers to Ying Pu, also called Ch'ing Pu (d. 196 B.C.), a general who abandoned Hsiang Yü to go over to the founder of the Han (*Shih chi* 91.1–19; Watson (6), I, 196–207). For his services he was made King of Huai-nan, but he too was eventually frightened into rebellion and killed. There was much duplication of allusions in sixth-century writings, but it would be a remarkable coincidence for Yü to arrive independently at the same obscure pair to describe the same man; it is simpler to take lines 133–4 as an announcement of the fulfilment of the Eastern Wei prophecy. Such writings were read for their literary value, and lines 339–40 below are a similar echo of a letter threatening Wang Seng-pien, the subject of the lines.

Lines 133–6 are all noun phrases in the original ('a fugitive criminal

who ..., a desperate bandit who ...'); I have made sentences out of them.
Lines 135–40 list omens. According to *Chin shu* 28.19a (Wu), in 307 A.D.
the ground caved in near Loyang, at the site of the ancient Ti-ch'üan. Two
geese emerged, one white, the other slate-gray. The gray one flew up into the
sky; the white one remained on earth. It was explained that white was the
color of metal, the element governing the Chin, and that gray symbolized the
barbarians. The interpreter refused to go on; no further explanation is
necessary if one recalls the subsequent destruction of the Western Chin. There
is an unidentified allusion in line 136, but the meaning is clear anyway;
it is proverbial in China, as elsewhere, that a cornered animal will turn and
fight. There were also many popular stories of large drum-shaped stones which
would sound as an omen of war; *Chin shu* 29.5b (Wu) mentions one which
gave the warning for Wu, the region around Chien-k'ang.

The Metal Star in line 138 is Venus, which governed warfare. *Tung* could
perhaps mean simply 'move', but it sounds like the technical term for
scintillation, generally a bad omen; movement is normally called *hsing* (Ho
Peng Yoke, pp. 40, 21). *Shih chi* 27.53 gives one case of a glittering Venus
signalling warfare. There are unidentified allusions in lines 139–40; the roar,
or song, of a dragon, though extraordinary, is not usually ominous.[61] According to *Huai-nan tzu* 3.2a (Wang), 'When unicorns fight, the sun and moon
are eclipsed.' This sounds alarming enough, but we still need some explanation
of the east mound; as Kuei suggests, the reference is almost certainly to a
story about stone unicorns at an imperial tomb (*ling*).

The Han had fought their endless wars against the Hsiung-nu on foreign
soil, in Mongolia; now the situation was reversed, with a foreigner attacking
the Chinese capital. In 18 B.C., Yang Hsiung submitted a memorial to the
throne, recounting the prolonged warfare against the Hsiung-nu, and asking
rhetorically, 'Was it because former rulers enjoyed spending immeasurable
sums and conscripting innocent men, because they were eager for the land
north of Lang-wang?' He replies that this was the only way to gain lasting
peace, and thus they were willing 'to transport the wealth of the treasuries
to fill up the gorges of Lu-shan' (*Han shu* 94B.16a, Wang). The Yellow
Map is one of the capital area, and Red Region was the fanciful name assigned
to China in the cosmology of Tsou Yen.[62]

Hou Ching, having requested brocade, had been supplied by the Liang
government with a quantity of green cloth to make robes for his troops.
He therefore made green his ceremonial color. During the attack he himself
wore green robes and rode a white horse with green silk reins, supposedly
because of a prophetic boys' song: 'Green silk and white horse come from
Shou-yang' (*Nan shih* 80.7a, Wang).

There is probably a missing allusion in line 147. Nothing in the records indicates that Emperor Wu did not hold court on New Year's Day, the most important occasion of the year. The day in question would have been February 13, 549; the city did not fall until April of that year. The New Year's court in Yü's time would normally be cancelled whenever some major disaster (a famine, the death of a high official, etc.) made such festivities inappropriate. Perhaps Yü has something of the sort in mind here, though the line does not seem to have been literally true in 549.

Line 148 suggests the Shan-yü Mo-tu's siege of Han Kao-tsu at Po-teng in Shensi in 200 B.C. (*Shih chi* 110.26), though I know of no reference to the Shan-yü's amusements in the Han case. The barbarian Shan-yü, ruler of the Hsiung-nu, is here the barbarian Hou Ching; the fact that Hou aspired to be emperor seems of doubtful relevance. The twin towers and thousand gates are set phrases for the imperial palace.

White rainbows are among the most commonly reported omens; as the *Chin shu* says, 'The white "rainbow" [which Ho defines as a parhelic circle] is the root of all calamities and the source of all chaotic events' (trans. Ho Peng Yoke, pp. 146, 164). There are records of white rainbows during the Liang, but it hardly matters. The events in lines 151–2 had been omens of the murders of high officials, *Chan-kuo ts'e* 3.27 (Wang). According to the *Shih chi* (trans. Chavannes, I, 169–70), Chieh, the evil last ruler of the Hsia, imprisoned the founder of the Shang in the Hsia-t'ai. Several early sources have Shun imprisoning Yao at Yao-ch'eng; the story, which shows the existence of other, less edifying versions of the ancient legends, is quite appropriate for Yü Hsin's purposes.[63]

Lines 155–6 evidently refer to the fratricidal warfare among the Liang princes; because of it, only limited help was available from the provinces. Line 155, an example of Yü's remarkable syntax, is based on a *Tso chuan* passage; cf. Legge (1), V, 193b (Wang): A Chou king, having fled to Cheng, sent a messenger to Lu to ask for help. Someone at that court said, 'Can we presume not to hurry to report to the officers?' (*Kan pu pen wen kuan-shou*). The officers are the rulers of the feudal states; the report was in fact sent to Ch'in and Chin, and Duke Wen of Chin rose to prominence as a result of his subsequent actions. We may note in passing that the Chou king is the regular symbol in the 'Lament' for any Liang Emperor (because of geography, Hsiao Yi often appears as ruler of Ch'u), and the feudal lords (*chu hou*) normally symbolize the Liang princes.

T'ao K'an (257–332) once appropriated government grain-transport ships (*yün ch'uan*) to put down a rebellion, *Chin shu* 66.4b.[64] Ku Jung was able to disperse the army of another rebel by signalling with a feather fan, *Chin shu* 68.2a7. The rice ships and feather fan are merely symbols of whatever means are used to put down a rebellion, and we need not search Liang history for specific references to either.

Line 159 was a common saying:[65] 'A general will die rather than retreat. He may advance a foot, but he will not withdraw an inch.' Line 161 is unlikely to mean merely that the great sweeps used to raise signal fires were lowered at dawn. The author would hardly stoop to such banality, and anyway for him *lo hsing* means 'falling stars', as in line 90 of the 'Lament' and *Works* 12.15a: 'When a unicorn perishes, the stars fall. When the moon dies, the pearl is afflicted.' If we have falling stars, an omen of war (Ho Peng Yoke, p. 137), we need a comparable signal. Some sort of pyrotechnic device would be ideal, but the sixth century seems a little early.

Hsiao Kang is reported to have tried to get a message out of the besieged city by attaching it to a paper kite, which the rebels shot down (*Nan shih* 80.12a, Wang). Given such an obvious reference for line 162, it is perhaps ungrateful to propose that the story fits the line almost too well, and may have been fabricated to explain it. Yü seldom refers specifically to such minor events, but no convincing alternative explanation suggests itself. Lines 161–2 clearly do indicate the impossibility of getting word out of the city.

The initial attempts to raise the siege met with disaster; two examples are given in lines 173–84 below. Line 163 refers to the dismemberment of Han and Chao by Ch'in in the third century B.C. The phrase seems to have been a stock figure for a disastrous defeat. A memorial written by Yü Hsin for someone else expresses a hope to 'partition Han and split up Chao' (*fen Han lieh Chao*, *Works* 7.14b), and a contemporary letter makes the same threat with enough additional detail to enable us to identify at least one of the battles involved, that at Ch'ang-p'ing in 259 B.C., ending in the supposed massacre of 400,000 Chao troops. See the commentary on line 214 below.

Line 164 gives standard symbols of defeat. Lines 165–6 contain *Tso chuan* references; two ancient generals had been able to tell that an enemy had retreated by listening in the night to separated horses whinnying at one another and examining the confused tracks left by chariots (Legge (1), V, 478b, 86a; Wang).

Lines 169–70 restate lines 167–8 in metaphor; I have supplied the 'as if'. Elephants make an appropriate metaphor for the warrior; despite their use of elephants, Wang Mang's army had been routed at the battle of K'un-yang in 23 A.D. (*Hou-Han shu* 1A.5a1, Wu). The cunning snake was a natural symbol for a strategist; the snake of Ch'ang-shan, which, when attacked at the head, would strike with its tail, and vice versa, had in fact been Sun tzu's metaphor for an able general (*Sun tzu* C.22b, Wang). Finally, the four lines introduce the hunting metaphor for war, one of Yü Hsin's favorite devices, which reappears in lines 216, 239, 301, 407–8, and 426. Both creatures were common prey for the hunters in earlier rhapsodies, for example Tso Ssu's 'Rhapsody on the Wu Capital': 'They butcher the snake of Pa' (*WH* 5.20a), and Chang Heng's 'Rhapsody on the Western Capital': 'They trunk [i.e. seize by the trunk] the red elephant' (*WH* 2.21a).

As Kao Pu-ying says, lines 171–2 are a general statement about the suffering of the people during the rebellion, and one should not take the numbers too literally. *Sou-shen chi* (2) 4.6a, pointed out by Kao, quotes a story of five men from different commanderies who had lost their families, apparently in the warfare at the end of the Han or in the Three Kingdoms period, and who joined together as brothers. A similar story, quoted in *T'ai-ping kuang-chi* 161.4b (Chang Ying), deals with three men from different Chin provinces who agreed that one of them should be treated as a father by the other two.

Line 173 opens a series of brief sketches of the men most important in the defense of the capital. Wei Ts'an, who was given the posthumous title of Protecting General, had been a major organizer of the first attempt to relieve Chien-k'ang. Shortly after his arrival there, he was killed in an attack by Hou Ching, together with a son, three brothers, and several hundred relatives (*Liang shu* 43.4b–5a, Wu). Wei Ts'an's only other recorded son was later killed by his own soldiers (*Liang shu* 43.5a7). Wei was of a distinguished family; both his grandfather Jui (442–520, *Liang shu* 12.4b–12a) and his father Fang (*Liang shu* 28.13b–15b) had been generals. A third-generation general was proverbially courting disaster (e.g., *Shih chi* 73.18–19, Wang); Wei Ts'an's fate would fully justify such a belief.

Chiang Tzu-yi, a native of Chi-yang *chün* in Honan (identified in line 177 by the toponym), was killed along with two brothers in a suicidal attack on Hou Ching undertaken to redeem himself after an earlier defeat (*Liang shu* 43.5a–6b, cf. *Tzu-chih t'ung-chien*, p. 4990). Chiang Tzu-yi had held the military position of *jung-chao chiang-chün*, a title not listed in des Rotours or the *Shih t'ung* index; we are probably safe in assuming that it was not an important one (line 178). Line 181, expressing the common belief that it is the duty of the subject to die to avenge his lord's disgrace, comes from *Shih chi* 41.25 (Wang). Line 183 refers to the *Tso chuan* story of Hsien Chen, who, to make amends for an earlier offense, took off his helmet and made a suicidal attack on the Ti barbarians (Legge (1), V, 225b–226a; Wu). The Ti returned his head; Hou Ching likewise was moved by Chiang's actions to return his body. The three armies is a standard term for a great army, for example in Legge (1), I, 198.

Yang K'an, the Minister of Justice (*tu-kuan shang-shu*), was an Eastern Wei general who had gone over to the Liang in 537 (*Liang shu* 39.5b–12b,

Nan shih 63.9a–13b, Wu). The author treats his death of an illness, on
January 20, 549, as ending all hope of effective defense. Lines 189–90
still await satisfactory explanation, but we can tell that *wo ch'iang* in the
latter line almost certainly means 'to topple a wall', not, as Ni Fan would
have us believe, 'to build a wall while ill'. Ni took the line as a reference to
a non-Chinese general who erected a wall shortly before his death, during
the internal warfare in the North after the fall of the Western Chin. Yü
Hsin does not seem to have been much interested in barbarians fighting
among themselves, at least not in such a late and unclassical source. The
only allusions to non-Chinese in the 'Lament' concern their contacts with
the Chinese, such as the murder of two Chin emperors by the barbarians
(Preface, line 63), the Ti in line 183, the flight of Fu Chien's troops after the
battle of the Fei River (line 209), and so on. There is a useful gloss on
lines 189–90 in a *fu* by Emperor Yüan of the Liang (Hsiao Yi): 'Duplicating
the reduction of the Ch'i army's fires, Imitating the toppling of the Yen
hosts's walls', where the first line refers to Sun Pin's trick of lighting fewer
fires each night to suggest large-scale desertion from his army.[66] Yü Hsin
himself substituted a later general's variation on Sun's ruse in a couplet
probably inspired by Emperor Yüan's lines (*Works* 9.5a): 'Sometimes
increasing the Ch'i fires, On occasion toppling the Yen walls.' The unidentified
allusion in lines 189–90 apparently involves a Ch'i general able to capture a
city in Yen; whatever the allusion, the lines must mean that if Yang K'an
had survived, Chien-k'ang would not have fallen.

Line 192 is taken from *Shih ching* 264. In the original *wang* may mean
'to flee', as interpreted by Karlgren (2), p. 237, following Cheng Hsüan:
'When people flee the country, the state is exhausted and distressed.' However, the line was commonly quoted with reference to a death, as by P'an
Yüeh (*WH* 20.9a–b) and Yü Hsin himself (*Works* 14.43a, 14.54b).

Lines 193–202 are believed to refer to the Liang general Liu Chung-li,
largely on the basis of *Hsiao ming lu* B.13b: 'Liu Chung-li was called Shen-
tzu as a child; thus Yü Hsin's "Lament for the South" says . . .' A passage
from the same work (not found in present editions) was the authority for
taking Lan-ch'eng in line 42 as a name for Yü Hsin. Here the reasoning is
circular; at most, this source may indicate a common view at the time of the
author, Lu Kuei-meng, who died in 881. We are not likely to improve on
this identification now; Yü has gone to some lengths to conceal the man's
name, the *Spring and Autumn Annals* way of condemning a character.
All that we can really tell is that the passage describes a military man who
suffered a major defeat, and whose resultant disgrace was serious enough
to wipe out a long, distinguished career. That could apply to Liu Chung-li,
though the sources for his life are poor and often contradictory.[67]

At the time of Hou Ching's rebellion, Liu had already earned enough
distinction as a general to be chosen Commander-in-Chief of the armies
attempting to raise the siege. On February 14, 549, learning of Hou's attack
on his first cousin Wei Ts'an (lines 173–6), Liu led a hundred cavalrymen
against the rebel. Despite initial success, he was badly wounded and escaped
with his life only because someone came to his aid (*Tzu-chih t'ung-chien*,
pp. 5000–1). This was, according to the histories, the only occasion when
he raised arms against Hou Ching; he thereafter shut himself up in his fortified
camp and refused to venture out, despite all the entreaties of the other
Liang generals. At one point, we are told, his father reviled him from the
walls of the besieged city, without effect (*Tzu-chih t'ung-chien*, p. 5008).
After the fall of the city, like all the other important Liang generals on the
scene (including Wang Seng-pien), he surrendered to Hou Ching. Emperor
Yüan later saw fit to give him a new command, and he finally died, apparently
in captivity, after a defeat by the Western Wei.

Line 195 is archaizing; for this sense of *shih* cf. *Shih ching* 300. *Yüan jung*
also occurs in the *Shih ching*, but there with the meaning of 'great war chariots',
Karlgren (2), pp. 120–1. Line 196 is a set phrase; it occurs in *Chin shu*
62.4a5 (Wu), and also in the *Liang shu* 43.6a9 description of Chiang Tzu-yi's
ill-fated sortie, lines 177–84.

Line 197 alludes to the *Tso chuan* story of a Duke of Lu, defeated in
battle, who lost his helmet to the enemy; the latter hung it on their Fish
Gate, Legge (1), V, 183a (Wang). Elsewhere, Yü Hsin says of a victorious
general, 'At his gate hung many helmets' (*Works* 14.38a5). The horse-watering
spring was by this time more or less synonymous with the battlefield; the
phrase originated in the ballads to the title 'Watering Horses at the Spring by
the Great Wall'.[68]

The *locus classicus* of *t'ung chung* in line 199 is in a description of Han
Kao-tsu's most serious wounds (*Shih chi* 8.59 commentary, Wang). Yü
seems to have associated the phrase with Kao-tsu's general Ts'ao Ts'an; a
couplet in *Works* 14.9b5–6 combines the same two allusions as in lines
199–200 and identifies the subjects. Ts'ao Ts'an is reported to have borne
the scars of seventy wounds, Watson (6), I, 128, but they are not described
as *t'ung chung*. *San-kuo chih* 36.2b–3a describes Kuan Yü's composure
when it became necessary to lay bare a bone and scrape it to remove poison
from an old arrow wound (Wu).

K'ang-ts'ang tzu 10a says that a quail dressed up in falcon's wings would
only deceive someone with poor eyesight (line 203, Lu). There was also a
famous parable about a fox which was able to convince a simple-minded tiger
that when the two walked together, the other animals were running away
from the fox, *Chan-kuo ts'e* 2.15–16 (Wang). Retreating after the battle

of the Fei River, the army of Fu Chien heard the wind and the cranes and concluded that the Chin troops were overtaking them, *Chin shu* 114.7b (Wang); Rogers, p. 170. A Chin general, besieged by the Hsiung-nu, played a Hsiung-nu flute to make them homesick; the enemy raised the siege and withdrew, *Chin shu* 62.7b (Wu).

Lines 211–14 revivify old clichés for the fall of an army by adding references to historical events; the prose sense of the passage is, 'They lost their halberds, abandoned their horses, crumbled like sand, broke up like tiles.' T'ai-shih Tz'u lost his halberd in combat with Sun Ts'e at a site made clear by Sun's later remark: 'Do you remember the time at Shen-t'ing? What if you had captured me then?' *San-kuo chih* 46.10a (Wu). Line 212 may refer to another story about Sun Ts'e, who once was struck by an arrow in the thigh, apparently in the area of Heng-chiang. Unable to ride a horse, he returned to his camp in a carriage, *San-kuo chih* 46.10a (Ni Fan).

In lines 213–14 I have followed Yen K'o-chün's reading *yü*[b] instead of Ni Fan's *yü*[a], on the admittedly remote chance that Yü Hsin is here using the word in the sense of *ju* ('like') or as an exclamatory *hu* (Morohashi, 252.6, 11). Chü-lu was the site of several battles; Yü was probably thinking of Hsiang Yü's great victory over the Ch'in there in 207 B.C. (Chavannes, II, 210–11; III, 64–5), of which the Liang emperor Chien-wen says, 'At Chü-lu the troops shook the heavens' (*Ch'üan Liang wen* 8.4a3). I am aware of no landslide of sand connected with that battle.

Line 214 looks at first like a reference to *Shih chi* 81.13 (Wang): The Ch'in army camped west of Wu-an, and their drums and shouts shook the tiles on the roofs of that city. It has been proposed to emend Ch'ang-p'ing to Wu-an, but there is no need of that. There was clearly a similar story at one time about the much more important battle at Ch'ang-p'ing in 259 B.C., when the Ch'in general Po Ch'i, Lord of *Wu-an*, was supposed to have massacred 400,000 Chao prisoners, *Shih chi* 73.5–8. Yü Hsin's contemporary, the Northern Chou regent, threatens to attack the Northern Ch'i: '[then it will be as in the ancient examples] when the tiles were shaken [by war drums] at Ch'ang-p'ing and the State of Chao was divided in two, or as when armies came out of Han-ku and Han was rent into three', *Chou shu* 11.11b–12a, trans. Dien (1), p. 50. Li Po furnishes additional information: 'They say of the general from Wu-an / That his rage shook the tiles at Ch'ang-p'ing', *Li T'ai-po shih chi* 11.6b–7a. The general here is clearly Po Ch'i, Lord of Wu-an; it is possible that Ssu-ma Ch'ien's anecdote is a telescoped version, with the Wu-an of Po Ch'i's fief becoming the place where the tiles shook.

Cassia Forest and Long Isle had appeared in Tso Ssu's 'Rhapsody on the Wu Capital' as parks of the Three Kingdoms Wu, *WH* 5.23b, 12b (Wang). One may grant that deer grazing in a capital or palace are standard symbols of desolation, as in *WH* 6.4a and 42.5a; they are, however, very much in place in an imperial park. There is no verb in line 216, literally: 'Long Isle was deered'; the odd syntax is not unparalleled in earlier *fu*. It almost certainly means that the inhabitants of Chien-k'ang were hunted down like deer, the two parks serving as symbols of the capital. The hunting metaphor for war has already appeared in lines 169–70, and it is noteworthy that Yü later, in line 426, uses exactly the same metaphor for the fall of the second Liang capital at Chiang-ling: 'The Yün-meng Park was the site of a mock hunt.'

The four states in lines 221–2 had been ruled by cadet branches of the Chou royal family; Chou is Yü's regular symbol for the Liang emperor, and the feudal lords (*chu hou*) represent the Liang princes. It had been said of the restoration of the Chou in the eastern capital, 'Our Chou's removal to the east was all through the help of Chin and Cheng', Legge (1), V, 21b. Again in the *Tso chuan*, someone objected to the growing breach between Lu and Wei: 'Of all the sons of T'ai-ssu [King Wen's queen] the duke of Chou and K'ang-shu were the most friendly', Legge (1), V, 763a (Wang). The Duke of Chou, ancestor of the Lu ruling family, had made his younger brother K'ang-shu ruler of Wei, *Shih chi* 37.3.

In lines 223–4, moving the Gate of Heaven and turning the axis of the earth are metaphors for the imperial rule; compare a memorial by Yü, *Works* 7.14a: 'I would observe that Your Majesty [two lines omitted] by his virtue moves the Gate of Heaven, by his majesty moves the axis of the earth.' The lines thus mean that the Liang princes, 'not in harmony', were fighting one another for the throne.

Lines 225–8 refer to the death of Emperor Wu; the murder of his heir, Emperor Chien-wen, appears below in lines 319–20 and 325–6. It appears from 225–6 that Yü accepted the popular theory that Hou Ching had starved him to death (as did Han Yü; see Birch, I, 251); he almost certainly believed that Wu had been murdered by some means. A king of Chao (line 225) had once been shut up alone in a palace; he survived for a time by eating young sparrows but finally starved, *Shih chi* 42.69 (Wu). A king of Ch'u, about to be murdered by a son, asked for a last meal of bear's paws, Legge (1), V, 230b (Wu). Duke Chuang of Ch'i was buried (*ts'e*) by his murderer in the northern suburbs; he was later given a more permanent burial, seven chariots being buried with him.[69] In 284 B.C., King Min of Ch'i was hung by the tendons from the rafters of his ancestral temple; he died the next day, *Chan-kuo ts'e* 2.38 (Wang).

Someone once dreamed of ghosts standing in the temple by the altar to the soil in Ts'ao discussing the destruction of that state, Legge (1), V, 814b (Wu). Shen Pao-hsü, who has already appeared in line 43 of the preface, stood and cried for seven days in the Ch'in court while awaiting a reply to his request for help for Ch'u. Since the earlier use of the allusion referred to Yü's peace mission to the Western Wei, it has been suggested that line 230 means that he left the capital looking for help for the endangered court. That is possible, but Yü is unlikely to have left Chien-k'ang until a year or two after its fall. It seems easier to take lines 229–30 as indicating only the threatened destruction of a state; that is what the two allusions have in common.

We have almost no specific information on Yü's flight from Chien-k'ang to Chiang-ling, but it appears from lines 231–2 that, like his father, he may have made his escape from the capital by pretending to go on a mission for the rebels. The allusion in line 233 has not been satisfactorily identified; Hsü Ling probably has the same one in mind when he says that, thanks to Ch'en Pa-hsien, 'The defile of O-pan has been opened', *Ch'üan Ch'en wen* 6.6a3–4. Wu Tzu-hsü's narrow escape from arrest, proposed by Ni Fan, took place at a different pass and had nothing to do with slander or ridicule.

A pre-*Ch'un-ch'iu* Duke of Sung had rewarded a man named Erh for services against the Ti by giving him the revenues of a customs barrier, which was thereafter called Erh's Gate, Legge (1), V, 258b (Wu); Erh's Gate in line 234 is thus simply a place where one has to pay taxes. The line does not indicate that the author was passing through Sung, then Eastern Wei territory, or even that he is necessarily complaining of taxes; lines 233–4 may indicate only general obstacles confronting the author.

That is almost certainly the point of lines 235–6, which are not likely to mean that he first rode a white horse and then a black mule. The famous proposition of the logician Kung-sun Lung, that a white horse is not a horse, inspired many anecdotes. There was one story of him being turned back at a pass while riding a white horse, since he had no permit (Huan T'an, *Ch'üan Hou-Han wen* 15.4b6–7); presumably he was unable to convince the guard that it was not a horse. On another occasion he was more persuasive; that is apparently the allusion in a poem by Yen Chih-t'ui on his flight down the Yellow River from the Western Wei to the Northern Ch'i: 'The color of my horse confused the guard at the pass' (Ting Fu-pao, p. 1524, line 8). Either story would do nicely for line 235; line 236 is more of a problem. Li Shao-chün, the famous Taoist adept and guide of Emperor Wu of the Han, re-appeared after his supposed death riding a black mule; his coffin proved to be empty ('Lu Nü-sheng pieh-chuan', *T'ai-p'ing yü-lan* 901.5b, Wu). Line 236 perhaps means that a wizard able to escape from his own coffin could not get past the rebels, but this may not be the right allusion.

As explained in Chapter 2, the 'Li sao' inspired many *fu* about real earth-bound journeys; the corresponding section of the 'Lament' is lines 231–52, almost entirely in *sao* meter. Saw-teeth and hook-claws, originally fierce animals (*Huai-nan tzu* 8.2b, Ni; *WH* 5.9a), here become metaphors for the rebels. *Hsi liu* in line 240 literally means skilled at sailing or at naval combat.

Chang Liao was an important general under Ts'ao Ts'ao and the Three Kingdoms Wei, but no source survives connecting him with the Red Cliff. It has been suggested that Red Cliff be emended to Ho-fei, the successful defense of which is the main subject of Chang's biography, *San-kuo chih* 17.1a–5a. The emendation seems unwise; Yü may have in mind a lost incident of Chang's campaigns against Wu, though it can hardly have been the famous battle at the Red Cliff ending in the defeat of Ts'ao Ts'ao, Chang Liao's patron. A victory is called for, something comparable to Wang Chün's great armada sailing down the Yangtze to wipe out the Wu. Emperor Wu of the Chin had sent him instructions to 'go down to the east and sweep away Pa-ch'iu' (*Ch'üan Chin wen* 6.1a5), and Wang Chün later said of the conquest, 'From the time I reached Pa-ch'iu, wherever I turned they bowed down as before the wind' (*Chin shu* 42.6b4). Hou Ching's siege of Pa-ch'iu, also called Pa-ling, marked the turning point of his upriver campaign; having failed to take the fortress, and growing alarmed at defeats elsewhere, he returned to Chien-k'ang.

The naval engagement of lines 245–6 is told in conventional terms. Ts'ao Ts'ao once shot so many arrows at a ship with Sun Ch'üan embarked that it grew lopsided and threatened to capsize. Sun, according to the story, turned the ship around to allow additional arrows to restore its balance (*San-kuo chih* 47.4b commentary, Wang).

Lines 247–8 seem to be a general reference to Liang casualties; Yü speaks of the deaths with regret, and it is unlikely that the lines can refer to the capture of rebel generals, as Wu suggested. Huang Kai, a Wu general, was wounded and fell into the water during the battle of the Red Cliff, of which he was the great hero. He was pulled out by the Wu forces, who mistook him for an enemy and threw him into a latrine. Gathering all his strength, he called out to a friend, who recognized his voice and rescued him (*San-kuo chih* 55.3a commentary, Wu). Tu Chi was testing a ship when it capsized and he was drowned. A companion had called out to a rescuer, 'First save Marquis Tu!' (*San-kuo chih* 28.11b commentary, Wang).

The place names in lines 249–50 are rather exceptional for Yü Hsin in that, for once, they are meant more or less literally. As Hu San-hsing points out, they are near one another and in the neighborhood of Chiang-hsia, *Tzu-chih t'ung-chien*, p. 5068. The lines clearly refer to the author's stay with Hsiao Shao. Although he had reached the middle Yangtze, he still looked toward the stars governing events in Chien-k'ang, *Chin shu* 42.11b10.

The subject of a given passage in the 'Lament' is usually not indicated, but it is only in lines 253–60 that this poses a real problem. Most

commentators have taken the passage as an account of the flight of the
defeated Hou Ching back down the Yangtze. Kao Pu-ying, on the other hand,
treats it as a continuation of the author's journey upriver. It is true that lines
259—60 do seem to be Yü's own observations, but the allusions in 253 and
256 are to a fleeing general, and the author was hardly building walls or
burning a camp, lines 257—8. I have followed the traditional view, especially
since the author's trip is dealt with below in lines 263—8. The heroic stature
of Hsiang Yü, the subject of lines 253 and 256, does not prevent him from
being used as a figure for Hou Ching; Hsiao Yi had already done that in so
many words: 'Hou Ching is a Hsiang Yü', *Ch'üan Liang wen* 16.3b12. One
must admit that Yü Hsin elsewhere uses the Wu-chiang allusion of line 256
to describe himself (*Works* 9.24a9—10); there, however, he means that he
cannot go back to the South from the Northern Chou, and the point of the
reference is clearer than it would be here.

   Lines 253 and 256 refer to the last days of Hsiang Yü. Fleeing after his
defeat at Kai-hsia, he lost his way at Yin-ling (Chavannes, II, 317; Wu);
sources differ, but it may have been about 110 miles WNW of Nanking. The
tiao-t'ai in line 254 is unexplained, like the one in line 45 of the preface;
there was one at Chiang-hsia, but in the absence of a suitable anecdote there
is no reason to select that one. In line 255 Ni Fan's edition has the Red Cliff
(Ch'ih-pi); this seems repetitive after line 243, and it would make no sense
anyway. There is no apparent reason why either Hou Ching or Yü Hsin (if,
like Kao, we consider Yü the subject of the lines) should be weeping at
Ts'ao Ts'ao's failure to conquer Wu. Hou Ching was by this time trying to
defend Wu against the conquering Liang armies. I have followed the better-
attested reading Ch'ih-an (in all three editions of the *Chou shu*, the *Wen-
yüan ying-hua*, and the *SPTK* edition of the works). The story involved here
is unknown, but Ch'ih-an is in a strategic position on the north side of the
Yangtze near Nanking.

   Hsiang Yü, finding Heaven clearly opposed to his designs, refused to cross
the Wu-chiang (apparently about 30 miles SW of Nanking) in the boat waiting
for him; he then committed suicide (Chavannes, II, 317, Wang). Lei-ch'ih
in line 257 is a lake just north of the Yangtze about 225 miles SW of Nanking,
and Ch'üeh-ling is an island in the Yangtze about 180 miles SW of Nanking.
No suitable story is known about either place, but it is clear from a letter
by Pao Chao (Chang Jen-ch'ing, I, 63) that Lei-ch'ih had been the site of many
battles.

   Line 261 reintroduces the Ch'u metaphor for Hsiao Yi, who was by then
the best chance for a restoration of the Liang. Hindsight makes the author
express his earlier hopes with strong reservations; line 262 is reminiscent of
a 'Li sao' passage on the infamous Orchid: 'I thought that Orchid was one to

be trusted', *Ch'u tz'u* 1.41b, trans. Hawkes (1), p. 32. Mounts Ching and Heng are the 'Tribute of Yü' boundaries of Ching-chou, synonymous with Ch'u, Legge (1), III, 112 (Lu). The able men who had gone from Ch'u to become ministers in other states had been compared to the willows and catalpas (or 'best timber') exported by that state, Legge (1), V, 521, 526 (Wang).

Line 263, again from the 'Tribute of Yü', gives the boundaries of Yang-chou, basically the lower Yangtze and associated particularly with Nanking, Legge (1), III, 108 (Wu). Chiang-ling is about 700 miles upriver from Nanking.

In line 265, I have emended *p'iao* ('to wash') to read *Li*, as suggested by Ku Yen-wu; the two characters are almost identical. With *p'iao*, the line would refer to Han Hsin, who as a young man was given food by a washer-woman near his home, *Shih chi* 92.2 (Wu), trans. Watson (6), I, 208. Emended, the line becomes a much more appropriate reference to Wu Tzu-hsü, who during his flight did in fact beg for his food at Li-yang, literally 'the sunny side of the Li', *Wu-Yüeh ch'un-ch'iu* A.15b (Kao). The fact that the author was not likely to pass through Li-yang on his journey upriver is irrelevant; line 234 does not mean that he was in Sung. Lines 275−8 all deal with Ssu-ma Ch'ien and his father T'an, so it is not surprising to find here paired references to Wu Tzu-hsü, who waited in the reeds for a boatman to take him across a river, *Wu-Yüeh ch'un-ch'iu* A.14b (Wu).

Toward the beginning of Ssu-ma Hsiang-ju's 'Tzu-hsü/Shang-lin Rhapsody', the spokesman for Ch'u says that he has heard 'in Ch'u there are seven marshes' or hunting parks, the smallest of them being the enormous Yün-meng (*WH* 7.18a, Wang); this established the seven marshes as a figure for Ch'u, for example in *WH* 27.4a. King Wu of the Chou, after conquering the Shang, was asked one night why he had not gone to sleep; he replied, 'I have not yet been assured of the protection of Heaven' (*Shih chi* 4.34, Wang; trans. after Chavannes, I, 242).

In lines 271−2, the author modestly disclaims any qualifications for office. Confucius expected 'lofty action' of all officials, whether the times were good or bad, Legge (1), I, 276 (Wang).

Lines 275−82 deal with the death of the author's father Chien-wu; the author identifies himself with Ssu-ma Ch'ien and Chien-wu with Ch'ien's father T'an. A similarity of dates is evidently the core of the comparison (Appendix V), so we need not put too much stress on lines 277−8. Line 277 is based on Ssu-ma T'an's dying quotation from *Hsiao ching* 1.2b, trans. Legge (2), 466−7; such a wish would come naturally to any dying man. Conceivably Chien-wu did tell his son to complete a book he himself had wanted to write, as in line 278, but so many coincidences would be surprising;

it seems most likely that Yü Hsin was simply in some way to carry on the life work of his father, as von Zach suggests.

In line 279, T'an Cheng-pi's text, followed by those of Chang Jen-ch'ing and Ch'ü Shui-yüan, has 'four generations' (*ssu shih*) instead of three. I know of no earlier text with such a reading, and 'three' makes better sense. The family of Ch'en Shih held ever-higher posts for four generations under the Han and Wei, despite a continual decline in virtue; there was supposed to be a popular saying that each man had been a disgrace to his father, even though he held a higher rank (*Po-wu chih* 6.1b–2a, Kuei); Yü obviously means that only he, the implied fourth generation, has brought shame on his family. Pan Ku commented with some wonder that the family of Chin Mi-ti, a Hsiung-nu, had been inner-court officials for seven generations under the Han, *Han-shu* 68.27a. Pan Ku's statement made seven generations a stock figure for a distinguished family, used for example by Shen Yüeh, *WH* 50.15b, and by Jen Fang, *WH* 38.21b. This being the case, it would be pointless to count generations of Yü's ancestors, particularly since line 279 has just given us a different, and equally conventional, number.

Tseng tzu was supposed to have written the 'Song of Liang-shan' to express his concern when trapped by a snowstorm and unable to return home to see his parents ('Ch'in ts'ao', quoted by Li Shan, *WH* 30.23b). Line 282 is based on an old metaphor for the brevity of one's parents' lives, *Shuo yüan* 3.3b–4a (Chang Jen-ch'ing).

Line 285 is derived from the 'Lady of the Hsiang': 'Sweet pollia I've plucked in the little islet / To send to my far-away Beloved', *Ch'u tz'u* 2.15a (Wang), trans. Hawkes (1), p. 39. Line 286 refers to a 'boys' song' predicting the death of Chu-ko K'o, Chu-ko Liang's nephew and a powerful general under the Three Kingdoms Wu: 'Chu-ko K'o! Unlined rush clothing and buckle of wicker work. Where shall we seek him? At Ch'eng-tzu-ko' (trans. Achilles Fang (1), II, 153–4). The historian goes on to explain Ch'eng-tzu-ko as a 'transversion' of Shih-tzu-kang (the name of a big cemetery at the Wu capital). Shortly afterward, having been accused of planning a coup, Chu-ko K'o was murdered on instructions of the emperor, Fang (1), II, 137. His body was wrapped in a mat, tied at the waist with wicker, and dumped in the cemetery. We are surely meant to ignore the circumstances of Chu-ko K'o's death; however bad Hsiao Yi may have been, Yü can hardly be saying at this point that he expected Yi to murder him because of slander. Such a suggestion would disastrously undercut the section immediately following, on Hsiao Yi's triumphant restoration of the Liang. Wang Yi, compiler of the *Ch'u tz'u*, considered the original sweet pollia a gift to win admission to a group of recluses; it here clearly symbolizes life in retirement. If we ignore the details

of Chu-ko K'o's death, the unlined garment of rushes suggests the simplest
of burials. This would be suitable for a recluse and also would fit well into
the dense vegetation of lines 283—6, which stresses how much of a recluse
the author intended to be.

Lines 287—306 describe the final Liang campaign against Hou Ching,
the recapture of Chien-k'ang, and Hou's death. Lines 287—8 are obscure;
the single statement is made up of three disparate elements, and it is difficult
to decide how to fit them together. Hsiang Yü, when granting fiefs to his
generals, took for himself the title Hegemon King of Western Ch'u (Chavannes,
II, 292). *Chien chi* in line 288 may perhaps come from a story of a ruler of
Ch'u who was so enraged at hearing of the killing of one of his envoys that he
rose from his seat and rushed out. In the terse language of the *Tso chuan*,
'His sword caught up with him [*chien chi*] outside the door of his chamber;
his chariot caught up with him in the . . . market' (cf. Legge (1), V, 323,
324b; Wu). The identity of the Fan-yang in line 288 is the greatest problem;
ideally it should have some connection with Hsiang Yü, the announced
subject of line 287, but I can find none. Morohashi (27849/136) lists five
places called Fan-yang; here are their locations in relation to Nanking, the
actual destination of the Liang armies:

(1)   230 miles WNW
(2)   350 miles NW
(3)   300 miles WNW
(4)   800 miles W
(5)   Same as (2) above.

Unless we are missing a Fan-yang nearer Nanking, the one in line 288 must be
intended metaphorically. (3) is the only likely possibility; it was the place
where the Wei accepted the forced abdication of the Han, *Hou-Han shu*
9.17b commentary (Lu). It was also a recognized allusion in Yü Hsin's time.
Wang Seng-pien sent Hsiao Yi a series of letters urging him to assume the title
of emperor; in one of his replies, Yi says that once the rebellion is put down he
intends to imitate ancient worthies who refused thrones, and not at all to
seek the throne for himself. The latter sentiment is expressed through references
to the Pavilion of a Thousand Autumns ([*Ch'ien*] *ch'iu t'ing*, where Emperor
Kuang-wu took the throne) and 'the stones at Fan-yang' (*Fan-yang chih shih*),
Liang shu 5.8a—b.

Line 287 clearly refers to Hsiao Yi, who at the time of the rebellion was
constantly spoken of as hegemon (*pa*), since he was not yet emperor but
only the leader among the princes. The line also includes the regular Ch'u
associations with Yi. Hou Ching on January 1, 552, had forced a Liang puppet
to abdicate in his favor and founded a Han dynasty. In view of this, and the

historical significance of Fan-yang, line 288 may possibly mean that Hsiao
Yi sent out an army to save his dynasty. This interpretation is too complicated to be very satisfying; it is offered only as a stopgap.

In line 292, von Zach has iron rudders. This is quite possible; I have
translated 'prows' because iron would seem more useful there, for ramming.
On the other hand, ivory on masts would presumably be only ornamental.
Line 293 has traditionally been taken as a reference to the oath sworn by
Wang Seng-pien and Ch'en Pa-hsien at the beginning of the attack on Chien-
k'ang, but that is a mistake; such an oath would require the *blood* of the
white horse (to be smeared on the participants' lips). This horse has been
thrown into a river as a sacrifice to a river god. The same thing, described
in identical words (*ch'en pai ma*), was done by the Second Emperor of
the Ch'in to stop nightmares caused by a river god (*Shih chi* 6.38a1, Po-na
edition), by Emperor Wu of the Han to end a drought (*Shih chi* 29.6b3—4,
Po-na edition), and by someone else during the Han to avert a threatened
flood (*Han shu* 76.29a5). When a white horse was used to seal an oath, it
would be killed in such a way as to allow the blood to be drawn off, e.g.
Shih chi (Po-na edition) 69.7a5, 70.6a9—10. It was customary for an attacking
army, when crossing or sailing on a river, to make a sacrifice to the gods of
the river and pray for victory. During the attack on the Ch'en, the Sui army
sacrificed both to the Huai and the Yangtze, though not horses in this case,
and the texts of the prayers survive, *Ch'üan Sui wen* 19.8b—9b. Yü Hsin
may well have in mind a specific allusion for this sacrifice, but the meaning
is clear even without one.

Similarly, the word *shih* in line 293 has nothing to do with an oath. It is
a harangue delivered to an army on the eve of a campaign, in the tradition
of the 'Great Declaration' ('T'ai shih') section of the *Shu ching*, the source
of the phrase *shih chung*: 'the king went round his six hosts in state, and made
a clear *declaration* to all [*shih chung*] his officers', Legge (1), III, 294. *Shih
chung* is used in the same sense in *Ch'üan Chin wen* 100.7b4.

The legendary sage Yü was once crossing the Yangtze when his boat was
lifted up by a yellow dragon, *Lü-shih ch'un-ch'iu* 20.7a (Wu). In line 294,
the yellow dragon indicates a favorable response to the sacrifice, and there is
also an overtone of divine approval of Hsiao Yi's claim to the throne. In the
text of the Liang abdication in favor of Ch'en Pa-hsien, Hsü Ling says of the
latter, 'A yellow dragon bears up his boat' (*huang lung fu chou*), *Ch'üan
Ch'en wen* 6.9a13—9b1.

Line 296 is another allusion to a good omen. King Chao of Ch'u was once
crossing the Yangtze when a number of objects as large as peck measures
struck his boat. He sent to inquire of Confucius, who explained that they
were the fruit of the *p'ing*, to be obtained only by the hegemon, *Shuo yüan*

18.17b—18a (Wang). These enormous fruits could have come from no ordinary water plant, so I have left them in Chinese. By *wang* one has to understand 'royal forces', since Hsiao Yi had remained behind in Chiang-ling.

Lines 297—8 are almost identical to a passage in Tso Ssu's 'Rhapsody on the Wu Capital': 'War chariots fill Shih-ch'eng; Spear-ships cover the rivers and lakes', *WH* 5.16a (Hsü Chiung). The author has reworked a general statement of military strength into an account of the battle to recapture Chien-k'ang, the old Wu capital, from Hou Ching. Shih-t'ou ch'eng was an old fortress just west of Chien-k'ang, still important under the Liang. Defeated by the Liang forces in a battle near there, Hou fled the capital. The Northern Ch'i, allied with Hsiao Yi, had been attacking the northern frontiers as suggested in line 298. The Northern Ch'i is perhaps meant in line 299; the 'leader of the covenant' in line 300 is certainly Hsiao Yi, who has already appeared in line 287 as hegemon. The Earl of Cheng had once arrived early at a conference called by Ch'u, which many of the other feudal lords were reluctant to attend, Legge (1), V, 597a (Wu). Line 299 may indicate that the Northern Ch'i was more willing to cooperate with Hsiao Yi (or 'Ch'u') than his brothers were. On another occasion, Hsün Ying arrived with the Chin armies at dusk to join in an attack; the ruler of Chin was at that time the leader of the covenant, Legge (1), V, 452b (Wang), and this allusion is particularly appropriate since Hsiao Yi did not himself command his armies in the attack but remained in his capital.

Line 301 is reminiscent of hunting scenes in earlier *fu*, such as Tso Ssu's 'Rhapsody on the Wu Capital' (*WH* 5.19b, Lu): 'They overturned their nests, Cut open their lairs.' The *ch'ih-mei*, a single word split here for parallelism, is a *Tso chuan* goblin, e.g. Legge (1), V, 283. Line 302 is very like the exorcisms in earlier *fu*; the *ch'ih-mei* is in fact exorcised in Chang Heng's 'Rhapsody on the Eastern Capital', *WH* 3.26a, trans. Watson (2), p. 6. Lines 303—4 were perhaps influenced by a letter of Hsiao Yi referring to Hou Ching's death in terms of the giant Ti and Ch'ih-yu, *Ch'üan Liang wen* 17.4a4—5, but both were common symbols for defeated enemies by this time. The giant Ti's head had been buried at the Tzu-chü Gate of Lu, Legge (1), V, 258a—b (Wang). Ch'ih-yu, the legendary first rebel at the time of the Yellow Emperor, died according to one account as Yü says here, *Shih chi* 1.8 commentary (Wang). The corpse of the Latter Han dictator Tung Cho was exposed in the marketplace; because of the heat, the fat of the corpulent man began to run off, and a guard lit a wick and stuck it into his navel. It is supposed to have burned for several days, *Hou-Han shu* 72.15b (Wu). The syntax in lines 305—6 is a little unusual; in the second line, for example, it would be more natural to say *yi ch'i t'ou wei yin ch'i*. However, such syntax can be paralleled in more straightforward prose passages, such as a statement in simple narrative

that a fourteen-year-old member of the Liang ruling family liked to ride on
the back of an over-indulgent official: 'He rode on his back as a horse' (*ch'i
pei wei ma*), *Tzu-chih t'ung-chien*, p. 5064.

The meaning of lines 307—8 is not clear. The two omens are evidently
used as symbols of actual events, as often in Yü's works; context suggests
the retaking of Chien-k'ang. Hu Wei-sheng supplies a reference which would
justify this reading of line 307, at least: if a white rainbow crosses the
south wall of a city, an attack at that point will be successful (*Huang-ti
chan-chün chüeh*, quoted in *T'ai-p'ing yü-lan* 14.9b). The commentators
have cited a number of stories about comets as omens of death, but none of
them seems to fit in here. There is an interesting parallel passage in one of
Yü's 'Yung-huai' poems (*Works* 3.37b): 'A straight rainbow shone over the
fortifications at dawn; a comet fell on the camp in the night.' It appears
from this that lines 307 and 308 both have military implications.

Chu-ko Liang once said that the hills of Chien-k'ang, coiling like dragons
and crouching like tigers, made it the seat of emperors, *T'ai-p'ing yü-lan*
56.3a (Wang). The phrase has become the classic description of the terrain
of Nanking; a map in the *Ching-ting Chien-k'ang chih* (*chüan* 5) has that
title. Fox and rabbit burrows are standard symbols of desolation. The banners
and clouds were auspicious vapors, also indicating an imperial capital, associated
with Chien-k'ang; see a letter quoted by Li Shan, *WH* 56.15b. Wind-blown
dust in line 312 is a symbol for rebellion, but Yü uses it with full consciousness
of the literal value; the auspicious vapors have disappeared in a sandstorm.

The Hanging Gardens, glossed by the ancient variant *hsüan* (Morohashi,
20814/326), are here not the legendary ones in the K'un-lun Mountains
but an actual imperial park northeast of Chien-k'ang. Established by the
Southern Ch'i (*Ching-ting Chien-k'ang chih* 22.49b), it belonged later to Hsiao
T'ung, the first Liang Crown Prince (*Ch'üan Liang wen* 19.4a4), and finally
to his younger brother Kang. Kang probably acquired it on becoming Crown
Prince after T'ung's death in 531; we find him lecturing there in *Liang shu*
4.9a and 37.7a. The Broadview Park (*yüan*), apparently a mile or two from
Chien-k'ang (though it is not clear in which direction), passed through the
same hands. It belonged in turn to a Southern Ch'i Crown Prince (*Ching-
ting Chien-k'ang chih* 22.48a), Hsiao T'ung (*Works* 15.45a2 and, most probably,
Ch'üan Liang wen 18.5a3, 5), and Hsiao Kang (*Works* 3.1b).

The lakes in line 316 are literally 'filled in' or 'leveled'. Compare a passage
by Huan T'an (*Ch'üan Hou-Han wen* 15.11a4—5): 'After a thousand autumns,
ten thousand years . . . [your] high towers will have toppled, and [your]
winding streams grown level [*p'ing*].' Old trees were sometimes admired,
but apparently not during that period. In *Works* 15.7b3—4, Yü pairs old
trees (*ku shu*) with withered flowers (*ts'an hua*). See also a poem by Hsiao

Kang on his imprisonment by the rebels, Ting Fu-pao, p. 941. This couplet
is particularly interesting; not only are the lines grammatically unparallel,
but they show contrasting situations, past glories in line 315, present con-
dition in line 316.

Lines 319–20 are glossed by the occurrence of an almost identical couplet
in a poem by Yü on a murdered emperor of the Northern Chou; one could
in fact use the same translation for both passages (*Works* 3.59a): *t'u hsüan
jen-shou ching*; *k'ung chü Mao-ling shu*. The mirror is literally that of 'the
longevity of the good', a phrase originating in Confucius's statement that 'the
good live long' (cf. Legge (1), I, 192) and considered auspicious as a mirror
inscription. There is an anonymous T'ang *fu* celebrating the discovery at
the beginning of the T'ien-pao period (742–56) of a natural stone 'mirror'
with the characters *jen-shou* clearly visible on its surface, *Wen-yüan ying-
hua* 86.4b–5b. One of the commentators on the 'Lament', Hsü Chiung,
quotes a Han mirror inscription: 'By hanging it up, may you gain the longevity
of the good; may the Emperor live ten thousand years!' (*hsüan chih jen-shou*;
T'ien-tzu wan nien). This inscription, presumably on a mirror intended for
an emperor, is the ideal reference for the allusion, but I have not located
Hsü's unspecified source. According to the *Han Wu-ti nei-chuan*, Emperor
Wu commanded that a number of Taoist works he had used in his quest of
immortality be buried with him in the Mao tomb (*ling*).[70] Lines 319–20
illustrate a common feature of the 'Lament', the last two lines of a rhyme
section used to introduce the subject of the new rhyme to follow. Compare
lines 329–30 and 423–4.

There were three ways to 'die without decaying': to be remembered for
one's virtues, deeds, or words, Legge (1), V, 507a (Wang). The omission in
line 321 is significant; one would not remember a puppet for his deeds.
Line 322 consists of two phrases from the *Shu ching*, Karlgren (1), p. 8;
Legge (1), III, 527–8 (Wang). Both were applicable to a meritorious subject,
not to an emperor; cf. *WH* 25.12b, 56.4a, 58.22b; *Ch'üan Hou-Chou wen*
7.6b5–6; and *Works* 13.52b2, 15.42b6.

Line 323 is a reference to a typical bit of 'pure conversation': A Taoist,
holding as usual that the classics contained only dregs and no ultimate truths,
was told that, according to the 'Great Appendix' of the *Yi ching*, 'The Sage . . .
appended explanations [*hsi tz'u*] to exhaust words' (*Chou yi yin-te* 44/
Hsi shang/12). He replied, 'Now, when it says, " . . . appended explanations
to exhaust words", that doesn't refer to what is outside the ties [*hsi piao*]',
San-kuo chih 10.13a commentary (Kao Pu-ying). This plays on the two senses
of 'tie' (*hsi*): 'appended', as in the title of the 'Great Appendix', and 'dependent,
contingent, restricted'.

Ho-shang Kung ('His Excellency of the River Bank') is the pen-name of

an anonymous commentator on the *Tao te ching*. Emperor Chien-wen seems
to have been particularly interested in Taoism; he lectured several times on
Taoist texts in the Hanging Gardens, *Liang shu* 37.7a.

Prince Ch'iao, already mentioned in line 41, was taken by Fu-ch'iu Kung
up Mount Sung-kao to become an immortal, *Lieh-hsien chuan* A.12b (Wang).
The same Prince, told by Music-Master K'uang that he would not live long,
replied that within three years he would 'go up and lodge with God' (*shang
pin yü Ti so*), *Yi Chou shu*, p. 293 (Ni). The phrase, sometimes a euphemism
for death, must here have its basic sense of attaining immortality; compare
Li Po: 'To go away with Prince Ch'iao, And live long as a guest [*pin*] in the
Jade Heaven', *Li T'ai-po shih chi* 24.14a. Lines 327–8 are explained in
Appendix VI.

Lines 329–30 involve unidentified allusions, but it is clear that the lines
represent a desirable situation. In one of a series of threatening letters, a
Liang prince trying to gain the throne boasts of his army: 'Dragon armor
and rhinoceros shields, all of them arms from Cloud Terrace' (*Yün-t'ai
chih chang, Ch'üan Ch'en wen 8.7a*). Tu Fu says with evident regret, 'There
were no longer the arms of Cloud Terrace [*Yün-t'ai chang*]; Useless to
build ships for naval warfare!' (*Tu shih yin-te* 335/42/13–14).

Wang Seng-pien, who had spent most of his life in the service of Hsiao
Yi, was rewarded with the title of Premier (*ssu-t'u*) on the latter's accession
in 552, *Liang shu* 45.9b (Wu). The author includes an account of him here
because of his greatest accomplishment, putting down Hou's rebellion, but
he anticipates Wang's death in 555. Hu Yen (line 332) said to Duke Wen of
Chin that the best way to attain hegemony over the feudal lords was to
'strive for the King' (*ch'in wang*), Legge (1), V, 195b (Wu).

There is a useful gloss on lines 333–4 in one of the author's grave inscriptions (*Works* 14.10b), where he says of a general:

> He always wanted to
> Hold a bronze drum and question the King of Wu,
> Grasp an engraved axe and get back the land from Ch'i.

We can tell from this that line 333 is a reference to Ts'ao Mei (perhaps
identifiable with Ts'ao Kuei), a defeated Lu general, who forced Duke Huan
of Ch'i (the first of the hegemons) to swear to return the land captured from
Lu (*Ch'un-ch'iu ching-chuan yin-te* 61/Chuang 13/4 *Kung*); he thus 'got
back the land from Ch'i'. Ts'ao Mei's weapon appears sometimes as a dagger
(*pi-shou*), sometimes as a sword or a 'three-foot blade'. It is conceivable
that the author has found him with an engraved axe in some undiscovered
version of this extremely popular story, which appears, for example, in
Shih chi 14.62, 32.20, 33.30, 62.5, 83.16–17, 86.3; *Chan-kuo ts'e* 2.9;

Huai-nan tzu 13.13b—14a; and the 'Li Ling' letter, *WH* 41.4b. However, Yü Hsin mentions him elsewhere with a dagger (*Works* 13.45a6), and it seems more likely that he has here dressed up the original a little, adding a more dignified weapon. An engraved axe (a *ko* is literally what the archaeologists call a 'dagger-axe') was a valuable, rather ceremonial object; this is undoubtedly why all the commentators, following Wu, have referred line 333 to Duke Mu of Ch'in (one of the hegemons), who 'grasped an engraved axe' during a meeting with an envoy of Chin, whose territory he had attacked (*Kuo yü* 9.4b). In that case, one would have to translate the line, 'He confronted the hegemon, though he [the latter] was grasping an engraved axe.' This would not make sense in the context: Wang Seng-pien was bold enough to speak up to a man who was his better, and armed too?

A Han general had held a bronze drum (*chih chin ku*) while interrogating the surrendered King of Chiao-hsi, one of the participants in the revolt of the seven kingdoms, *Shih chi* 106.28 (Wang).[71]

Tu Yü (T. Yüan-k'ai) was one of the commanders of the Chin forces which conquered the Three Kingdoms Wu; Wang Seng-pien's victory over Hou Ching was a close parallel. Wen Ch'iao (T. T'ai-chen, 288—329) is represented in his biography as primarily responsible for recapturing Chien-k'ang from the rebel Su Chün (*Chin shu* 63.6b, Wang); the Emperor wrote that because of him, 'the royal house, endangered, has been made secure again', *Chin shu* 63.7a.

In lines 337—8, Yü uses two place names for their literal meaning as descriptions of Wang Seng-pien's career and death. 'Total Devotion' is mentioned in P'an Yüeh's 'Traveling West', *WH* 10.12b (Wang); Li Shan explains it as the site of the death of a Han Crown Prince implicated in the supposed conspiracy to murder the Emperor by sorcery. 'Innocent Victim' is the name of a mountain in Honan, supposed to have been the scene of the last Shang king's murder of Prince Pi-kan (Ni). After the fall of Chiang-ling, Wang Seng-pien put a surviving son of Emperor Yüan on the throne in Chien-k'ang. The Northern Ch'i attempted to put their own pretender on the Liang throne, Hsiao Yüan-ming, a favorite nephew of Emperor Wu, captured years earlier while leading the Liang forces supporting Hou Ching against the Eastern Wei. Wang Seng-pien, defeated by the Northern Ch'i forces, was forced to consent to their plan. Ch'en Pa-hsien accused Wang of treason and seized and 'executed' him and a son.

While his army was marching south, Hsiao Yüan-ming had sent a series of threatening letters to Wang; a line from one of them has already been quoted in the commentary on line 330. Another passage is remarkably similar to lines 339—40 (*Ch'üan Ch'en wen* 8.8a10—11):

The yellow dog at the east gate, you will surely long lament;
The commoners' clothes [*pai yi*] of Nan-yang, how can you get
   them again?

The first line, like line 340, refers to Li Ssu, the great Ch'in minister, who
said to his son as they were on their way to execution, 'Even if I and you
wished once more to lead a yellow dog and go together out of the east gate
of Shang-ts'ai in pursuit of the crafty hare, could we indeed do so?' (Bodde,
p. 52, Wang). Line 339 and the second line of the letter also seems to involve
the same allusion, but it has not been identified. As Kao Pu-ying says, the
story of Wen Chung's death, which is generally cited, says nothing about
collating texts (*Wu-Yüeh ch'un-ch'iu* B.65b); it also fails to mention life as
a commoner. Wu Chao-yi takes the second line of the letter as a reference to
Chu-ko Liang, but there is no mention of him collating texts either. There is
a very good chance that lines 339–40 were inspired by the letter. The original
had been a threat: 'Don't do something you are going to regret!' Lines
339–40, like 133–4 above, are a statement that the prediction came true.
Here there is the additional irony that Wang had most reason to regret yielding
to the earlier threat; his agreement to put Hsiao Yüan-ming on the throne
cost Wang his life. Yü would have been in the Western Wei when the letter
was sent, but Hsü Ling, the author of it, was an old friend of Yü, and the two
met again at least once later in the North (*Works* 4.60a–b). Lines 339–40
are quite odd prosodically, a two-line rhyme section.

Lines 341–8 deal with Hsiao Lun, who was driven to his death by Hsiao
Yi's forces. We can tell that Lun is the subject from a *Sui shu* anecdote
fabricated to explain line 345 (Appendix VI). The story, though apocryphal,
is welcome; Hsiao Lun is supposed to have held the title of General Defending
the East (*chen-tung chiang-chün*, *Liang shu* 29.7a), not the North. It is
possible that there is a mistake in line 341 or in Lun's biography; on the other
hand, Lun may well have held both titles, with only one appearing in the
somewhat incomplete sources remaining.

Lines 343–6 are an extended metaphor; none of the statements is literally
true, but taken together they present a picture of a man punished by the
gods for his crimes. The histories depict Lun as a monster; on one occasion
he is said to have held a mock funeral for his father, Emperor Wu (*Nan shih*
53.15b). The rebel Hou Ching may have this in mind in his denunciation of
the Liang ruling family (*Tzu-chih t'ung-chien*, p. 5007, lines 8–9). Lun's
life was a series of failures. He was defeated in battle by Hou Ching when he
tried to relieve the siege of Chien-k'ang; by Hsiao Yi's general Wang Seng-
pien when he again raised an army, supposedly to fight Hou Ching but

perhaps to attack Hsiao Yi, as the latter thought; and finally by a Western
Wei army which took the city to which he had fled and killed him. One
might surmise divine opposition, the explanation (or at least metaphor)
Yü Hsin offers.

Lines 343–4 are references to the First Emperor, Ch'in Shih-huang. The
mountain spirits of 344 are the stones whipped to make the bridge in line
65 above (Wu). Attempting to reach the islands of the immortals, Ch'in Shih-
huang shot a sea god in the guise of a great fish; this is presented as the
cause of his death soon afterward, *Shih chi* 6.65–66 (Ni). The allusion in
345 is unidentified, since the *Sui shu* story is clearly apocryphal; the one in
line 346 could be the story of the two dragons (*chiao*, as in Yü's text) sent
by God in 419 A.D. to sink the ships of two greedy merchants who had
angered him (*T'ai-p'ing kuang chi* 425.4b–5a).[72]

Hsiao Lun had at least three sons: Chien, Ch'üeh, and Chih. The first
two, both of whom have biographies in *Nan shih* 53.19b–21b, were killed
by Hou Ching. The third appears only in incidental references (*Nan shih*
53.18a9; *Tzu-chih t'ung-chien*, p. 5052, lines 2, 7); his fate is unclear, but he
had accompanied his fleeing father and was perhaps killed together with him
(*Tzu-chih t'ung-chien*, p. 5061, lines 14–15). Hsiao Ch'üeh is treated as a
hero in his biography, and Hsiao Chien as a wastrel who caused the fall of
Chien-k'ang. It is most unlikely that Yü intended line 347 to apply only to
Hsiao Ch'üeh, as opposed to that worthless Hsiao Chien; we have no way
of telling what he thought of the sons. Lines 347–8 are simply the author's
general comment on the fate of the family of a major figure in the 'Lament';
compare lines 175–6, 327–8, and 473–4.

After the death of Empress Lü of the Han, the future Emperor Wen,
then King of Tai, went to Ch'ang-an. After discussions in the Palace of
Tai, his residence in the capital, he agreed to take the throne (Chavannes,
II, 448–51; Wang). The allusion is obviously appropriate to Hsiao Yi, also
a *wang* (King/Prince) and restorer. Restoring Ancestor, an emperor's temple-
name, would have suited Emperor Yüan of the Liang (cf. line 472); it actually was given not to him but to the earlier Emperor Yüan who restored the
Chin in the South. Line 352 is evidently a reference to Yao, who is supposed
to have been Marquis of T'ang before succeeding his brother on the throne
(*T'ai-p'ing yü-lan* 80.2a, Wang). The specific story has not been located, but
it must have been one about popular appeals in the outskirts of T'ang for
Yao to take the throne; Wang Seng-pien refers to it in urging the same course
on Hsiao Yi, *Liang shu* 5.8b9. Yao is appropriate in line 352, not because
Hsiao Yi was a sage, but because he too was succeeding a brother, Emperor
Chien-wen.

The future Emperor Kuang-wu of the Latter Han went ahead as Governor of the Capital to prepare Loyang for the coming of his cousin Liu Hsüan, most commonly called the Keng-shih Emperor because of his reign-title. The old Han officials are said to have wept on seeing Kuang-wu's followers, since they had thought that such majesty was lost forever (*Hou-Han shu* 1A.9a–10a, Wang).

The Cheng-shih period (240–9) was the Golden Age of 'pure conversation' and a subject of much nostalgia for the later Chinese exiles in the South (e.g., Mather, p. 103). Yü is not praising Emperor Yüan as a conversationalist, but as the restorer of something thought lost. Any period viewed with nostalgia would probably have done equally well; Hsü Ling chooses to praise Ch'en Pa-hsien for bringing back the T'ai-shih and Yung-p'ing periods, respectively 96–93 B.C. and 58–75 A.D. (*Ch'üan Ch'en wen* 6.7b1–2).

It should be clear from Chapter 1 that Emperor Yüan was more than merely suspicious. Line 358 is taken, slightly modified, from the *Tso chuan,* Legge (1), V, 699a (Wu). The feudal lords are Yü's regular metaphor for the Liang princes, and they were indeed shaken after all these years of civil war with Hsiao Yi, or Emperor Yüan. King Huai of Ch'u was warned in 313 B.C. that if he followed a certain course, 'in the West you will arouse enmity with Ch'in and in the North break off relations with Ch'i, so that the armies of both countries will be sure to come here', *Shih chi* 40.56 (Wu). Any ruler of Ch'u might serve as a metaphor for Hsiao Yi; King Huai, the 'bad last ruler' associated with Ch'ü Yüan, was particularly appropriate, and the old prediction also fit the current situation. The Western Wei ('Ch'in') and Northern Ch'i were both threatening Hsiao Yi by this time.

Ssu-ma Ch'ien lists it among the mistakes of Hsiang Yü that, instead of making his capital in the well-protected Kuan-chung area, he chose to return to Ch'u, *Shih chi* 7.76 (Wang). That is the source of line 361, with which we may compare Yü's statement of someone's flight to Chiang-ling during Hou Ching's rebellion (*Works* 15.50a7–8): 'Turning his back on the Pass and longing for Ch'u, he traveled there in a little boat.' T'ai-po, the founder of the ancient state of Wu, is supposed to have gone there in order to allow a younger brother (the father of the later King Wen) to succeed to the Chou throne. Yü did not, of course, expect Hsiao Yi to give up the throne to a younger brother; he is referring here to Yi's failure to return to 'Wu', or Chien-k'ang. I have supplied the name of T'ai-po, identified in line 362 by his ceremonial clothing, Legge (1), V, 813b (Wu).

The soldiers of Green Wood (line 363) were a group of bandits who took refuge on a mountain of that name about fifty miles northwest of Chiang-ling; they were instrumental in overthrowing Wang Mang (*Hou-Han shu* 11.1b, Wang). Runaway conscripts from Ch'in Shih-huang's tomb at Li-shan ('Black Mountain') were also important in the fall of the Ch'in; the most famous of these are the ones set free by the eventual founder of the Han, who had been supposed to escort them to the tomb site. See Watson (6), I, 80. The place-names serve only to identify the allusions; Yü Hsin means weak armies sent out against rebels.

In 689 B.C., Ch'u, attacking the small state of Sui (Herrmann, p. 5 C3), 'opened a road, bridged the Cha, and camped its army overlooking Sui' (trans. after S. Couvreur, I, 134; cf. Legge (1), V, 76, 77a; Wu). During his initial war with his nephew Ch'a, Hsiao Yi had lost among other places two cities irresistibly suggesting this *Tso chuan* passage: Hsia-cha and Sui-chün (*Tzu-chih t'ung-chien*, pp. 5031, 5033); as Hu San-hsing points out, the place-name Hsia-cha refers to the Cha River bridged during the Ch'u attack on Sui. Ch'a, in alliance with the Western Wei, finally killed Hsiao Yi and his sons (lines 395, 473–4).

Hsiao Yi was forced to resort to sorcery in his war against his brother Chi, as explained in Chapter 1, but Chi was eventually captured and killed (lines 366–9). A Duke of Sung who had sacrificed the ruler of another state was warned that such an offering to an 'unclean and dark spirit' would not help him attain his goal of hegemony (Couvreur, I, 321; cf. Legge (1), V, 175, 177a; Wang). In line 368, the reading *wu* 'shaman' is better attested than Ni's *fu* 'talisman, spell' (*Chou shu*, *Yi-wen lei-chü*, *Wen-yüan ying hua*, and the SPTK edition of the works). Either word would rhyme satisfactorily.

Yü's place-names tend to be meaningful only as identifications of analogous ancient events; in lines 369–70 he supplies both the ancient and the contemporary sites involved. The allusions are, quite appropriately, to two succession disputes of the *Spring and Autumn* period. A younger brother of a Duke of Cheng had been seizing Cheng territory for himself, including Lin-yen; according to the *Tso chuan*, he was finally driven into exile, Legge (1), V, 2, 6 (Wang). Yü combines that account, the source of the Lin-yen, with the *Kung-yang Commentary*, where the Duke kills his brother (*Ch'un-ch'iu ching-chuan yin-te* 2/Yin 1/*Kung*). A member of the ruling family of Lu was poisoned by a brother because of another succession dispute and died at K'uei-ch'üan, Legge (1), V, 120, 121 (Wang). Hsiao Chi was captured and beheaded in August of 553 near Ching-men, a mountain on the south side of the Yangtze about forty miles west of Chiang-ling (*Tzu-chih t'ung-chien*, p. 5103). Hsiao Lun, the subject of lines 341–8, was killed by Western Wei troops near Hsia-k'ou in February of 551. It is irrelevant that Lun was not actually killed by his brother's forces, as the allusion in line 370 would suggest. Wang Seng-pien's army was hunting him down, and if they did not kill him, it was only because the Western Wei got there first.

Line 371 is based on *Hsiao ching* 5.3a; cf. Legge (2), p. 478. The original context requires Legge's translation: 'The sages proceeded from the [feeling of]

. . . affection to teach [the duties of] love.' Yü here adapts the original to mean 'to teach love by his own behavior toward relatives'.

For 'fraternal feeling', line 372 says literally 'peaceful happiness', from *Shih ching* 164: 'When brothers are concordant, they are peacefully happy and steeped in joy', trans. Karlgren (2), p. 108 (Wu). The preface to the original (*Mao Shih Cheng chien* 9.3b), which explains it as a lament on the rebellion of the brothers of the Duke of Chou, adds depth to Yü's quotation from it. It is apparent from the context that the phrase 'drew back his bow' refers to a *Mencius* parable about fratricide.[73]

An ancient general of Lu, criticized for meddling in matters that the 'meat-eaters' were discussing, replied, 'The meat-eaters are poor creatures, and cannot form any far-reaching plans'; cf. Legge (1), V, 85, 86a (Wang).

Lines 375—88 indicate that Hsiao Yi, blind to everything except the throne he hoped to gain, had destroyed his own state. It had been predicted that an ancient Prince of Ch'u would be unable to take the throne because of five difficulties; these included such things as poor planning, hostile relatives, and the prince's own vices (Chavannes, IV, 369; cf. Legge (1), V, 644, 650a; Wang). The Ch'u Prince had in the end ruled only ten days; Hsiao Yi, who had similar difficulties, only about two years.

In line 375, Ni Fan and all three editions of the *Chou shu* read 'two' (*erh*), instead of the 'three' (*san*) of the *Wen-yüan ying-hua*, SPTK edition of the works, and many of the modern texts. 'Three' would give a senseless reference to the *Han Shih wai chuan*: 'the superior man avoids the three points (*san tuan*): he avoids the brush-point of the literary man; he avoids the spear-point of the military man; he avoids the tongue-point of the sophist' (trans. Hightower (3), p. 227; Wu). I have followed the *Chou shu* reading and the interpretation of the editor of the 1971 Peking *Chou shu* (p. 749, note 27).

Yang-ch'eng (line 377) is a mountain in Honan, mentioned in the *Tso chuan* as one of the steepest in China, Legge (1), V, 596b (Wang). Ti-chu is a peak in the middle of the Yellow River in Honan. Lines 377—8 are interesting because of the chance survival of a fragrant of an old commentary on the 'Lament', quoted in the *Lei yao* by Yen Shu (991—1055). The anonymous commentator cites a passage from the *Shih tzu*: 'Pi-kan protested to Chou [the evil last king of the Shang], "Your danger today is no different from climbing Yang-ch'eng . . .",', the remainder being identical to lines 377—8. This passage is not found in modern texts of the *Shih tzu*;[74] what makes it interesting is the fact that the metaphor was originally applied to King Chou.

Line 379 is taken, with an added *yü*, from an ancient judgment on the future Duke Hui of Chin, then attempting to gain the throne for himself, Legge (1), V, 153, 155b (Wang). Line 381, with small differences in wording, is a common expression for opportunistic fence-sitting. Line 382, like line 372, is a reference to *Shih ching* 164: 'Brothers hurry [in aid] in difficulties', trans. Karlgren (2), p. 107 (Wang).

Chia Yi once said that the small state of Huai-yang, compared to the larger states, was like a mole on a face, *Han shu* 48.26a (Wang); 'mole' would be ambiguous in English, hence the paraphrase 'wart'. A crossbow pellet is also an old metaphor for restricted territory, as in *Shih chi* 76.14 (Wu).

To make sense of line 385, we must adopt Wang's suggestion that this *tu* is borrowed for a phonetically identical word in the *Tso chuan* phrase *yüan tu* (two occurrences in Chao, 8; Legge (1), V, 620, 622a). Line 386 is based on an ancient play on words. The ruler of Wu had asked for the renewal of an agreement (*hsün meng*, the normal phrase for this, with twenty-nine occurrences listed in *Ch'un-ch'iu ching-chuan yin-te*, pp. 1120b—1121a). He was told that if a covenant can be renewed (*hsün*, or 'warmed up', Karlgren (4), number 662a), it can also be made cold, Legge (1), V, 827, 829a (Wang).

A daughter of the Fiery Emperor, drowned in the Eastern Sea, was transformed into a bird, most commonly called Ching-wei but with the alternate name 'Vengeful Bird'. She continually carried sticks and pebbles from West Mountain to fill up the sea (*Shu-yi chi* A.4a, Wang; *Shan-hai ching* 3.16b, Ni; cf. Hightower (4), pp. 241—2). According to another legend, a man almost ninety years old decided to move a mountain from an inconvenient location; the impossible project was finally completed with divine assistance, *Lieh tzu chi-shih*, pp. 99—101; trans. A. C. Graham, pp. 99—101.

In line 389 read *hsiao* 'night' (as in the Po-na edition of the *Chou shu* and the *Yi-wen lei-chü*) instead of *chao* 'dawn, morning'. The latter appears below in line 391, and there is no necessity for the banal antithesis *day/night*. Line 390 sounds ominous enough as it stands, but the author was perhaps thinking of the famous shower of stars in the seventh year of Duke Chuang of Lu, already the subject of line 90; the *Tso chuan* account of that could have provided the word *yün* 'fall'.

Clouds like a flock of red birds flying around the sun for three days were taken as an omen of the death of a king of Ch'u, Legge (1), V, 808, 810b (Wang). The clouds of line 392 served to warn another king of Ch'u that the rulers of seven states were planning his death, *Pei-t'ang shu-ch'ao* 55.3b (Kao Pu-ying). Given Yü's constant use of Ch'u as a symbol for Emperor Yüan, the meaning of such passages is obvious. It was supposedly predicted in 509 B.C. that Yüeh would destroy Wu within forty years; the prediction came true in 474, Legge (1), V, 738, 740a, 854 (Wu). A similar prediction of the arrival of the conquering Wu armies in Ying, the Ch'u capital, in a *keng-ch'en* year also came true in 505 B.C., Legge (1), V, 736, 738b, 749, 753 (Wang). Chiang-ling, of course, was on the site of Ying.

Chou is the author's regular metaphor for any Liang emperor, and here for Emperor Yüan. Cheng, ruled by a branch of the Chou royal family (line 221), symbolizes a Liang prince, here Hsiao Ch'a, who has already appeared in line 365 and who joined with the Western Wei ('Ch'in') in attacking Chiang-ling. Lines 395—6 are examples of Yü's unusual syntax, glossed by the parallel passage in one of his 'Yung-huai' poems (*Works* 3.38a): 'The Chou king met with the wrath of Cheng; the ruler of Ch'u encountered the vengeance of Ch'in' (*Chou wang feng Cheng fen*; *Ch'u hou chih Ch'in yüan*). Line 395 is perhaps a reference to a Cheng attack on Chou in 719 B.C., Legge (1), V, 11, 13a. Line 396, an obvious allusion to the third-century B.C. destruction of Ch'u by Ch'in, may be without more specific reference.

Music-Master K'uang once predicted the defeat of a Ch'u army because, having sung the airs of the South, he found them 'without strength', Legge (1), V, 477, 479b (Wu). Line 398 is based on another prediction, that Chin would be defeated by Ch'in, the 'neighbor to the west', Legge (1), V, 165, 169a (Wu).

In line 399 I have followed von Zach's interpretation of *t'i-ch'ung* as 'Sturmleitern'. The phrase is normally glossed as two separate things, scaling ladders (*yün-t'i*) and a wheeled vehicle with soldiers inside used somewhat like a battering ram (*ch'ung-ch'e*), Morohashi, 14881/21. If the vehicle was as low and cumbersome as it appears in Morohashi's illustration (34069/31), it could not possibly dance wildly, nor could it attain the heights reported in a Latter Han description of an attack: '*T'i-ch'ung* danced above our towers', *Hou-Han shu* 73.15a (Wu). Everything, including the parallel with 'Horses of Chi', suggests that *t'i-ch'ung* means one thing, not two; Morohashi himself explains the two words in opposite order (*ch'ung-t'i*) simply as 'tall ladder' (34069/48).

Chi, in Hopeh, had been famous for its horses, Legge (1), V, 592, 596b. *Hou-Han shu* 74.19a has a passage identical to line 400 except for word-order (Wang), and in Wang Seng-pien's report of the victory over Hou Ching even the word-order is the same, *Liang shu* 5.17b.

As explained in Chapter 1, Yü Hsin went on his mission to Ch'ang-an on May 27, 554; this mission is clearly the subject of lines 409—10. There was nominally peace between the Western Wei and the Liang until November of 554. We must therefore take lines 399—404 as referring to threatening gestures rather than actual warfare; that certainly is the effect of lines 401—4, at least. A shallow body (*chien shou*) and protruding wheel-naves (*ch'ang ku*) appear as characteristics of war chariots in *Shih ching* 128, one of the 'Airs of Ch'in';

cf. Karlgren (2), p. 82 (Wang). The Gate of Thunder, mentioned in *Han shu*
76.23b (Wu) is explained by Yen Shih-ku as a gate of K'uai-chi, the site of
a large drum which could be heard in Loyang, about 600 miles away.

Lu notes that Chu-ko Liang once besieged Ch'en-ts'ang (without capturing
it, one must add; see Fang (1), I, 286, note 36d) and that he is said at the end
of his biography to have invented a *lien nu* (apparently a repeating crossbow[75]), *San-kuo chih* 35.15a. That will not do as an explanation of line 403;
we need a specific incident. In the absence of that, I have followed Morohashi's
interpretation of Yü Hsin's *lien nu* as verb and object (38902/236.2); that is
grammatically easier and fits the parallel with line 404 better. Han Hsin once
tricked an enemy into expecting him to cross at Lin-chin but actually moved
his troops across elsewhere, Watson (6), I, 213 (Wu). The place-names in
lines 403—4 may be significant; both were in Shensi and fairly near Ch'ang-
an.

We have already seen the seven marshes as a symbol of the great size of
Ch'u in line 267. Hsiang Yü's uncle was told of a prophecy that 'though but
three houses be left in Ch'u, it is she who will destroy Ch'in', Watson (6),
I, 41 (Wu). Lines 407—8 reintroduce the hunting metaphor for war. During
one of those ideally chivalrous battles in the *Tso chuan*, someone being pursued
by the enemy saw six deer and shot one of them, which he presented to his
pursuers; they broke off the chase. This same passage provides the unusual
meaning of *li* 'to hit', Legge (1), V, 313, 319a (Wang). The anonymous
commentary on the 'Lament' in Yen Shu's *Lei yao* quotes a story of a Ch'u
royal hunt in Yün-meng, the drums rumbling like thunder, where nine tigers
simply lay down and died (Wu).

Lines 409—10 are adapted from the 'Nine Hymns': 'Gently the wind of
autumn whispers; On the waves of the Tung-t'ing lake the leaves are falling',
Ch'u tz'u 2.12a, trans. Hawkes (1), p. 38; 'Gazing at the distant Ts'en-yang
mooring/I waft my magic across the Great River', *Ch'u tz'u* 2.8a—b, trans.
Hawkes (2), p. 73. Next to the title, these two lines are the most conspicuous
Ch'u tz'u references in the 'Lament'; with them Yü announces his departure
on his ill-fated mission to the North. Since he left in May, the falling leaves
are not to be taken literally; they serve rather as a warning of the great
winter coming for the Liang.

Lines 411—12 are based on divination about a battle between Ch'in and
Chin in 644 B.C. The ruler of Chin having consulted the *Yi ching*, the results
were explained to him: 'The fire burns the flags: — our military expeditions
will be without advantage', Legge (1), V, 169a (Wu). Ch'in obtained the
hexagram *Ku*, composed of the trigram symbolizing wind in the lower or
chen position and that for mountain in the upper position; this indicated
three victories over Chin and capture of the Chin ruler, *Ibid.*, 164, 167b.

Emperor Yüan had gathered in Chiang-ling the largest library in China.
He set fire to it just before going out to surrender to the conquering Wei
army, and on his way out of the city he is said to have struck the gate with
his sword, *Nan shih* 8.15a. The *Tzu-chih t'ung-chien* version (p. 5121) has
improved on the story a little; here the Emperor has to be restrained from
throwing himself into the flames, and he takes his sword and hacks at a pillar
until the sword breaks, thus showing his rage at the failure of both learning
and military means to save him. Lines 413—14 are difficult to interpret. It
is possible that 413 refers to the burning of the library, an event which
horrified contemporaries as much as the destruction of the one at Alexandria.
It is most unlikely, on the other hand, that line 414 means that 'Emperor
Yüan also hacked at a pillar with his sword'; this would make an appalling
anticlimax. 'Dragon-Pattern' can mean various things, among them a sword
made for a king of Wu, *Po-wu chih* 4.3a—b (Wu). Columns covered with carved
dragons are quite common, and in view of Yü Hsin's syntax the line could
equally well mean, 'They hacked at the dragon-patterned columns.' In either
case, as long as Dragon-Pattern does not have to be a single sword belonging
to a ruler, there is no problem. The line would remind us of Han Kao-tsu's
drunken followers, who hacked at the pillars of the Han palace with their
swords (Watson (6), I, 293), and also of the rebels in line 317, who had
'propped bows against Jade-girl windows'.

As von Zach says, the places in lines 415—16 have to be the topics of lines
417—18, either under siege themselves or trying to relieve a siege somewhere
else. It is a reasonable hypothesis that the place under siege is Chiang-ling,
and the allusion in line 415 would justify this interpretation. At the end of
the reign of Wang Mang, a group of rebels rose in the general area of Hankow;
they then moved west and established themselves at Nan-chün, where they
assumed the title of Troops from the Lower Yangtze (*Hsia-Chiang ping*),
Hou-Han shu 15.6a. This was presumably because they had originated farther
down the Yangtze, as the commentator Chin Cho suggests. There is thus no
evidence for Lu's claim that Hsia-chiang was the name of a place in what
would be Wu-ning *chün* (north of Chiang-ling) under the Liang. Nan-chün,
where the rebels established themselves, had its capital at the later Chiang-ling,
and (as pointed out earlier) Emperor Yüan calls Yü Chien-wu a native of
Nan-chün to indicate Chiang-ling. This suggests, not too surprisingly, that
the 'old fortress of the troops from the lower Yangtze' is simply Chiang-
ling, at least for Yü Hsin's purposes. The *yü* and *ku*, synonymous in this
context, indicate that the author is speaking of the actual places, not simply
using them as metaphors (as he does so often). The Ch'ang-lin in line 416
is more of a problem. It is true, as Lu says, that the Chin established a Ch'ang-
lin *hsien* in what would be the Wu-ning *chün* of the Liang, but the 'former

camp' requires some story about an army, which we do not have. We cannot be sure that this army, possibly rebels, were at or even from the Ch'ang-lin founded by the Chin, if line 415 is any guide. It is simpler to hypothesize that at some unknown time a 'Ch'ang-lin' army had had a camp somewhere near Chiang-ling.

Line 417 refers to a kind of psychological warfare used by inhabitants of an ancient besieged city. They put food before their horses, to suggest to observers that there were ample provisions, but first they blocked the horses' mouths so that they could not eat (*Ch'un-ch'iu ching-chuan yin-te* 202/Hsüan 15/2 *Kung*, Wang). The Warring States general T'ien Tan, surrounded by a Yen army, gathered a thousand oxen, tied weapons to their horns and oil-soaked reeds to their tails, and set fire to the reeds. The maddened animals broke through the besieging forces, *Shih chi* 82.5–6 (Wu).

Line 419 involves a Chinese equivalent of the Trojan horse. Someone wishing to attack a small state found the roads inadequate; he therefore presented the ruler of the state with a set of large bells mounted on a big wagon. The delighted recipient set out to open a road wide enough to permit the wagon to pass, despite the objections of Ch'ih-chang Man-chih, who felt that the gift was suspiciously lavish in view of the size of their state. His warnings going unheeded, he cut off the wheel-naves of his chariot (apparently to permit passage down the narrow road then existing) and fled. Soon after-wards his state was in fact destroyed, *Lü-shih ch'un-ch'iu* 15.6b (Wang). Yü has amputated part of the man's name to match the name in line 420.

Kung Chih-ch'i advised against allowing a Chin army to pass through his state to attack a third state, knowing that his own would then fall to the returning Chin army. This did happen as predicted, but not before he him-self had fled with all his family, Legge (1), V, 143, 145b–146a (Wu). It seems best to ignore the unheeded warnings and concentrate on flight, which is what lines 419–22 have in common. Emperor Kuang-wu of the Latter Han, fleeing with his army, was told by a scout that there was neither solid ice nor boats to get them across a river ahead. He sent someone to check, who reported (falsely) that the ice was solid, simply to avoid a panic and keep the army moving. By the time they reached the river, the ice was indeed solid enough to permit crossing by all but the last few cavalrymen, *Hou-Han shu* 20.5a (Wu).

Line 422 refers to the famous story of a man who by imitating a cock-crow enabled Lord Meng-ch'ang to get through the Han-ku Pass and thus escape pursuing Ch'in forces, *Shih chi* 75.9 (Wang).

For lines 423–4 we are again helped by the anonymous commentator quoted in Yen Shu's *Lei yao* (*chüan* 9, 'Mediocre Rulers', according to Kao

Pu-ying). Line 423 is taken verbatim from the king of Yüeh's denunciation of the king of Wu, *Kuo-yü* 21.3b; line 424 is identical to a passage from the *Shih tzu* (not in present reconstructed texts) describing the results of having a 'little man' on the throne. Both *chieh ku* and *t'un sheng* admit two interpretations (Morohashi, 35067/99, 3329/29); I have taken lines 423—4 as anticipating what follows, still another couplet at the end of a rhyme-section announcing the subject of the following section.

The Chang-hua Tower, built by King Ling of Ch'u (Legge (1), V, 611, 615), was almost as much a symbol of that state as the hunting park, Yün-meng. The *wang* sacrifices are also associated with Ch'u, for example in Chavannes, IV, 367. It might be possible to take line 425 as meaning that Emperor Yüan was praying for deliverance, but context suggests making lines 425—6 references to the slaughter of the defenders, human sacrifices (line 425) and human prey in a hunt, again the hunting metaphor for war (line 426). Each of the two lines has to make a complete statement in itself; we cannot, as with lines 415—16, take them as the topics of what follows. Han Kao-tsu, told that Han Hsin, King of Ch'u, was planning to rebel, 'pretended to be going on an excursion' (*wei yu*) in Yün-meng; the purpose was to induce the rebel to come out to meet him, as etiquette required (*Shih chi* 8.70, Wang). An excursion in Yün-meng could only mean a hunt, hence my translation.

Lines 427—8 are taken almost intact from a *Tso chuan* account of the aftermath of a disastrous defeat of a Ch'u army, brought about largely by the folly of its commander, the Mo-ao. The only change the author has made is in word-order; in the original the people are at the beginning of each line, and the place-names at the end (adapted from Legge (1), V, 60, 61a; Wang). This couplet is the most famous example of Yü's syntax, but not the most remarkable; lines 395—6 are much stranger. Both Legge and Couvreur (I, 113), following Tu Yü (*Ch'un-ch'iu CCCC* 2.14a), treat the Mo-ao's death as suicide. The original is ambiguous, but in line 427 a killing makes better sense.

Line 429 is corrupt. Ni's *Hsing-ku* (the site of Ch'in Shih-huang's massacre of the scholars) would make no sense here. The Po-na edition of the *Chou shu* has *chou ching* 'province and pitfall', a phrase with nothing to recommend it. I have therefore restored the *hsing ching* of the other texts, equally meaningless but at least well-attested. In 429 we are apparently missing a pair of savage animals or birds, something to parallel line 430. Hawks and falcons are common symbols of ferocity; as Wu notes, they appear twice in the *Tso chuan* in this sense, Legge (1), V, 282b, 517b.

Tsou Yen, despite total loyalty to his ruler, was imprisoned because of slander. He looked up at the heavens and wailed; as a sign of his innocence there came a frost, though it was summer. Li Shan, *WH* 39.19b, attributes this to the *Huai-nan tzu*, but, as Kao notes, it is not found in the present text.

Line 432 seems to be a reference to the general Keng Kung. Once, when his water supply was cut off by the besieging Hsiung-nu, he dug a deep well but could still find no water; he then prayed before the well and water gushed out, *Hou-Han shu* 19.21b (Ni). When Ch'i Liang was killed in battle, his widow wailed over his body at the foot of a city wall; after she had continued in this way for ten days, the wall fell down, *Lieh nü chuan* 4.13a (Wu). The spots on a certain kind of bamboo[76] were popularly explained as caused by the tears of the two Ladies of the Hsiang, mourning their late husband Shun (*Po-wu chih* 10.2a, Wu).

Lines 435–42 describe the plight of the Liang captives, numbering some tens of thousands, who were carried off into slavery in the North. The Ching River, a tributary of the Wei in Shensi, was supposed once to have been poisoned by Ch'in to prevent an attack by Chin, Legge (1), V, 460, 464b (Wang). Mount Ching-hsing, famous for its precipitousness (Lu), is located about 270 miles southwest of Peking on the border of the ancient state of Chao. Lines 435–6 could also be comparative: '. . . more poisonous than . . . higher than . . .'

Lines 437–8 measure the captives' progress in terms of post stations, a major one every ten *li*, a minor one every five *li*. There was a popular belief that swallows hibernated underground in winter (Morohashi, 33537/2 – swallows do not, but whippoorwills do), and we read that at the time of Emperor Yüan of the Chin (*reg.* 317–23), the starving people would dig up these hibernating swallows and eat them, *Chin shu* 67.8a (Wu). A fleeing emperor is said to have made his way by the light of fireflies, *Hou-Han shu* 8.23a (Wang).

Lines 441–2 play on place names. Black Water was a river in Ch'in, mentioned in the 'Tribute of Yü', Legge (1), III, 135, cf. 119 (Wang). Green (or Blue, or Black) Mud was the name of a mountain and fortress in that same area, Morohashi, 42564/419, 420.

The Tzu and Sheng are both rivers in Ch'i; there was a saying that someone with a good sense of taste would be able to tell them apart, even if they were mixed together (A. C. Graham, p. 166; Wang). Line 446 is a metaphor for the indiscriminate enslavement of the upper and lower class. The great families thought of themselves as the 'pure stream' (*ch'ing liu*) and those of lower birth as the muddy or turbid stream (*cho liu*). Shen Chiung uses the same metaphor for the same purpose in his 'Returning Soul', which has been proposed as a model for the 'Lament'. In Shen's *fu*, the two rivers are the Ching and Wei (*Ching Wei hsiang luan*, *Ch'üan Ch'en wen* 14.3a10); Shen's was the traditional phrase, and Yü's the more original.

In line 447, one would expect 'Snow white as sand'. The author is thinking

of the North as the land of sandstorms and snowstorms, and combining both
ideas in a single line. Compare his poem 'On Hearing Them Beating Cloth at
Night' (*Works* 3.56b), dealing with women preparing cloth to make winter
clothes for their husbands away at the frontier: 'By the jade steps, the wind is
getting strong; The Great Wall must be dark with snow' (*Ch'ang-ch'eng
hsüeh ying an*). Lu Chao-lin (*c.* 634–84) was evidently thinking of lines
447–8 when he wrote his 'Song of the Falling Snow': 'The snow seems dark
as the Tartar sands [*hsüeh ssu Hu sha an*], The ice as bright as the Chinese
moon' (trans. Stephen Owen (2), p. 97).

   Lu Chi, a native of the Three Kingdoms state of Wu, was forced to go to
the Chin capital at Loyang after the fall of his own state, *Chin shu* 54.4a
(Wu). The phrase 'hurrying to Loyang', which implies the imperial command
involved, is taken from the titles of two series of poems written by Lu on that
occasion, *WH* 26.18b–19a, 26.20a–b (Wu). Wang Ts'an (177–217), who
fled south to escape the warfare at the end of the Han, wrote about his homesickness in the famous *fu* 'Climbing the Tower' (*WH* 11.1b–3a, trans. Watson
(2), pp. 52–4). The Lung River in Ch'in was a standard symbol for exile;
according to a popular song, it had such a mournful sound that it would break
your heart to listen to it (*T'ai-p'ing yü-lan* 50.1b, Wang).

   Literally, lines 453–4 say, 'You [my husband] are in Chiao-ho, and I
[your wife] am in Ch'ing-po.' The style is that of the popular poems about
rejected or abandoned women; a similar passage, with different place names,
had also appeared in an earlier *fu*, Chiang Yen's 'Separation' (*WH* 16.29b,
trans. Watson (2), p. 99). Chiao-ho (Herrmann, p. 16 F2) was a fortress in
modern Sinkiang; Ch'ing-po was apparently in Honan. Line 455 refers to a
woman who stood looking after her husband, who was going off to war, until
she turned to stone (*Ch'u-hsüeh chi*, p. 108; Wang). A fragment of the *Shu-
yi chi* quoted in *T'ai-p'ing yü-lan* 178.4b mentions a Watching-for-Son Ridge
(*Wang-tzu ling*, Lu). Unfortunately, the passage is missing from the present
text of the *Shu-yi chi*, and the *T'ai-p'ing yü-lan* quotation breaks off before
explaining the origin of the name.

   Line 457 is normally referred to a Hsieh T'iao poem about a palace woman
of Han-tan married to a groom, *Hsieh Hsüan-ch'eng chi chiao-chu*, p. 462.
This is not satisfactory; Han-tan was the capital of Chao and had nothing to
do with Tai. More promising is a passage in one of the author's autobiographical
'Lien chu' where he speaks of 'the grief of the widow in Liao-tung, the sobs
of the bereaved wife of Tai-chün' (*Works* 9.9a). The context of that passage
is similar to this section; it goes on to speak of the falling wall and the stained
bamboos, the same allusions as in lines 433–4. Ni's explanation of the 'Lien
chu' passage might do for line 457: A sister of a king of Chao was married
to a king of Tai. After her brother murdered her husband and annexed Tai,

she committed suicide (*Shih chi* 43.29–30). The only problem, and it is a major one, is that the sister of a king of Chao, presumably the principal wife of the king of Tai, could hardly be called what I have rendered as 'Palace Woman'. This was not a distinguished title; literally 'talented person', it was normally given to concubines skilled in music.

The Chin Princess of Ch'ing-ho, carried off into slavery at the fall of Loyang, was treated with great cruelty by her new masters. Emperor Yüan rescued her and executed her oppressors, *Chin shu* 31.11b (Wang).

Yü seems to have made a mistake about an allusion in line 459, which is based on an entry in the 'Essay on Bibliography', *Han shu* 30.23b: *Pieh Hsü-yang fu wu p'ien*. As Ku Yen-wu points out (21.20a), in the *Han shu* context Pieh has to be a surname (not the verb 'to part') and Hsü-yang a given name: 'Five *Fu* by Pieh Hsü-yang'. Line 460 is based on another entry in the 'Essay on Bibliography', *Han shu* 30.24a–b: *Lin-chiang wang chi ch'ou-ssu chieh-shih ko-shih ssu p'ien*. Here it is the present *Han shu* text that is corrupt; it should say, not 'Four Songs *about* the King of Lin-chiang, Sorrow, and the Man of Honor', but 'Four Songs *by* the King of Lin-chiang about Sorrow and the Man of Honor'. The word 'and' (*chi*) has slipped into the text from one of the neighboring entries, where it appears frequently when two authors' works are combined under one title (for example, the entry immediately after the Lin-chiang one). No one has discovered any other reference to a 'Song of Sorrow' by the King of Lin-chiang, but both Lu Chüeh and Li Po wrote poems to the *yüeh-fu* title 'The King of Lin-chiang's Song of the Man of Honor' (Ting Fu-pao, pp. 841–2; *Li T'ai-po shih chi* 4.15a; Wang Ying-lin, Wang Hsien-ch'ien). Tu Fu himself asks, 'Are the men of honor of Lin-chiang worth counting?' (*Tu shih yin-te* 225/2/21).

Wu-wei (line 461) was in Kansu, and Chin-wei a mountain in Mongolia; all these places are merely hyperboles for the remoteness of Ch'ang-an. Pan Ch'ao, the great Latter Han general, after spending most of his life in Central Asia, wrote a letter to the Emperor saying that he hoped only to come in alive through the Yü-men Pass, *Hou-Han shu* 47.16a (Wu). Wen Hsü, another Latter Han general in the Western Region, was buried next to the wall of Loyang in a site granted by the emperor. His ghost appeared to his oldest son in a dream saying that he felt homesick, and the son resigned his post to return the body home, *Hou-Han shu* 81.10a (Wang).

In one of the apocryphal Li Ling-Su Wu poems, the two men are compared to a pair of ducks flying north, only one (Su Wu) to return south, *Yi-wen lei-chü* 29.4a (Wang). Su Wu was supposed to have forced the Shan-yü to release him by arranging for a Han envoy to report that the Emperor, hunting in the Shang-lin Park, had shot down a goose with a note tied to its leg telling where Su was (*Han shu* 54.20b, Wu).

Lines 467—78 recapitulate the fall of Chiang-ling. Lines 479—86 trace
its consequences in the return of the capital to Chien-k'ang and the abdication
of the last Liang ruler, and lines 487—94 are general observations on the fall
of the Liang. The disaster at Chin-ling (a literary name for Chien-k'ang, as
in line 4 of the preface) was the abdication leading to the founding of the
Ch'en.

The unusual phrase *chung p'i* in line 467 may have been taken from a
dirge by Yen Yen-chih, *WH* 57.12a (Yang). Line 469 imitates a *Tso chuan*
passage, Legge (1), V, 480, 483a (Wu). *Hsiao ch'iang* in line 470, from the
Lun yü (Legge (1), I, 309), was commonly used of discord within a family.
Hsiao Lun warned his brother Yi that unless he could end the fratricidal
warfare 'within the enclosure', the Liang must surely fall, since it would be
unable to deal with its external enemies, *Ch'üan Liang wen* 22.10b5.

As often happens with antithetical couplets, lines 471—2 make sense
only if we read them together, in this case combining the last words of the
two lines in a single statement: Emperor Yüan's 'sacrifices were cut off
abruptly'. Yü seems to be thinking of a *Tso chuan* passage where, with the
fall of two states, their common ancestor's 'sacrifices were cut off abruptly'
(*pu ssu hu chu*), cf. Legge (1), V, 240, 241b. He has replaced *hu chu*, a
hapax legomenon, with *hu yen*; apparently he considered the two phrases
interchangeable.[77]

However bad Emperor Yüan may have been, he had put down Hou Ching's
rebellion and thus could legitimately claim the titles in lines 471—2. However,
Yü is certainly playing on the irony of a restorer destroying his dynasty.

Lines 473—4 are actually a single line, one of the very rare lines of 'prose'
in the 'Lament', though it still ends in a rhyme. I have divided the two phrases
in order to preserve the line numbering, with odd/even couplets. The 'elder
and younger' is taken from *Shih ching* 37, where it appears in the opposite
order, Karlgren (2), pp. 23—4. 'Uncles', the apparent meaning of the original,
would make no sense in this passage; Yü is following Mao, who explains them
as indicating only elder and younger, *Mao Shih Cheng chien* 2.11b—12a. In
line 474, *yu tzu* 'like a son' is a set phrase for a nephew, coming perhaps
from the *Li chi* statement that the nephews of the dead man wear the same
kind of mourning 'as his sons' (*yu tzu*), *Li chi cheng-yi* 8.3a (Wu). The phrase
was a cliché by this time; a nephew of Emperor Wu, for example, is referred
to as his 'like-a-son', *Tzu-chih t'ung-chien*, p. 5127, line 12. Lines 473—4
are the familiar general comment on the fate of the sons of a principal figure
in the 'Lament'. There is little information about Emperor Yüan's sons,
but we do now know that his nephew Hsiao Ch'a killed at least two of
them, and probably more (*Tzu-chih t'ung-chien*, pp. 5122—3).

The basic idea of lines 475—6 is that good men are like pearls and jade.

By Yü Hsin's time, no self-respecting writer could use such a cliché, at least
not without reworking it. Elsewhere, writing of the death of Wang Pao, Yü
calls him 'Capable of restoring moisture to withered trees; Able to make
flowing water form circular ripples' (*Works* 4.21b10—22a1). The old metaphor
is barely recognizable here, but the first line describes the supposed effect
of jade, and the second that of pearls; in short, Wang Pao was like jade and
pearls. In lines 475—6, the metaphor is embedded in allusions to two of the
most famous treasures of ancient China, a disk carved from a jade block
found by Pien Ho on Mount Ching (Liao, I, 133; Wang) and the great pearl
of the Marquis of Sui. The latter was supposed to have treated the injury of
a snake, which later gave him the pearl out of gratitude (*Huai-nan tzu* 6.3b
commentary, Kao). The next step comes naturally; if good men are like jade
and pearls, a pointless sacrifice of them is like throwing away the two
treasures. In the *Debates on Salt and Iron* someone argues that only rarity
makes things valuable: 'Around the K'un-[lun] Mountains they throw jade
blocks at magpies' (*Yen-t'ieh lun* 7.2a, Wang). It would probably be quibbling
to demand an equivalent saying about Mount Ching, particularly with an
author capable of line 476, where the pearl, instead of being presented by
the snake, is thrown at it. This twisting of the original allusion is quite
deliberate; compare line 37 of the preface, where only the association between the general and the tree remains from the source. The pearl, incidentally,
can die because pearls were thought of as living things in a way, waxing and
waning with the moon (cf. Schafer, pp. 7—8).

Ghost fire in line 477 is a name of the will-o'-the-wisp, thought to be caused
by the blood of men killed in battle (*Shuo-wen chieh-tzu ku-lin*, p. 4521a;
Wu). Bands of men from P'ing-lin (about 140 miles northeast of Chiang-
ling) and Hsin-shih (about 90 miles northeast of Chiang-ling) had joined in
the armies overthrowing Wang Mang (*Hou-Han shu* 1A.3a, Wu), but a more
specific reference would be desirable. Yü may be thinking of a ghost story;
he was fond of them.

Lines 479 and 480 both invert their sources. Line 479 reverses an obscure
statement in *Shih chi* 8.19: *Feng ku Liang hsi*, which Chavannes translates:
'[La population de] *Fong* se compose d'anciens émigrés de *Leang*' (II, 338).
It is explained, with the help of *Han shu* 1B.22a, as a reference to the transfer
of the Warring States Wei capital from Ta-liang to Feng, after a major defeat
by Ch'in. It is far too late in the poem for the author to be talking about
the move from Chien-k'ang to Chiang-ling; in fact, he means the opposite.
He has inverted the original to say, in effect, that the Warring States Wei
went from Feng back to its old capital at Ta-liang. This can only refer to the
reestablishment of the Liang at Chien-k'ang after the fall of Chiang-ling,
defeated by 'Ch'in'. Line 479 would make equally good sense whatever

the dynasty; the fact that it was the Liang is merely a bonus, as in the case of the 'grain of Chou' in line 26 of the preface.

Line 480 refers to the prophecy that even though there were only three households left in Ch'u, it was she who would destroy Ch'in; compare line 406. Here again the original is reversed, for obvious reasons.

A man who by several murders had secured the accession of a Marquis of Chin was asked by his new lord, 'Is it not a difficult thing to be your ruler?' This was a broad hint that he should commit suicide. He replied, 'If others had not been removed, how could you have found room to rise?' (*pu yu fei yeh, chün ho yi hsing*), Legge (1), V, 156, 157a (Wang). The word *fei* here has nothing to do with deposing a ruler. After the death in battle of his eldest son, whom he disliked, Emperor Yüan is supposed to have quoted the *Tso chuan* murderer's reply to 'console' his second son, now become his heir (*Liang shu* 44.9a).

Lines 483—4 are also based on the *Tso chuan*. Someone was trying to decide whether to give his daughter in marriage to Ch'en Wan, a member of the ruling family of Ch'en. He was told: 'The posterity of this scion of the Kuei [surname of the House of Ch'en] will be nourished among the Chiang [surname of the House of Ch'i]. In five generations they will be prosperous, and the highest ministers in Ch'i; in eight, there will be none to compare with them for greatness', Legge (1), V, 102, 103a—b (Wu). The ruling family of the ancient state of Ch'en, like later people of the Ch'en clan, claimed descent from the legendary Shun, one of whose 'surnames' was Kuei (Chavannes, IV, 169). As Legge indicates, the founder of the ancient Ch'en is supposed to have had the surname Kuei; later it was changed to · Ch'en, from the name of the state. Ch'en Wan was forced to flee to Ch'i; his descendants there at some point changed their name to T'ien (Chavannes, V, 228), and one of them finally seized the throne of Ch'i (Chavannes, V, 239).

Line 485 borrows a tag from *Tao te ching* A.15a: 'The empire is a sacred vessel' (trans. D. C. Lau (1), p. 87).

Lines 487—8 are from the *Yi ching* (*Chou yi yin-te* 45/*Hsi hsia*/1). As usual in references to that passage, the stress is on the second line; Wang Seng-pien, for example, had quoted the two *Yi ching* lines in urging Hsiao Yi to take the throne, *Liang shu* 5.9a.

It was said of the King of Wu who led the rebellion of the seven kingdoms early in the Han that he had been able to attract to himself only 'worthless young men [*wu-lai tzu-ti*] who had fled for their lives', *Shih chi* 106.19 (Wu). Wu Chao-yi takes lines 489—90 as criticism of Emperor Wu's failure to instruct his own family, but *tzu-ti* (literally 'sons and younger brothers') is used here in its more general sense of 'young men', as in the *Shih chi* original. As we can tell from the 'employing' (*yung*), the lines are about bad officials. Line 490 is quite similar to an earlier observation on the fall of the Three Kingdoms Wu: 'Now the Last Ruler has taken the whole South [*Chiang-nan*] and thrown it away', *San-kuo chih* 51.9b (Wu). Strictly speaking, Yü's *Chiang-tung* ('east of the Yangtze') refers to the lower Yangtze region, but he uses it here as synonymous with *Chiang-nan*. Yang Fu-chi notes the *Li chi* statement that 'the sage is able to make of the empire a single household', *Li chi cheng-yi* 22.2a.

According to a popular story, while Duke Mu of Ch'in was in a trance, his spirit feasted with God (Ta ti); the latter, being drunk, gave him the possession of the land later to be ruled by Ch'in, governed by the astronomical Quail's Head (*WH* 2.4a and Li Shan's commentary; Chavannes, V, 25–6; Wang). Yü Hsin here shows remarkable courage; anyone who had read this far in the 'Lament' would surely realize that Ch'in meant the Western Wei.

The closing lines of the poem are quite direct; in that respect, they are reminiscent of the conclusion of the preface. Lines 497–8 refer to Yü T'ao, already the subject of lines 14–18 of the 'Lament' proper. The Eastern River in line 498, apparently an allusion, has not been satisfactorily explained. It may refer to the South in general, or perhaps specifically to Chiang-ling, where Yü T'ao had moved the family.

There is a certain similarity between lines 501–2 and P'an Yüeh's description of his journey to take up office in Ch'ang-an: 'Supporting old and young, I entered the Pass', *WH* 10.4a (Wang). The author's father had already died during Hou Ching's rebellion (lines 275–82), but his mother joined him in Ch'ang-an. The Northern Chou sources are too tactful to say how she got there; she was perhaps among the captives carried away after the fall of Chiang-ling, Yü's home. At least one of the author's sons survived to become his heir, *Chou shu* 41.18b; this son was finally murdered during the Sui (*Tzu-chih t'ung-chien*, p. 5746, line 6).

Line 503 is taken from *Shih ching* 31: 'In death and life [we are] separated and far apart', trans. Karlgren (2), p. 19. Line 504 is based on Wang Yi's theory that the *Ch'u tz'u* piece is called 'Heavenly Questions' ('T'ien wen') rather than 'Questioning Heaven' ('Wen t'ien') because 'Heaven is august and may not be questioned', *Ch'u tz'u* 3.1a. The line means here, as usual, that one has every justification for questioning heaven, if it were not for this prohibition; Yü has been questioning heaven as recently as line 494: 'How could God have been so drunk!'

Line 505, based on a metaphor of autumn leaves, was used regularly for the deaths of friends; Wang points out one of the three occurrences in the *Wen hsüan*, differing only in the word for 'almost' (*WH* 30.27b–28a, 41.21b,

42.9a). Wang Yen-shou says in the preface to his 'Rhapsody on the Ling-kuang Palace in Lu' that the other Former Han palaces have all been destroyed, and 'the Ling-kuang, soaring, alone remains' (*Ling-kuang k'uei-jan tu ts'un*), *WH* 11.13b (Wu). *K'uei-jan* could mean either soaring or solitary (Morohashi, 8622 and 8622/6); Yü is obviously thinking of the 'alone remains' of the original, and I have translated that instead. Lines 505–8, important evidence for the question of the date of the 'Lament', are discussed in Appendix IV.

Lines 511–12 are quite reminiscent of P'an Yüeh's tour of Ch'ang-an in his 'Traveling West'; both the place-names appear there, *WH* 10.17b, 10.7a. Li Shan's commentary explains Everlasting Joy as the name of Han Kao-tsu's palace at Ch'ang-an, and Universal Peace as one of the eastern gates of that city. The difference is that P'an Yüeh's work was a travelogue interspersed with comments on historical figures; Yü has selected two place-names for their ironic contrast with his own feelings.

Lines 513–14 refer to Ch'in Shih-huang, who built the O-fang Palace on the south side of the Wei and connected it with Hsien-yang by covered roads over the river (Chavannes, I, 174–5; Kao); as a result, the Wei did indeed pass through the Heavenly Gates, a term for the imperial palace. As Lu notes, Ch'in Shih-huang's tomb on Mount Li was called the 'underground market' because of the richness of its contents (Morohashi, 4890/192).

The phrase I have translated as Commandant in line 515, literally 'military headquarters', is a title closely analogous to *k'ai-fu* and dating back at least to the Former Han. Here the author may be thinking of Wei Ch'ing, a Grand General of the Former Han; compare a poem by Tu Fu: 'Wei Ch'ing established his military headquarters' (*Tu shih yin-te* 363/27/1). The Former Han Prime Minister and Marquis of P'ing-chin, Kung-sun Hung, set up a special residence for honored guests and went so far as to open a gateway facing east (rather than south) in order to welcome them with special politeness, *Han shu* 58.6b (Wang). The four families in lines 517–18 are stock figures for the great ones of the land, for example in *WH* 21.4b, 45.11a.

Line 519 refers to the Former Han general Li Kuang. During one period in disgrace, having been reduced to a commoner, he was hunting at night and came to the Pa-ling pavilion near Ch'ang-an, where he was stopped by a drunken guard. Warned that he was stopping the former general Li, the guard replied that even a present general could not travel at night, much less a former one, and detained him for the night (*Shih chi* 109.9, Wu). The enraged Li Kuang killed the guard at the first opportunity.

Line 520 alludes to a Crown Prince of Ch'u who was sent as a hostage to Ch'in. When the King of Ch'u fell ill, Ch'in still refused to return the Prince. It was told that if he was returned immediately and succeeded to the throne, he would be sure to show his gratitude. If he was kept there any longer, someone else would be chosen to replace him as heir, and he would become merely a commoner in Hsien-yang (the Ch'in capital), of no further use to Ch'in (*Shih chi* 78.13, Kao).

APPENDIX I:
HISTORICAL AND BIOGRAPHICAL SOURCES

The best overall source for the period of Yü Hsin's life is the *Tzu-chih t'ung-chien*, by Ssu-ma Kuang (1018–86) *et al.* The work has the advantage of drawing on a number of sources now lost and provides, in convenient chronological arrangement, a good deal of information not to be found in the official histories (for example, the date of Yü Hsin's mission to the Western Wei). Even Ssu-ma Kuang could not make bricks without straw. Many of the earliest sources had disappeared long before him, and also, especially for the Northern Chou (557–81), the records were apparently never very complete. The *Tzu-chih t'ung-chien* has the additional advantage of an excellent commentary by Hu San-hsing (1230–1302).

Yü Hsin's life is divided into two periods: that under the Liang, down to 554; and that under the Western Wei/Northern Chou. For each period there are two complementary works among the official histories. The earlier period is the better documented, with the *Liang shu*, compiled by Yao Ssu-lien (d. 637), and the *Nan shih*, by Li Yen-shou (*fl.* 629). The Liang had been the subject of a number of contemporary or near-contemporary histories, some of which are discussed in *Erh-shih-wu shih pu-pien*, pp. 5252a–53a, 5265c–67c. Most of these survived long enough to be used by the T'ang historians. It is, of course, difficult to judge now exactly what use they made of them, but, probably as a result of this rich documentation, the *Liang shu* is much the best of the four official histories that concern us here. Even it does not give an altogether coherent picture of the period; often one can tell that, for a given historical figure, it was drawing on at least two contradictory sources, one favorable and one hostile. The result is more often confusing than balanced; this sort of thing is perhaps inevitable with any period when it is so important to find villains to blame for a series of disasters.

The *Nan shih* has been much admired; for example, see the official Republic of China college textbook *Chung-kuo shih-hsüeh shih*, p. 72. It has the obvious advantage of brevity, allowing the reader to cover the history of the four dynasties from the Southern Sung through the Ch'en much more quickly than would be possible with the separate dynastic histories. Because of this, the *Nan shih* and the companion *Pei shih* (by the same author) for hundreds of years drove the separate histories almost completely out of

circulation, and there was a real danger that some of them would be lost.[1]
Li's two works are not simply condensations of the dynastic histories; on a
given event, the *Nan shih* account is sometimes independent and occasionally
more detailed. This is a result of the circumstances of composition and also
of the personality of the author. Li Yen-shou was allowed access to the
other histories while they were being written at the beginning of the T'ang.
He was also able to examine the vast body of sources which had been gathered
for the compilers, including a great deal of anecdotal and unofficial material,
and he made his own copies of the things that interested him. Much of this
ended up in his own histories. The problem, to paraphrase Chao Yi (p. 205),
is that Li was very fond of a good story. Quite often, the additional details
in his work are simply anecdotes, at least suspect if not demonstrably false,
and much of the *Nan shih* must be considered historical fiction. Still, it
should be consulted for what independent information it does contain.

For the period after 554, the two official histories are the *Chou shu*,
compiled by Ling-hu Te-fen (583–666) *et al.*, and the *Pei shih*, by Li Yen-
shou. The *Chou shu* is the only one of the four to have been compiled by a
team of government history-writers; it was a bête noire of Liu Chih-chi
(661–721), who criticized it for a paucity of facts, even in cases where unused
potential sources still survived to be pointed out, and for a tendency to gloss
over the realities of the Northern Chou.[2] One can only applaud Liu's judgment.
The *Chou shu* makes unpleasant reading, largely because of the efforts of
the Northern Chou rulers (later abetted by the T'ang historians) to make a
generally depressing period sound like the ancient Chou dynasty. This is also
a problem in the *Pei shih*, which seems to contain less independent information
than the *Nan shih* but still suffers from the compiler's weakness for anecdotes.
Fortunately, the failings of these histories of the North need not concern us
much here. For our purposes, what is most important is the last decade of
the Liang, the period covered in the 'Lament', and the surviving sources for
that are quite adequate.

Besides his own works, there are four main sources for Yü Hsin's biography.
First, Yü-wen Yu's preface to the collected works of 579 A.D. This is basically
a eulogy of the man himself, but it contains an account of Yü's career and a
little additional information. In the strictest sense, it is the only primary source
we have for this (aside from the works, of course). It was written by a friend,
during Yü's lifetime, and presumably from information supplied by him. Ni
Fan quotes Yü-wen Yu's preface and adds his own commentary; see the first
volume of the *Works*, where it is separately paginated 1a–14b.

Second, a biography in *Chou shu* 41 (*lieh chuan* 33). 6a–18b. This was
based partly on Yü-wen Yu's preface but also on other sources now lost, as
we can tell from the numerous differences in details. The biography is not as
informative as its length might suggest; rather more than ten folios are taken
up by a text of the 'Lament'.

Third, a biography in *Pei shih* 83 (*lieh chuan* 71). 17a–18a. This is a much-

abridged version of the *Chou shu* biography; the only significant difference
is in one office title. Ni Fan quotes this and adds his own commentary,
separately paginated 1a–4b in the first volume of the *Works*.

Fourth, Ni Fan's chronological biography (*nien-p'u*) of Yü Hsin, separately
paginated 1a–27b in the first volume of the *Works*. This should be treated
with the greatest caution. At his best, Ni is extremely careless; see, for example,
notes 59 and 62 to Chapter 1. At his worst, Ni is capable of manufacturing
evidence where it suits his purpose; see note 5 to Appendix II. Unfortunately,
most later biographical sketches of Yü are based on Ni's *nien-p'u*, either
directly or indirectly.

APPENDIX II:
YU HSIN'S CAREER

As often happens with early Chinese writers, what little biographical information there is for Yü Hsin mostly concerns his official career. What we have is a list of titles — a relatively long list, since he was unusually successful as writers go. His biographies, as usual, are vague about the dates when he held a given post; at best, we may be told that it was during a certain reign. Theoretically the annals section of the histories should help in such cases, since appointments to important positions are normally recorded there under a specific date. Unfortunately, Yü's positions under the Liang were too low to be mentioned in the relatively complete annals for that dynasty. He rose rather high under the Northern Chou, but those annals are fragmentary and remarkably uninformative. We are thus forced to rely on inference; the following is confined to what the available evidence will reasonably support.

Yü Hsin (T. Tzu-shan, also known by his title *k'ai-fu*), was born in 513. We know almost nothing about his education except that he was particularly interested in the *Tso chuan*. His writings do show a fondness for that work, as well as an extraordinarily wide range of reading in general and an exceptional memory. We should remember that this was still the age of the manuscript, and that there were very few large collections of books anywhere in China. Unquestionably the best was the Liang imperial library; officials would sometimes ask permission for their sons to study there. Most of Yü's reading must have been done in it, during his years of service of the Liang ruling family. There were no very good libraries in the Western Wei/Northern Chou, where Yü wrote almost all his surviving works; it is disturbing to think that he would have had to rely on his memory for most of his allusions, in the 'Lament' for example.

Our earliest specific information is that in 527, at 14, he attended the classes of the Liang Crown Prince, Hsiao T'ung (501–31). The latter was then 26, and this was about the time when he compiled the *Anthology* (*Wen hsüan*).[1] Yü took the palace examinations and, according to Yü-wen Yu, placed first in them.[2] He began his career as Regular Attendant (*ch'ang-shih*) to Hsiao Yi, the Prince of Hsiang-tung. During this period he would have been back at home in Chiang-ling; Hsiao Yi, then Military Governor (*tz'u-shih*) of Ching-chou, had his capital there. A Regular Attendant to an emperor's son ranked on the second level of the Liang eighteen-level civil hierarchy.[3] Yü was then transferred to Acting Military Consultant to the General Pacifying the South (*an-nan fu hsing ts'an-chün*, on the third level). This can be dated, since the post of General Pacifying the South seems to have been filled only once during this period; Hsiao Hsü, Emperor Wu's fifth son, held it from 535 to 537 (*Liang shu* 3.17a–b, 3.20a).

From there, Yü went to the capital as a Compiler (*ch'ao-chuan hsüeh-shih*) for Hsiao Kang, who had succeeded his elder brother T'ung as Crown Prince on T'ung's death in 531. After a period as Senior Secretary of the Bureau of Public Revenue in the Imperial Secretariat (*shang-shu tu-chih lang-chung*, fifth level), with the title of Surrogate Regular-Quota Attendant[4] (*t'ung-chih cheng-yüan lang*), he returned to the provinces as Adjutant to the Military Governor of Ying-chou (*Ying-chou pieh-chia*, sixth level). This last post is also datable, since Yü-wen Yu's preface says that at that time there was a rebellion along the Yangtze, and that Yü was sent to discuss naval warfare with Hsiao Yi. The passage was evidently written with one eye on line 57 of the 'Lament' proper. As Ni Fan suggests, this must have been the rebellion in 542 of Liu Ching-kung, against whom Hsiao Yi sent troops (*Tzu-chih t'ung-chien*, pp. 4910–11). We thus can tell that the Military Governor of Ying-chou under whom Yü was serving was Hsiao Lun, Emperor Wu's sixth son, who received that title in 540 (*Liang shu* 3.22b); Lun is the subject of lines 341–8 of the 'Lament'. Sometime after 542, Yü was sent on an embassy to the Eastern Wei, with the additional title of Surrogate Grand Counselor (*t'ung-chih san-chi ch'ang-shih*, eleventh level).[5]

On his return he was made, depending on the source, either a Scholar in the Crown Prince's Palace (*Tung kung hsüeh-shih*) or a Regular-Quota Attendant (*cheng-yüan lang*) and finally Acting Magistrate of Chien-k'ang' (*ling Chien-k'ang ling*).[6] He was in this post in December of 548, when Hou Ching attacked Chien-k'ang. We know very little of his activities for the next three years. Yü's father Chien-wu remained at the capital in office under Hou's puppet Emperor Chien-wen; he finally was able to escape in 550 on the pretext of a mission for Hou Ching, as explained in Chapter 1. Yü Hsin may also have continued in office; if so, none of his titles are recorded. We know only that he is supposed to have visited Hsiao Shao and quarreled with him in Chiang-hsia (Herrmann, pp. 22–3 G2), sometime after August 21,551.[7] Continuing up the Yangtze, he arrived at Chiang-ling probably in the autumn of 551. Hsiao Yi, who had established a rival court there, made him Vice Censor-in-Chief (*yü-shih chung-ch'eng*, eleventh level). Yü's father died about this time, and the 'Lament', lines 283–6, speaks of a period of mourning. The duration is unclear.

Hsiao Yi, having put down Hou Ching's rebellion, took the throne in December of 552. Sometime after that, Yü was made General of the Right Guard (*yu-wei chiang-chün*, twelfth level). Hsiao Yi moved the imperial library from Chien-k'ang to Chiang-ling, and Yen Chih-t'ui mentions that Yü,

as General of the Right Guard, was engaged in collating the belles lettres
section, Albert E. Dien (2), pp. 63–4. Yü was also made Marquis of Wu-k'ang
hsien, with the honorific epithet 'Capable of Founding a State' (*k'ai-kuo*).
Finally, on May 27, 554, he was sent on his ill-fated mission to the Western
Wei. At that time he had the title of Grand Counselor (*san-chi ch'ang-shih*,
twelfth level).

Yü was detained in the North for the rest of his life. Here we must digress
for a brief explanation of the Northern Chou system of offices, which was
actually put into practice under the Western Wei in 556. Like much else
established by that dynasty, it was archaizing, based in theory on the ancient
Chou. Put in its simplest form, it ranged from 'nine commands' (*chiu ming*),
the highest level, down to a low of 'no commands'. There could also be a
higher rank on a given level, such as an 'upper six commands' position (*cheng
liu ming*).[8] The system covered both honorary and functional titles, and, of
course, a given person's honorary titles tended to be higher than his functional
ones; that was certainly true of Yü Hsin. The Western Wei abdicated in favor
of the Northern Chou on February 14, 557. By that time Yü had been given
four honorary titles, all extremely high but involving no real power: Credential-
Bearing General Controlling the Army (*shih ch'ih-chieh fu-chün chiang-chün*,
eight commands), Right Palace Grandee with Gold Seal and Purple Cord
(*yu chin-tzu kuang-lu ta-fu*, eight commands), Grand Governor-General (*ta
tu-tu*, eight commands), and Credential-Bearing Great General of Chariots and
Cavalry Ceremonially Equal to the Three Authorities (*shih ch'ih-chieh chü-chi
ta chiang-chün yi-t'ung san-ssu*). The last, as its length might suggest, was a
nine-command title.

After the founding of the Chou in 557, Yü was made Viscount of Lin-
ch'ing *hsien* (upper six commands), with income from five hundred households. This was not bad, at least in terms of households; only a member of
the ruling family or an important general would get much more. He was also
given his first functional position in the North, that of Lower Grandee in
the Ministry of Water Control (*ssu-shui hsia ta-fu*, upper four commands). Here
the sequence of positions becomes a little unclear. According to the biography
of a cousin (*Sui shu* 78.3a3), Yü in 560 was a Scholar in the Lin-chih Hall
(*Lin-chih hsüeh-shih*). It was probably after that, in the early 560s, that he
became Prefect of Hung-nung *chün*; Hung-nung was a major city, strategically
important, so it was most likely an upper-six or seven commands position.
From about 566 to 573, Yü was back in Ch'ang-an, holding a series of mostly
honorary positions while engaged in literary work. As explained in Chapter 1,
Yü had a hand in the composition of the Chou ritual hymns during that period
and wrote a congratulatory memorial when they were completed in 573.
During the period at Ch'ang-an, Yü was made Great General of Doughty
Cavalry, Palatine Ceremonially Equal to the Three Authorities (*p'iao chi ta
chiang-chün k'ai-fu yi-t'ung san-ssu*, nine commands). Before 573, when the
title was abolished, he had become Vice Censor-in-Chief (*ssu-hsien chung ta-fu*,

upper five commands). He was also made Marquis[9] of Yi-ch'eng *hsien* (upper eight commands). By 577 he rose to the most important position he ever held, that of Military Governor of Lo-chou (probably upper seven); see note 67 to Chapter 1. Sometime after August 21, 578,[10] he was brought back to Ch'ang-an as Middle Grandee in the Directorate of the Imperial Family (*ssu-tsung chung ta-fu*, upper five commands). He retired from government work in 579, pleading illness, and died in 581.

APPENDIX III:
EDITIONS AND COMMENTARIES

Yü Hsin's works were originally collected during his own lifetime by his friend Yü-wen Yu, the Northern Chou Prince of T'eng. This first collection, of 579, no longer survives; all current editions of the works are reconstructions from quotations in encyclopedias, etc.[1] A good deal has certainly been lost, but almost all the surviving works are apparently intact, not fragmentary. There is also a problem with false attributions, but this involves only a few minor pieces.[2] The 'Lament' itself is as surely by Yü Hsin as *Paradise Lost* is by Milton.

The standard edition of the works is the *Yü Tzu-shan chi*, with commentary by Ni Fan;[3] it appears in the *Ssu-pu pei-yao* series, among other places. Because of its ready availability, I have used this as my basic text and have cited as *Works* the *Hu-pei hsien-cheng yi-shu* facsimile reprint of Ni's first edition of 1687.[4] Ni's text is generally good, but his commentary is less satisfactory. It is, admittedly, of staggering length, about 50,000 words on 3400 or so words of text of the 'Lament', for example, but a great deal of it is irrelevant or forced.

The modern scholar Kao Pu-ying used Ni's work as the basis for his 'Commentary on "The Lament for the South"' ('Ai Chiang-nan fu chien'). More capable than Ni, Kao added much valuable information from other commentators as well as his own corrections. He also deserves gratitude for tracking down hundreds of citations; sometimes this meant only identifying the specific *chüan* in a common work, but often the search led to obscure and almost unobtainable texts. Kao's work was set from movable type and contains a great many misprints, including some in the text of the 'Lament' itself.

There was especially widespread interest in Yü Hsin in the seventeenth and eighteenth centuries; *Chao-tai ts'ung-shu ting chi* 14.1a–72b contains the collected commentaries on the 'Lament' of several dozen scholars of that period. The work is inconvenient to use, since one must check not only the basic work but also three supplements (14.4a–45a, 14.45a–68a, 14.68a–70b, 14.70b–71a). Still, this collection is far superior as a whole to the work of Ni Fan. Kao quotes some of it, but occasionally omits something of real importance. The major figures in it are the brothers Wang Hui and Wang Hsü (indistinguishable, so I have cited both as 'Wang'), Wu Chao-yi, Lu Fan-ch'ao, Hsü Chiung, and Yang Fu-chi.

There are a number of popular commentaries on the 'Lament', such as those of Chang Jen-ch'ing, pp. 286–351; T'an Cheng-pi and Chi Fu-hua, pp. 1–52; and Ch'ü Shui-yüan (2), pp. 201–44. All are derivative, but each has something to offer, particularly Chang's. Ch'ü's is the most uneven, sometimes quite good, but on occasion capable of altering proposed allusions to make them fit Yü Hsin. These tailor-made allusions must in every case be checked with the original source.

The Preface to the 'Lament' is a popular anthology piece in its own right, and there are innumerable commentaries on it. Kao makes considerable use of Li Hsiang's 'Collected Commentaries on Yü Hsin's "Lament for the South"', of which I have seen only the opening section dealing with the Preface (perhaps the only part ever printed). Li's traditional scholarly work is often not as useful as the more popular commentaries, the best being Wang Li, pp. 1101–11.

Professor Florence Chao (Chao Yeh Chia-ying) of the University of British Columbia has very kindly made available to me recordings of a series of her lectures, prepared in 1963 for broadcast by the Taiwan Educational Radio program. Nominally limited to an explanation of the Preface, these broadcasts, more than seven hours long altogether, include extensive discussions of the 'Lament' proper. They are especially noteworthy for their coherent presentation of the work as a whole.

There are two translations of the 'Lament' in print: a vernacular Chinese one by Wang Li-ch'ing, and a German paraphrase by Erwin von Zach, pp. 1047–66. Wang's is of little use. That by von Zach, based largely on Ni Fan but sometimes improving on Ni, is important as a first translation.

Peter M. Bear's doctoral dissertation on Yü Hsin's lyric poetry includes a translation of lines 21–6 and 31–4 of the Preface but is more important for its sketch of Yü's life, critical analysis of a few poems, and useful bibliography. I am grateful to Professor Bear for making this available.

I have used a number of texts for collation. The earliest surviving text of the complete works, a late Ming edition by T'u Lung (*chin shih* 1577) reprinted in the *Ssu-pu ts'ung-k'an*, is quite similar to Ni's text; where the two differ, Ni's is almost always better. The 'Lament' is quoted in entirety in Yü Hsin's biography in the *Chou shu*. The text in the Po-na edition (41.7b–18a) is extremely poor, with many misprints and some grotesque phonetic borrowings, such as *fei* 'fly' instead of *fei* 'not' in line 348 (15a8). The Palace[5] and Chung-hua[6] editions of the *Chou shu* are somewhat better, and the latter has the excellent textual notes characteristic of that series of punctuated reprints of the standard histories.

The 'Lament' circulated independently at least as early as the T'ang; unfortunately none of these early texts survive. The oldest surviving one is the much abridged version in *Yi-wen lei-chü* 34.12a–13a, a Sung edition of the period 1131–62. This contains about a fourth of the whole work; it is of very uneven quality but sometimes has interesting readings. *Wen-yüan ying-hua* 129.779d–783b has a complete text, but it is not an important one.

I have made frequent reference to Yen K'o-chün's collection of pre-T'ang prose. Since in most cases such references are intended only to clarify a point of grammar or an obscure allusion, I have generally omitted the title and author of the specific work quoted and given only the folio and line in Yen's work, e.g. *Ch'üan Liang wen* 2.8a13 (in other words, *Complete Prose of the Liang, chüan* 2, folio 8 *recto*, line 13). Throughout the book, citations in general are reduced to the essentials (author or title and page number); details are given in the Bibliography.

APPENDIX IV:
THE DATE OF THE 'LAMENT'

The late Professor Ch'en Yin-k'o (2) suggested the Chinese year corresponding
to 578 A.D. as the date of composition of the 'Lament'. His reasoning is as
follows: Line 8 of the Preface mentions the fall of Chiang-ling in the year
chia-hsü, or 554. The phrase *chou hsing* in line 11 seems to indicate the
passage of a 12-year Jupiter cycle between that and the composition of the
poem (e.g. Morohashi, 3441/314). This would suggest the date 566 (= 554 + 12)
for the 'Lament'. Yü Hsin would have been 53 years old then, and could
reasonably have spoken of his 'twilight years', as in line 510. On the other
hand, he says in lines 505–6, 'The rest have almost all withered and fallen,
And, another Ling-kuang, I alone remain.' He could hardly consider that he
'alone remained' in 566, since Wang Pao, the other great Southern writer
exiled in the North, was then still alive and would die only eleven years later,
in 577. If, however, we add still another 12-year Jupiter cycle to 566, we arrive
at 578. Wang Pao would have died the year before, and Yü, then 65, would
indeed have been the only one left.

I agree with Professor Ch'en that a date would be welcome, and my own
subjective feeling is that the 'Lament' probably was written around the time
he suggests. It seems to me, however, that the critical phrase in line 11
makes better sense if we reject the idea of the Jupiter cycle. The best clue
to the meaning of that passage is in lines 507–8: 'The sun is entering its last
conjunction; The year is about to begin again.' These lines are based on the
'Monthly Ordinances' ('Yüeh ling'), a text which appears in a number of
ancient works: in the last month of winter, 'the sun has gone through all
its mansions, the moon is entering its last conjunction with the sun' (*Li
chi cheng-yi* 17.13b, *Lü-shih ch'un-ch'iu* 12.2a, *Huai-nan tzu* 5.14a). For
our purposes, what is most interesting is the text immediately following this
in the 'Monthly Ordinances'; in the *Huai-nan tzu* version it reads, 'The stars
are completing their circuit of the heavens' (*hsing chou yü t'ien*). The *Lü-
shih ch'un-ch'iu* and *Li chi cheng-yi* both read *hui* instead of *chou*, but the
wording of Cheng Hsüan's paraphrase in the latter suggests strongly that
his text actually had a *chou* too, like the *Huai-nan tzu*: 'It says that the sun
and moon and the other heavenly bodies in their movements *all come full
circle to their old positions* [*chieh chou tsa yü ku ch'u*] in this month.'

The 'Monthly Ordinances', in all three versions, goes on to say, 'The year is about to begin again', providing the basis for line 508. Line 11, then, means simply that, at the end of the year, the heavenly bodies are completing their circuit of the heavens, whereas human history is linear. This interpretation gives particular point to line 64 of the Preface, 'And now, as the seasons pass, I always grieve for what is gone', and to the author's constant references to old age; the Chinese got one year older on New Year's Day. Finally, it relieves us of the necessity of reading, not one, but *two* Jupiter cycles into line 11. One may admit that the Chinese do commonly use a reference to the Jupiter cycle as an elegant way of indicating the passing of twelve years (though more often in a phrase such as *yi hsing yi chou, Ch'üan Liang wen* 2.8a13); still, if that was what Yü Hsin had in mind in line 11, one would wish for some indication that *two* cycles are involved.

As for the question whether Wang Pao was still alive when the 'Lament' was written, I would suggest that people getting old rather tend to think of themselves as last survivors after the death of any contemporary. Dating the work as late as 578 does not solve that problem anyway. Wang Pao would have died the year before, as Professor Ch'en says, but the conquest of the Northern Ch'i in 577 had brought a large influx of originally Southern Chinese to the Northern Chou court (including Yen Chih-t'ui), so that Yü might well have felt less isolated in 578 than earlier.

APPENDIX V:
YU HSIN AND SSU-MA CH'IEN

Lines 275–8 are the most extended allusion in the 'Lament'. They clearly involve a comparison between the author and Ssu-ma Ch'ien; the problem is to tell what the two writers had in common. All that is known about Ssu-ma Ch'ien's birth is that, as he himself says, he was born in Lung-men (*Shih chi* 130.15; Chavannes, I, xxv). On the other hand, the historian gives us considerable information on his father T'an's death: returning from a journey, he found his father dying at Loyang. T'an urged him to write the history he himself had longed to write, and to serve in the hereditary post of Grand Recorder (or 'Historian') in such a way as to reflect credit on his family. Yü Hsin's father died, not at Loyang, but at Chiang-ling; then where among all these details is the similarity?

The answer is suggested by the very lack of information about Ssu-ma Ch'ien's birth. Since Yü Hsin was obviously not born at Lung-men (in Shensi), the only other possibility that suggests itself is that Yü felt that the dates of their births were somehow similar. We can calculate from Yü-wen Yu's preface to the collected works that Yü Hsin was born in 513 A.D., the year *kuei-ssu* of the 60-year cycle. We note that 148 B.C. was also a *kuei-ssu* year. Ssu-ma Ch'ien's birthdate is unknown. The earliest surviving source is a statement by Chang Shou-chieh in his *Shih chi cheng-yi* (dated 737) that in the first year of T'ai-ch'u (104 B.C.) Ssu-ma Ch'ien was 42 *sui* (quoted in *Shih chi* 130.19, line 7); in other words, that he was born in 145 B.C. Chang gives no proof of his assertion, but it has been widely accepted. A millenium later, Wang Ming-sheng[1] reasoned that in the first year of Yüan-feng (110 B.C.), Ssu-ma Ch'ien must have been about 40 *sui*; in other words, that he was born about 149 B.C. 148 B.C., we remember, was the year corresponding in cyclical terms to that of Yü Hsin's birth.

This is certainly suggestive, but not very compelling taken alone; let us see if something similar is going on in line 276. It is well established that Ssu-ma Ch'ien's father T'an died in 110 B.C. (Chavannes, I, xxxii), a *hsin-wei* year, as was the year corresponding to 551 A.D. (actually ending February 10, 552). The date of Yü Chien-wu's death is nowhere specifically stated, but Chiang Liang-fu, following Ni Fan, has him dying in 551; Morino Shigeo has '?552'. All these authorities may ultimately agree, if one allows for the overlap between the Chinese and Western year. Our last solid date is some-time after August 20, 551, for Yü Hsin's visit to Chiang-hsia while enroute to Chiang-ling (lines 249–50). It appears from the *fu* that the author lost his father soon after his arrival in Chiang-ling, and before the final campaign against Hou Ching (March–April 552). We can probably assume that Chien-wu died sometime before February 10, 552, in the Chinese *hsin-wei* year corresponding in the main to 551, and thus in the same year of the cycle as Ssu-ma T'an.

The basis of the comparison is thus clearly a matter of dates; a similarity of birth-dates alone might very easily be a coincidence, particularly since Ssu-ma Ch'ien's is uncertain, but it is impossible to accept both lines as coincidences. We need not, of course, consider Ssu-ma Ch'ien's birth in 148 B.C. proven, but only allow that Yü might reasonably have believed it. A great many early sources have been lost, and it is difficult to imagine that no one in the 800 years before Chang Shou-chieh had ever wondered about the great historian's dates; they have been the subject of endless controversy since then.

Such consciousness of similar dates is not uncommon in China. To give only one example, Ch'en Yüan notes in the preface of his *T'ung-chien Hu-chu piao-wei* that he completed the book in 1945, an *yi-yu* year like 1285, the year in which Hu San-hsing finished the commentary on which Ch'en's work is based. Westerners tend to note birthdays or centennials, but in traditional China, where birthdays were seldom recorded (except for princes) and there was no comparable zero-year of the calendar, cyclical anniversaries were the only ones likely to be noticed.

APPENDIX VI:
TWO *SUI SHU* ANECDOTES

The 'Lament' was much admired from the time of its completion. We can get some indication of its popularity from the fact that two of Yü Hsin's metaphors for contemporary events have made their way into the official histories as if literally true. In both cases, the historian responsible was Wei Cheng (580–643), the chief compiler of the *Sui shu*.

In line 345 of the 'Lament', Yü Hsin says of Hsiao Lun, 'A hibernating bear injured his horse'. *Sui shu* 22.23b3–4 duly records that while Lun was on his way to the capital during Hou Ching's rebellion, 'a hibernating bear all at once came up and bit the horse Lun was riding'. This comes from the 'Treatise on the Five Elements', the repository in the official histories for omens and portents. These *Sui shu* treatises had originally been prepared to accompany the history of the dynasties before the Sui, and that explains how Hsiao Lun can appear in the *Sui shu* despite his death in 551. Yü's original line had been an allusion, as yet unidentified, used as a metaphor for divine punishment for Lun's crimes. The two lines before it had involved allusions to the First Emperor; it is quite likely that line 345 also refers to another story about the same man, or at least some similar ancient figure surrounded by legends. It is hardly necessary to point out that hibernating bears do not all at once come up and bite one's horse; anyone but a poet had better be prepared to explain the circumstances.

Wei Cheng's story about the bear is obviously apocryphal; his second fabrication, more plausible, has gained wider circulation. Lu Fan-ch'ao and other commentators identify the source as the *Sui shu*; I have not found it earlier than the *Tzu-chih t'ung-chien*, p. 5017: Shortly after the fall of Chien-k'ang to Hou Ching on April 24, 549, Hsiao Kang, a prisoner of the rebels, is said to have sent his infant son Ta-yüan away to Hsiao Yi in Chiang-ling. The story was inspired by lines 327–8 of the 'Lament', which say of Hsiao Kang: 'He had entrusted his beloved sons/son to others; Though knowing of the western mound, who was there to look toward it?' This, like the bear story, is based on an allusion, but in this case the source has been identified (by Lu): According to Lu Chi, the dying Ts'ao Ts'ao commanded his older sons to care for his infant son and daughter, and to go frequently to 'look toward my western mound' or imperial tomb; Lu Chi comments on how sad it was that one who had earlier been able to bear the weight of the entire empire 'must now entrust his beloved children to others', *WH* 60.17a—b. At first sight, the touching story of Hsiao Kang's parting with his son seems like the perfect contemporary reference for the allusion, but that is not the way Yü Hsin's allusions function. Hsiao Ta-yüan in fact remained in or near Chien-k'ang for the next three years, and was finally discovered living in a Buddhist monastery there in 552 and only then sent to Chiang-ling (*Chou shu* 42.7b—11b and *Pei shih* 29.21a—b). Obviously still in rebel hands, on November 13, 550, something like eighteen months after the anecdote has him sent to the rival court, he was given a fief by the puppet Hsiao Kang, recorded under that date in the annals of that emperor, *Nan shih* 8.2b, and also in the *Tzu-chih t'ung-chien*, p. 5055. Dealing with a period of some complexity, the compilers of the *Tzu-chih t'ung-chien* understandably, if carelessly, failed to notice that they were here contradicting their earlier account of the child's departure.

If we took the *Sui shu* story seriously, we would have to see in line 328 the author's comment that, being out of town, Hsiao Ta-yüan unfortunately could not visit his father's grave. The reason for the lack of visitors there was that at least twelve of Ta-yüan's brothers, identifiable by the character *Ta* as the first element of their given names, had been slaughtered by Hou Ching (*Tzu-chih t'ung-chien*, pp. 5071, 5072), and at least two more were killed after the fall of Chiang-ling to the Western Wei (*Nan shih* 54.5a). Lines 327—8 are simply another of Yü's general statements about the fate of the family of a principal character in the 'Lament', like, for example, lines 473—4: 'Elder and younger Alike were killed by one like a son.' There was a tragic irony inherent in the fact of Hsiao Yi's sons being killed by his nephew, 'one like a son'. Hsiao Kang's sons were killed by outsiders; the author here provides an allusion which gives the same tragic irony to the events.

APPENDIX VII:
GENEALOGY

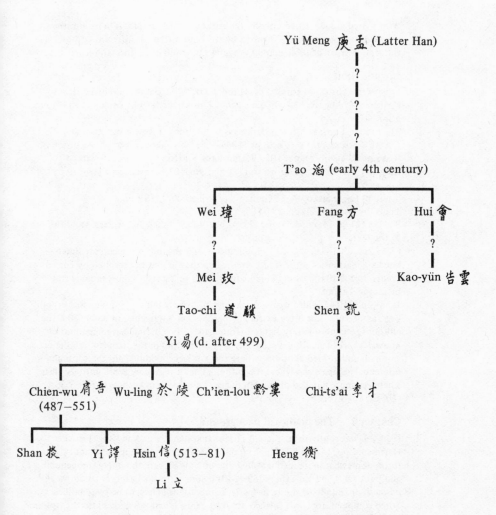

NOTES

Works cited are identified only by the author or title. Numbers in parentheses are used to indicate different works by the same author or different editions of the same work. The bibliography provides more detailed information.

Introduction

1 Prospective writers of parallel prose today are still urged to imitate Yü Hsin by Chang Jen-ch'ing, II, 538. On Yü's parallel prose, see Suzuki Torao (2) and Wang Yao.

2 The broadest range of *fu* translations is to be found in Erwin von Zach and Burton Watson (2). Von Zach, pp. 1047–66, has a German paraphrase of the 'Lament'; Watson (2), pp. 102–9, translates Yü Hsin's *fu* 'A Small Garden'.

3 'Hen fu', *WH* 16.24a–27a. Watson (2), pp. 96–101, translates a similar *fu* by Chiang Yen.

4 'Ch'ih pi fu', trans. by A. C. Graham in Cyril Birch, I, 381–2.

5 Trans. by Watson (2), pp. 29–51.

6 Watson (2), p. 44; cf. Hervouet (1), p. 112. I have bracketed Watson's additions to the text.

7 Chao Yeh Chia-ying, pp. 122–3, points out the absurdity of elaborate line-by-line explanations of songs (*tz'u*), even when they are clearly inspired by current events. Her criticism would apply equally well to Yü Hsin's most famous commentator, Ni Fan.

8 Juan Chi (210–63) also wrote about current events, but only in the most cryptic way; as a result, 'it is often extremely hard, often impossible, to understand the allusions to contemporary figures' (Holzman, p. 1). Given a certain amount of knowledge of Liang history, the only real difficulties in the 'Lament' are the occasional unidentified allusions (where the source is in doubt, not the contemporary reference) and passages where the author's line of reasoning is not entirely clear.

9 There is a more detailed discussion of the 'Lament' in my article in *HJAS* 36 (1976), 82–113.

Chapter 1   The historical background

1 Hsin-yeh was south of the present city of that name. For Nan-yang, see Albert Herrmann, pp. 14–15 E3. The Yü family of Hsin-yeh was apparently not related to the somewhat more distinguished one of Ying-ch'uan; the important general and political figure Yü Liang (289–340) belonged to the latter. *Erh-shih-wu shih pu-pien*, pp. 6058–61, quite properly distinguishes between the two families. Some commentators have mistakenly read Ying-ch'uan references into the opening lines of the 'Lament' proper; by this term I mean the rhymed section as opposed to the unrhymed preface, whose lines are separately numbered 1–72.

2 Wang Yü-ch'üan, pp. 147–50, discusses the post of Imperial Secretary. Yü Meng
 does not appear in the *Combined Indices to Hou Han-shu and the Notes of Liu
 Chao and Li Hsien*. To the best of my knowledge, the earliest surviving source
 that mentions his name is *Yüan-ho hsing tsuan* 6.20a (preface dated 813), the basis
 (along with *Yüan-ho hsing tsuan ssu chiao chi*, pp. 592–3) of the genealogy in
 Appendix VII. The lateness of the source is a little disturbing, and so are the gaps
 in the genealogy before and after such a distinguished figure, but we should remember several things. First, Meng's absence from the *History of the Latter Han*
 (*Hou-Han shu*) proves nothing. The work was compiled from poor sources,
 much poorer than those for the *Han shu*, for example. Many of the holders of
 'Three Lords' (*san kung*) positions in the Latter Han have no biographies in the
 Hou-Han shu; see tables in *Erh-shih-wu shih pu-pien*, pp. 1959–62, where those
 with biographies are marked. Second, the *Yüan-ho hsing tsuan* was an imperial
 compilation, done in a period when genealogies were still given great weight and
 careful scrutiny (David Johnson, p. 6). It does indicate something if the compilers
 were satisfied that someone in the Yü family had held the same post as, for example,
 Tung Cho (in 189) and Ts'ao Ts'ao (from 196 to 208), *Erh-shih-wu shih pu-pien*,
 p. 1962a–b. Third, the present text of the *Yüan-ho hsing tsuan* was reconstructed
 from fragments; see Teng and Biggerstaff, p. 263. The original may not have had
 the gaps. Fourth, and most important, Yü Hsin himself believed that an ancestor
 in the Han had been one of the Three Lords; that is clearly implied in line 2 of
 the 'Lament' proper.
3 Of Sui-ch'ang *hsien* in Chekiang. He appears in lines 11–18.
4 A contemporary, Emperor Yüan of the Liang, calls Yü Hsin's father a native of
 Nan-chün, equivalent to Chiang-ling (*Ch'üan Liang wen* 17.13a6). Others might
 view the matter more conservatively; for example, Yü Hsin is still a native of
 Hsin-yeh in his biography, *Chou shu* 41.6a.
5 Wolfram Eberhard, pp. 155–6.
6 Such offices, called 'pure' (*ch'ing*), were not limited to the higher ones; any office
 under the crown prince was considered pure, probably because of its potential
 if he later became emperor, and particularly the literary one of *hsien-ma*. This
 was only on the sixth level under the Liang, the highest being the eighteenth, but
 the question was raised whether one of Yü Hsin's uncles was of sufficiently pure
 family to hold such a position (*Liang shu* 49.6b2–4). For the Liang rank system,
 see note 18 to Chapter 1.
7 The word 'recluse' should not summon up visions of *Great Expectations*; as
 applied to China, it means only a person who refuses to take office. He may be
 living in the middle of the largest city, though there is some suggestion of a rustic
 life, as in Yü Hsin's portrait of his grandfather (lines 27–32).
8 For an introduction both to the atmosphere of the period and to the life of T'ao
 Ch'ien, see J. R. Hightower (4), pp. 1–6.
9 Yi's son Ch'ien-lou was made a magistrate at the beginning of the Yung-yüan
 period (499–501) and abandoned his post almost immediately because of fears
 for his father's health. Yü Yi died not long afterward, *Liang shu* 47.5b5–6a2.
10 Hightower (4), p. 3, points out the surprising but important fact that T'ao Ch'ien
 'is grouped with the Recluses, not with the poets'. It is less surprising in the case
 of Yü Yi (*Nan-Ch'i shu* 54.19b9–20a1), who dabbled in literature but left no
 surviving works.
11 As L. S. Yang says ((2), p. 11), 'tradition recognizes a close relationship between
 successful emperors and long-lived emperors'. Emperor Wu was a problem, since
 his reign ended badly and traditional historians were very much concerned with
 ends, whether of lives or of careers. Still, as Professor Yang says (p. 12), 'On the

whole, there seems to be a rather close correlation between a long reign and success, because in most cases *at least a part* of the long reign did constitute a peak in the configuration' (italics added).

12 Eberhard, p. 160, notes the failure of the system under the Southern Ch'i. There were minor problems with it throughout the Liang; for example, there were always a certain number of children in office, and the adults appointed to run things for them might find it difficult to control anyone with such exalted relatives. The real problem with such a system is that relatives are not necessarily more loyal than others, and may in fact be less so, since they are near enough to the throne to aspire to it. It was only around 548 that this became the major problem of the Liang dynasty.

13 Okazaki Fumio, p. 556.

14 Okazaki, p. 556.

15 Biographies in *Liang shu* 49.7a–9b and *Nan shih* 50.11b–13a. The date of his birth is calculated from the statement of the Liang Emperor Yüan that Chien-wu was 48 *sui* in 534 (*Ch'üan Liang wen* 17.11b10, 12a2, 13a6). The date of his death is discussed below in Appendix V. His brothers were Ch'ien-lou (biographies in *Liang shu* 47.5a–6b and *Nan shih* 50.10a–11a) and Wu-ling (biographies in *Liang shu* 49.6a–7a and *Nan shih* 50.11a). Both brothers were a good deal older than Chien-wu. Ch'ien-lou had already held several offices by the beginning of the Yung-yüan period (499–501). Wu-ling, the second son, held his first post in the period 490–4, when the Southern Ch'i prince Hsiao Tzu-lung was in Chiang-ling as Military Governor of Ching-chou (*Nan-Ch'i shu* 40.25b–26a). We can probably assume 20 as the earliest age for beginning a career; Yü Chien-wu was at least 22 when he first took office. The older brothers would thus have been born around 470, or somewhat earlier; both would have died before 520, Ch'ien-lou at 45 and Wu-ling at 47 in Western reckoning. One suspects that the recluse Yü Yi must have been born before 450, but this would be basing conjecture on conjecture.

16 For Hsiao Kang, see *Liang shu* 4.1a–9b and *Nan shih* 8.1a–5a. For Hsiao Yi, *Liang shu* 5.1a–32a and *Nan shih* 8.5a–16a. On their activities as patrons, Morino Shigeo, pp. 99–104. There is also a separate study of Hsiao Kang, John Marney (1); and an article on a fragmentary *fu* by Hsiao Kang, Marney (2).

17 If all three of Yü Yi's sons were born to the same mother, she would have been in her eighties by this time.

18 Here and in Appendix II, I have followed the account of the Liang hierarchy in Hu San-hsing's commentary, *Tzu-chih t'ung-chien*, pp. 4576–80. One source makes this Yü's second position.

19 See Chao Yi, pp. 266–9; and Peter M. Bear, pp. 11, 31 note 25, 211. Yü Hsin's 554 embassy to the Western Wei took place under a threat of war; given the Liang weakness then, diplomatic approaches were probably useless.

20 The 'Lament' insists on Hou Ching's foreign origins; see lines 84, 115–16, 121–4, 129, 135, 143–4, 148, and 183. His biographies (*Liang shu* 56.1a–41a and *Nan shih* 80.1a–25b) tell us nothing about this except that Hou's grandfather had the decidedly non-Chinese given name Yi-yü-chou (*Nan shih* 80.20b). Yao Wei-yüan, p. 84, suggests that Hou belonged to the Chieh, a group associated with the Hsiung-nu; for our purposes, the specific non-Chinese ancestry is unimportant.

21 Even after going over to the Liang, Hou continued to intrigue with the Western Wei, *Tzu-chih t'ung-chien*, pp. 4952–3.

22 According to one anecdote, Hou Ching forged a letter from the Eastern Wei offering to exchange a captive nephew of Emperor Wu for Hou, and Emperor Wu consented, *Tzu-chih t'ung-chien*, p. 4977. The story is probably apocryphal; Hou could have guessed his future without going through all this.

23 It is difficult to judge motivations now, but that was the general view at the time, held by Yü Hsin himself (lines 155–6, 221–2, 469–70) and by his younger contemporary Yen Chih-t'ui (531–after 590). See Albert E. Dien (2), p. 52.

24 Arthur Waley (3), p. 132, says of one T'ang emperor: 'what went on in the Palace was very imperfectly known even to the contemporary world, and we cannot hope at this distance of time to discover how Hsien Tsung died'. That is particularly true of a death in captivity; no one has any idea what really became of the sons of Edward IV of England, for example.

25 The standard histories generally refuse to go beyond a vague statement that the captive emperor grew ill from rage and grief (e.g., *Tzu-chih t'ung-chien*, p. 5017), but one of Hou Ching's biographies has Emperor Wu dying of illness and hunger (*Nan shih* 80.16a). The starvation story has always been a popular one; the fullest version I know is that of Chang Tun-yi (preface dated 1160), 11.6b: After the fall of the city (April 24, 549), Hou Ching had empty food containers presented to the emperor for seven days from *keng-ch'en* through *ping-hsü*, presumably May 7–13; he died on the last day. Chang gives no source for the story, and elsewhere (1.16a) contents himself with the more orthodox theory.

26 Biography in *Liang shu* 55.9a–10b.

27 Biographies in *Liang shu* 29.6a–12b and *Nan shih* 53.15b–19b.

28 The full story, which appears in *Tzu-chih t'ung-chien*, p. 4986, is written with real malice. Yü Hsin is supposed to have fled to the gate after removing only a single pontoon. He was chewing a piece of sugar cane, a sign of composure in a general in other stories of the period; when an arrow struck the gate, he dropped the cane, abandoned his army, and ran. It is impossible to be completely certain of this, since all the original sources are lost, but there is a strong probability that the story originated with Hsiao Shao, whose *Record of the T'ai-ch'ing Period* (*T'ai-ch'ing chi*) was the main contemporary account of Hou Ching's rebellion. According to *Nan shih* 51.10b–11a, Yü Hsin visited Hsiao Shao late in 551 and quarreled with him; the quarrel is supposed to have arisen from an earlier homosexual relationship between the two. The accusation need not be taken too seriously; Li Yen-shou, the compiler of the *Nan shih*, was notoriously fond of such anecdotes, and the great Ch'ing scholar Ch'ien Ta-hsin (1728–1804) mentions this particular one in his indictment of Li for including false stories which have no place in a historical work (quoted in Hsü Hao, p. 153). It does seem likely that there was ill feeling between Yü Hsin and Hsiao Shao, for whatever reason, and that the fact was generally known. Li Yen-shou's anecdote would have no point except as an attempt to explain the origins of the hostility.

29 *Liang shu* 49.9b. *Nan shih* 50.13a has a more eventful account of Yü Chien-wu's flight, and one particularly silly anecdote of Yü being forced to compose a poem in order to save his life.

30 *Liang shu* 49.9b says 'not long', but *Nan shih* 50.13a has two posts given him after his arrival in Chiang-ling: Military Governor of Chiang-chou (through which he had passed earlier) and Prefect of Yi-yang in Szechwan. He seems never to have assumed the duties of either post. It is possible that he was assigned to the Chiang-chou post during the brief period early in 551 when it was in Hsiao Yi's control (from March to about July – it was retaken in November), but that it had been lost before he could go there. Hsiao Yi had no control over Szechwan by this time. He may have had second thoughts about sending an official there, or else Chien-wu may have died in the meantime. On the date of Chien-wu's death, see Appendix V.

31 From his biographies, we can tell only that he was given additional titles sometime between December 552, when Hsiao Yi assumed the title of emperor, and May 27, 554, when Yü went on his mission to the Western Wei.

32 L. S. Yang (1), pp. 24–5 and note 17.
33 This was Jen Yüeh, *Tzu-chih t'ung-chien*, p. 5101, line 2.
34 Lu Fa-ho, biography in *Pei-Ch'i shu* 32.1a–7a.
35 *Tzu-chih t'ung-chien*, p. 5098.
36 *Tzu-chih t'ung-chien*, p. 5094.
37 For example, *Tzu-chih t'ung-chien*, pp. 4980–1, 5112.
38 On one occasion, Hsiao Yi is supposed to have struck Wang Seng-pien with a
    sword and imprisoned him for delaying a campaign, *Liang shu* 45.2b–3a.
39 *Tzu-chih t'ung-chien*, pp. 5104–5.
40 *Tzu-chih t'ung-chien*, pp. 5111–12.
41 *Tzu-chih t'ung-chien*, p. 5113. This is the only exact date we know in Yü's entire
    life, and it appears only in this source, not in the standard histories.
42 For example, the last of the government slaves from Chiang-ling were freed in
    572, *Tzu-chih t'ung-chien*, p. 5312. Yü Chi-ts'ai, a distant cousin of Yü Hsin, is
    recorded as buying freedom for his relatives and friends, *Sui shu* 78.2b–3a.
43 Ch'en Yin-k'o (1), p. 42.
44 *Ch'ao-yeh ch'ien tsai* 6.14b–15a.
45 Eberhard, pp. 148–50.
46 I have followed the views of Ch'en Yin-k'o (1), pp. 61–4. For a different interpret-
    ation, see Chauncey S. Goodrich, pp. 1–12.
47 Mou Jun-sun, pp. 60–1.
48 According to line 10 of the Preface, after the fall of Emperor Yüan, or Hsiao Yi
    (killed January 27, 555), 'For three years I was imprisoned in a detached lodging.'
    However, Yü is known to have held four official titles in the North by the end of
    the Western Wei (February 14, 557).
49 To give only one example, Yü's contemporary Yen Chih-t'ui, author of the
    Family Instructions of Mr. Yen (*Yen-shih chia-hsün*), held office successively
    under the Liang, Western Wei, Northern Ch'i, Northern Chou, and Sui dynasties;
    see his biography, *Pei-Ch'i shu* 45.22a–32b.
50 *Works* 1.23a–28b.
51 *Hsin hsü* 5.14b–15a.
52 One should discount the cliché about Yü Hsin's friendship with two Northern
    Chou princes being 'like that between commoners' (i.e. equals, *Chou shu* 41.7b).
    This means only that their relationship was somewhat closer than that between
    ruler and subject.
53 *Chou shu* 2.18a; *Tzu-chih t'ung-chien*, p. 5153.
54 The title had been used in the first year of the *Spring and Autumn Annals* (*Ch'un-
    ch'iu*); see Legge (1), V, 3.
55 In the ancient Chou, *kung* (later equivalent to duke) was only an honorific, not
    a rank of enfeoffment. The highest enfeoffment was as a *hou*, normally translated
    'marquis'. It is therefore strictly incorrect to speak of the Duke of Chou or Duke
    of Sung, though the custom is too firmly established to be changed now. By the
    time of Yü-wen Hu, the situation had changed; calling him the Duke of Chou
    would have meant giving a subject the entire nation as a fief. He had to be content
    with 'Duke of Chin'. There is a useful study of Yü-wen Hu, Albert E. Dien (1).
56 Legge (1), III, 399–412.
57 *Sui shu* 78.3a3.
58 *Chou shu* 5.12a.
59 The second year of Chien-te, *Chou-shu* 5.22a. Ni Fan's 'third year' (*Works* 7.4b) is
    a mistake.
60 *Works* 7.4b–8b. Yü's hymns make up *chüan* 6 of the *Works*.
61 Suzuki Torao (2), p. 346.

62 Fourth year of T'ien-ho, *Chou shu* 5.15a. Ni Fan's 'third year' (*Works* 1.47b2) is again a mistake. Yü's rhapsody appears in *Works* 1.47b–51a.

63 *Works* 1.1a–12b; it is dated, but only in terms of the heavenly stem *kuei*, so the date could be 563. Ni Fan thinks the reference is to the stem *hsin*, which would mean 561 or 571; however, see Morohashi, 13855/183. I know of no record of this archery contest in the Chou histories.

64 *Chou shu* 5.24a1–3. He commanded the Crown Prince to take charge of the government during this period.

65 Lü Ssu-mien, pp. 1067–8.

66 *Tzu-chih t'ung-chien*, pp. 5313, 5379. Rulers commonly burned fur coats, but seldom palaces; Lü Ssu-mien, pp. 1063–8.

67 *Tzu-chih t'ung-chien*, p. 5335.

68 Yü's memorial on the capture of Yeh in 577 expresses regret that his position as military governor prevents him from offering congratulations in person (*Works* 7.4a8).

69 These deaths are the subject of Yü's 'Heartbreak' ('Shang-hsin fu'), *Works* 1.38a–47a.

70 *Tzu-chih t'ung-chien*, p. 5746. I am indebted to Dr. Hon-chiu Wong for pointing out this reference.

Chapter 2 The *fu* in the Six Dynasties

1 There are excellent introductions to the history of the *fu* in Hightower (6), pp. 22–9; and Watson (2), pp. 1–18, 111–22. Much of the following is nothing more than footnotes to these two works, and in it I have assumed a background knowledge equivalent to that provided there. Suzuki Torao (1) is most useful on technical features such as meter.

2 The 'Treatise on Bibliography' of the *History of the Former Han* contains an entry: 'Twenty-five *Fu* by Ch'ü Yüan' (*Han shu* 30.22a); judging from this, the 'Li sao' itself was arranged among the *fu* in the Former Han imperial library.

3 For example, the 'Shang-lin', like the 'Li sao', has a flight through space. There is also an obvious kinship between the two 'Summonses' in the *Ch'u tz'u* and Mei Sheng's 'Seven Stimuli', and the *Ch'u tz'u* poem 'In Praise of the Orange Tree' (Hawkes (1), pp. 76–7) is quite simply an allegorical *fu*, one of the first of these.

4 Hightower (6), pp. 22–3. The amount of allegory in the *Songs* has been over-stated, but some of them are unquestionably allegorical, such as 113, on the rat; see Watson (4), p. 217. The merging of *Songs*, elegies, and rhapsodies warns us to expect allegory even in the 'descriptive' rhapsodies; it does occasionally appear there.

5 Watson (2), pp. 3–4.

6 Watson (1), p. 106.

7 Hightower (6), pp. 43–5.

8 With Lu Chi (261–303) and Liu Hsieh (6th century). See Achilles Fang (2), p. 541, couplet 86; Watson (2), pp. 120–1; and Hightower (6), pp. 43–5. Chih Yü (d. 311), a contemporary of Lu Chi, makes feeling the critical factor in judging *fu*; *Ch'üan Chin wen* 77.8a.

9 In his biography of Ch'ü Yüan, trans. David Hawkes (1), p. 12. The idea of poetry as the expression of legitimate personal feeling also underlies Mencius's reply to the charge that one of the *Songs* is 'plaintive' and therefore unacceptable; see D. C. Lau (2), pp. 172–3, and note 73 to Chapter 4 below.

10 Trans. Watson (2), pp. 49–51.

11 My translation; cf. Knechtges (1), p. 95.

12 Quoted in Ch'en Ch'ü-ping, I, 7.

13 'Erh ching fu', *WH* 2–3, trans. von Zach, pp. 1–37, and (in part) Watson (2), pp. 5–7.

14 'San tu fu', *WH* 4.12a–6.31b, trans. von Zach, pp. 44–92.

15 'Ch'i fa', *WH* 34.1a–13b, trans. Knechtges and Swanson. The following figures, based on the texts in Yen K'o-chün, are rounded off to the nearest hundred; they include prefaces or introductions where appropriate.

16 The 'Li sao' does not appear in Yen K'o-chün, and it is difficult to find an edition without commentary. Ch'en Ch'ü-ping, I, 2, estimates that it is something over 2490 words long.

17 Some *fu* are in fact labeled as *sung*, literally 'hymns', like the fourth section of the *Songs*. The *fu* genre presents problems of demarcation. Throughout this book I have used content as the deciding factor, including, for example, Liu Ling's 'Hymn to the Efficacy of Wine ('Chiu te sung') but rejecting obvious imitations of the *Songs* in four-word meter and archaizing language.

18 'Tai tu fu' by Kao Yün (390–487), now lost; see *Ch'üan Hou-Wei wen* 28.1a.

19 The 'Pei tu fu' and 'Nan tu fu' by Yang Ku (467–523), now lost; see *Ch'üan Hou-Wei wen* 44.1a.

20 'Ch'ien-tu fu' by P'ei Po-mao (d. *c.* 537, now lost; see *Ch'üan Hou-Wei wen* 39.9b.

21 'Hsin kung fu' by Hsing Shao (d. after 561), *Ch'üan Pei-Ch'i wen* 3.1a–b.

22 'Huang lung ta ya fu', by Hu Tsung (183–243), *Ch'üan San-kuo wen* 67.5b–6a.

23 'P'ing-Wu sung' by Chang Tsai (*c.* 285), *Ch'üan Chin wen* 85.3b–4a.

24 'Chung-hsing fu' by Wang Yi[a] (?276–322). Only the memorial presenting it to the throne survives; see *Ch'üan Chin wen* 20.11a–b.

25 'Nan cheng fu' by Lu Yün (262–303), the younger brother of Lu Chi; see *Ch'üan Chin wen* 100.6b–8a.

26 Lu Yün, for example, uses the same phrase 'address the army' (*shih chung*) as in line 293 of the 'Lament'; see *Ch'üan Chin wen* 100.7b4.

27 'Huang yin fu' by Hsia-hou Hsüan (209–54), on the birth of an heir to Emperor Ming of the Wei in 231, *Ch'üan San-kuo wen* 21.2a–b; see also Achilles Fang (1), I, 339. This was a natural subject for a rhapsody. Mei Sheng's son Kao had written one on the birth of an heir to Emperor Wu of the Han (*reg.* 141–87 B.C.), *Han shu* 51.26b.

28 'Tsan-shu t'ai-tzu fu', *Ch'üan San-kuo wen* 30.10b–12a. Pien Lan, the author, was a nephew of Ts'ao Ts'ao's wife, the Empress Dowager Hsüan, *née* Pien. Ts'ao P'i was thus his first cousin.

29 'Cheng hui fu' by Wang Ch'en (d. 266), *Ch'üan Chin wen* 28.1a–b.

30 A relatively good one is the 'Rhapsody on Dancing Horses, Written on Imperial Command' ('Wu ma fu ying-chao') by Hsieh Chuang (421–66), *Ch'üan Sung wen* 34.7a–8a.

31 For example, the 'Instruction in Warfare' ('Chiang-wu fu') by Yü Shih-chi (d. 618), *Ch'üan Sui wen* 14.1a–3a. The misleading title was a cliché regularly applied to hunts and archery contests.

32 See note 31.

33 Watson (1), pp. 107–8.

34 The original story is translated in Watson (3), pp. 187–8.

35 It is quoted in his biography, *Chin shu* 89.4a.

36 'Ying-wu fu', *WH* 13.20a–23b, biography in *Hou-Han shu* 80B.24a–29b. The work is translated and discussed in my article 'Mi Heng's "Rhapsody on a Parrot"', to appear in *HJAS* 39 (1979).

37 Li Shan's commentary, *WH* 13.21b10.

38 As explained in my article (note 36), Mi's own 'Parrot' seems too long (100 lines), too original, and too polished to have been written impromptu; on the other

hand, some of the more conventional imitations mentioned there may well have been improvised. The latter are only fragments, so it is difficult to judge them.

39 'Shan fu', *Ch'üan Chin wen* 51.5b–6a.

40 Watson (1), pp. 94–5, translates the supposed Lady Pan poem, which he believes to be of the second century A.D.

41 'Hsüeh Liang wang T'u-yüan fu', *Ch'üan Liang wen* 33.11a–12a.

42 Chang Jung's 'The Sea' ('Hai fu') appears in *Ch'üan Ch'i wen* 15.1a–3b; Mu Hua's, in *WH* 12.1a–8b, trans. Watson (2), pp. 72–9.

43 *Nan-Ch'i shu* 41.1b–6b.

44 Ch'ü Shui-yüan (1), p. 14. Ch'ü on pp. 13–15 has an extremely perceptive discussion of different categories of *fu*.

45 'Yao ch'üeh fu', *Ch'üan San-kuo wen* 14.5a–b.

46 Translated in Hans H. Frankel (1), pp. 249–58.

47 'Teng-t'u tzu hao-se fu' (*WH* 19.9b–11b), attributed to Sung Yü by Hsiao T'ung, who does show his disapproval by placing such erotica at the very end of the *fu* section. There is a partial translation of this in Waley (4), pp. 43–4. A Liu Ssu-chen, whom Yen K'o-chün can date only as pre-T'ang, wrote a *fu* on his own 'Ugly Wife' in imitation of the 'Master Teng-t'u', *Hsien-T'ang wen* 1.1b–2a. She is even uglier than Master Teng-t'u's: 'Skin like old mulberry bark, Ears like two hands sticking out'.

48 'Ping fu', *Ch'üan Chin wen* 87.2b–3b, trans. Waley (2), pp. 75–6.

49 'Ch'üan-nung fu', *Ch'üan Chin wen* 87.2a–b.

50 In his *fu* 'The Poor Family' ('P'in chia fu'), *Ch'üan Chin wen* 87.1a–b.

51 According to his biography, *Chin shu* 51.13a2. Shu Hsi was by no means the sort of disreputable figure one associates with the third century, but an orthodox Confucian and a distinguished scholar. He also claimed a much more distinguished ancestor, one of the men later immortalized in T'ao Ch'ien's poem 'In Praise of the Two Tutors Surnamed Shu', which is translated in Hightower (4), p. 215. The family were supposed to have changed the character of their surname slightly, eliminating the left-hand part, while in hiding at the time of Wang Mang. Shu's other works include a *fu* on 'Studies' ('Tu-shu fu', *Ch'üan Chin wen* 87.1b) and 'Nearby Wandering' ('Chin yu fu', *Ch'üan Chin wen* 87.2a), the latter a Confucian reply to the Taoist 'Distant Wandering' ('Yüan yu', trans. Hawkes (1), pp. 81–7).

52 Mather, pp. 194–5.

53 'Tsao shih fu'. The preface, which is all that remains, is quoted in his biography, *Nan-Ch'i shu* 52.5a9–5b8.

54 Trans. by Hightower in Birch, I, pp. 162–6; see especially p. 164.

55 *Nan-Ch'i shu* 52.5b9.

56 'Chin ch'un fu', *Ch'üan Liang wen* 8.7a–b.

57 For example, Chang Tsan's (499–549) 'Parting' ('Li-pieh fu'), *Ch'üan Liang wen* 64.7a–b.

58 The opening of Yü Hsin's 'Spring' ('Ch'un fu', *Works* 1.51b–52a) is indistinguishable from seven-word lyric poetry. This is the only such case in Yü's *fu*, and it may be considered a marginal example since up until the T'ang the seven-word meter was associated with songs rather than with *shih*, for example in Ts'ao P'i's (187–226) 'Song of Yen' ('Yen ko hsing'), trans. Frodsham (1), pp. 33–4. Other *fu* writers of the Six Dynasties also used the five-word lyric meter.

59 'Kan-liang fu', *Ch'üan Chin wen* 51.2a.

60 'K'un-je fu', *Ch'üan Chin wen* 65.3b–4a.

61 'The May-You-Have-Sons Flower' ('Yi-nan hua fu'), *Ch'üan Chin wen* 65.5b. Only the preface survives.

62 'Cold-Food Powder' ('Han-shih san fu'), *Ch'üan Chin wen* 65.5a. This was a combination of five minerals, taken with warm wine and cold food; see Mather, p. 20.

63 'Chieh fu', *Ch'üan Chin wen* 51.6a.
64 'Ching fu', *Ch'üan Chin wen* 51.6b.
65 'Ying-huo fu', *Ch'üan Chin wen* 51.11b–12a.
66 'Ch'uan fu', *Ch'üan Chin wen* 67.5b–6a.
67 'Kua fu', *Ch'üan Chin wen* 45.8b–9a.
68 *Ch'üan Chin wen* 45.9a1.
69 'Ying fu'[a], *Ch'üan Sui wen* 20.3a–4a.
70 'Pitchpot' ('T'ou-hu fu') by Fu Hsüan (217–78, *Ch'üan Chin wen* 45.7a), a tiny fragment; and a much longer work of the same title by Han-tan Ch'un (b. 132, *Ch'üan San-kuo wen* 26.1a–b).
71 For example, in the 'Wei-ch'i fu' by Emperor Wu of the Liang, *Ch'üan Liang wen* 1.7a–8a.
72 'Ch'i pu fu', *Ch'üan Chin wen* 81.9a.
73 'Mei-hua fu', *Ch'üan Liang wen* 8.8a–9a, trans. Frankel (2), pp. 1–3.
74 'Ts'ai-lien fu', *Ch'üan Liang wen* 8.9a.
75 'Yüan-yang fu', *Ch'üan Liang wen* 8.9b.
76 *Ch'üan Liang wen* 15.8b–9a.
77 *Works* 1.61a–62b.
78 Achilles Fang (1), I, 229, 241.
79 'Tang-tzu fu', *Works* 1.62b–64a.
80 Liu K'ai-yang, p. 70.
81 'Tui-chu fu', *Works* 1.57a–58b.
82 'Ch'un fu', *Works* 1.51a–55a.
83 'Ch'i hsi fu', *Works* 1.55a–b.
84 'Teng fu', *Works* 1.55b–57a.
85 'Ching lun', *Ch'üan Chin wen* 53.11b1.
86 'Jade' ('Yu fu'), *Ch'üan Chin wen* 51.8b.
87 'Hsüeh fu', *WH* 13.8a–11b, trans. Watson (2), pp. 86–91. For another translation and extended discussion, see Owen (1).
88 'Fu-niao fu', *WH* 13.16a–20a, trans. Watson (2), pp. 25–8.
89 'Ti tu fu', *Ch'üan Chin wen* 60.3b. Sun Ch'u, by a slip of the tongue, gave China the classic description of the recluse: 'I'll rinse my mouth with rocks and pillow my head on the streams.' See Mather, p. 402.
90 'Chiao-liao fu', *WH* 13.23b–26b, trans. von Zach, pp. 201–3.
91 Trans. Watson (3), p. 32.
92 'Yi feng fu', *Ch'üan Chin wen* 51.9b–10a.
93 Trans. Waley (1), p. 144. As Waley suggests, the text should probably say 'do not fade'.
94 'Sung po fu', *Ch'üan Chin wen* 13.2a.
95 'Hsiu po fu', *Ch'üan Ch'i wen* 6.8b.
96 *Nan shih* 43.10a.
97 'Tung ts'ao fu', Ch'ü Shui-yüan (2), pp. 199–200.
98 'Ying fu'[b], *Ch'üan Hou-Wei wen* 18.1a–b.
99 Trans. Hawkes (1), p. 70, line 13.
100 Hawkes (1), p. 156, line 15: 'Since the filth of the bluebottle cheats the eye with its hue.' Compare *Songs* no. 219, trans. Karlgren (2), p. 172: 'The green flies go buzzing about, they settle on the fence; joyous and pleasant lord, do not believe slanderous words.' Karlgren's green flies are my bluebottle.
101 *Wei shu* 19B.29a–35a.
102 'Ch'ing ying fu', *Ch'üan Chin wen* 51.11a–b.
103 He was thinking of *Songs* no. 219, translated above in note 100.
104 'Chiu fu', *Ch'üan San-kuo wen* 44.9a–b; trans. Holzman, pp. 19–20.
105 'Mi-hou fu', *Ch'üan San-kuo wen* 44.9b–10a; trans. Holzman, pp. 56–7. Holzman's

suggestion that the captive monkey is, to some extent, Juan Chi himself (p. 58), would make the 'Monkey' rather like Mi Heng's 'Parrot', a work Juan Chi presumably knew.

106 Holzman, p. 1, calls them 'some of the most obscure poetry ever written in China'. Chao Yeh Chia-ying, especially pp. 114–25, says a number of valuable things about the interpretation of allegory in *tz'u*; her remarks apply equally well to *fu*.

107 'Ch'i fa', *WH* 34.1a–13b, trans. Knechtges and Swanson.

108 Hsiao T'ung places them separately in *WH* 34–5; see Hightower (7), p. 531. The critic Chih Yü (d. 311) also devotes a separate discussion to the question of the didactic value of 'Sevens', *Ch'üan Chin wen* 77.8b–9a. Hsiao T'ung includes only three of the many 'Sevens' written, and he himself did his own version, *Ch'üan Liang wen* 20.3b–6b.

109 'Huai fu' by Tu T'ai-ch'ing, *Ch'üan Sui wen* 20.6b–7a.

110 The Liang Emperor Chien-wen's 'Regret' ('Hui fu', *Ch'üan Liang wen* 8.3a–4b), a disagreeably smug reflection on the lessons to be learned from history, is quite inferior to Chiang Yen's 'Regret' ('Hen fu'), though obviously inspired by it.

111 'Feng fu', *WH* 13.1b–4a, trans. Watson (2), pp. 21–4.

112 'Teng fu', *Ch'üan Liang wen* 34.3b–4a. The attendant is also the putative author of the 'Summons for a Gentleman Who Became a Recluse' in the *Ch'u tz'u*, trans. Hawkes (1), pp. 119–20.

113 'The Wild Goose' ('Yeh e fu'), *Ch'üan Sung wen* 46.6a–b.

114 'Yu ssu fu', *Ch'üan Sung wen* 46.1b–2a. This characteristic of some Six-Dynasties *fu* is pointed out by Hightower (6), p. 28.

115 'Ch'ing t'ai fu', *Ch'üan Liang wen* 34.5a–6a. The passage translated here appears in 34.5b11.

116 'Ch'iu hsing fu', *WH* 13.4a–8a; trans. von Zach, pp. 193–5.

117 'The Four Seasons' ('Ssu-shih fu'), *Ch'üan Liang wen* 33.2a–b.

118 'Hen fu' and 'Pieh fu', *WH* 16.24a–31b. The latter is translated by Watson (2), pp. 96–101.

119 'Wu ch'eng fu', *WH* 11.10a–13a; trans. Watson (2), pp. 92–5. Some of the following is taken from my more detailed discussion of the 'Lament' in *HJAS* 36 (1976), 82–113.

120 'K'u shu fu', *Works* 1.31b–38a.

121 There has been a tendency among critics to see a personal significance in Yü's 'Dead Tree', 'Bamboo Cane', and 'Cane of Ch'iung Bamboo' ('Ch'iung-chu chang fu', *Works* 1.28b–31b). That is certainly true of the 'Bamboo Cane', which is discussed in Chapter 1, and probably also of the 'Cane of Ch'iung Bamboo'. The latter begins very much like the rhapsodies on musical instruments, but the later section on the cane cut down and carried away from its home in the South (Chiang-nan) does remind one of Yü's biography. The 'Dead Tree', on the other hand, seems to be an objective description intended only to evoke a mood.

122 *Ch'ao-yeh ch'ien-tsai* 6.14b–15a, pointed out by Ni Fan.

123 *Ch'ao-yeh ch'ien-tsai* 4.17b has an anecdote of a four-year-old child challenged to recite the 'Dead Tree' from memory. One may question the details of the story, but it is normally only very famous literary works that inspire such anecdotes.

124 'Yü-lieh fu', *Ch'üan Han wen* 51.7a–9b.

125 Such as Yü's 'Heartbreak' ('Shang-hsin fu', *Works* 1.38a–47a). An earlier work of this type, by Hsiang Hsiu (third century A.D.), is translated in Watson (2), pp. 61–3.

126 Holzman, p. 24.

127 According to Confucius's own words; Waley (1), p. 135.

128 Trans. in Watson (2), pp. 64–71.

129   Hightower (2), p. 96 and n. 303. Yü's mournful 'Small Garden' is even more
       atypical of the genre of *fu* on life in retirement.
130   Hawkes (2).
131   'Yüan yu', trans. Hawkes (1), pp. 81–7.
132   'Ta jen fu', trans. Hervouet (1), pp. 185–203.
133   'Tan-sha k'o hsüeh fu', *Ch'üan Liang wen* 34.1b–2b.
134   'Yu T'ien-t'ai shan fu', trans. Watson (2), pp. 80–5. Li Po treats the same subject
       of an imaginary journey in a lyric poem, trans. in Watson (1), pp. 151–3.
135   Hawkes (1), p. 34.
136   For example, Chang Heng's 'Meditation on Mystery', *WH* 15.19a.
137   The *Shih ching* allegory had been much less complicated, and the same thing is
       generally true even of the 'Li sao' imitations.
138   They are generally identifiable by the word *cheng*[b] ('Journey') in the title; three
       are included in *WH* 9–10. Watson (2), p. 8, mentions the popularity of the form;
       I am thinking particularly of one by P'an Yüeh, *WH* 10.
139   Hsieh Ling-yün's 'Record of a Journey' ('Chuan-cheng fu', *Ch'üan Sung wen*
       30.4a–10a) is one of the longest *fu* of the Six Dynasties, with about 4000 words.
140   Hawkes (1), p. 22. The original was quite short; imitations are invariably longer
       and more detailed, as in the 'Lament'.
141   Liu Chih-chi 9.3a–b.
142   'Ssu-hsüan fu', *WH* 15.
143   *Hou-Han shu* 59 (l.c. 49).17b.
144   Trans. in Hightower (2), pp. 80–5.
145   'Chiao chü fu', *Ch'üan Liang wen* 25.2b–6b; the work is about 2600 words long.
146   *Ch'üan Liang wen* 25.5a13–5b3.
147   'Shih-ch'ing fu', *Ch'üan Hou-Wei wen* 33.7a–9b.
148   'Shu-shen fu', *Ch'üan Hou-Wei wen* 35.5b–7b.
149   *Wei shu* 36.16a9.
150   'Kuei hun fu', *Ch'üan Ch'en wen* 14.1a–3b. The suggestion is made in Ch'en Yin-
       k'o (2).
151   For example, a work by Ssu-ma Hsiang-ju on the Second Emperor, trans. in
       Hervouet (1), pp. 181–4; and one by Fu Hsien on the First Emperor, *Ch'üan
       Chin wen* 51.4a.
152   For example, the works grouped in *Wen-yüan ying-hua* 129–30 (including the
       'Lament' and Yü's 'Heartbreak') have nothing in common except a word such as
       'grief' or 'sorrow' in the title. The same approach led Hsiao T'ung to create a
       category of *tz'u* (synonymous here with *fu*) for T'ao Ch'ien's 'Return'.
153   What Hawkes (1), p. 7, represents as '*tum tum tum tee tum tum* hsi *tum tum tum
       tee tum tum*'. The particle *hsi* at the end of the first hemistich, common enough in
       Han and early Six-Dynasties works, tends to be omitted later.
154   'Shang-shih fu', *Ch'üan Sung wen* 46.2b–3a.
155   Most of this section on the T'ang is based on an article by Mou Jun-sun, listed in
       the bibliography. The theory of regional factions at the early T'ang court, which
       originated with Ch'en Yin-k'o, has been much disputed recently, for example by
       Howard J. Wechsler, pp. 101–20.
156   *Chou shu* 40.21a.
157   Wei Cheng (580–643), who was particularly hostile to *fu* (Mou Jun-sun, p. 55),
       quotes repeatedly without acknowledgment from the 'Lament' in his general
       assessment of the Liang emperors, *Liang shu* 6.10a–12b. It is also amusing to
       note that his misreading of the 'Lament' led to the fabrication of anecdotes;
       see Appendix VI.
158   For example, see William Hung (2), pp. 51, 236.
159   Hsü Shih-tseng (author's preface dated 1573), p. 101.

160   Mou Jun-sun, pp. 65–6.
161   By Wang K'ai-yün (1833–1916), pp. 1–12.
162   Quoted in Ch'en Ch'ü-ping, II, 102–3. Chang felt similar embarrassment about his enthusiasm for songs (*tz'u*); his attempt to find a saving virtue of allegory in them is the subject of Chao Yeh Chia-ying's article, listed in the bibliography.
163   Hsü's reminiscences appear in the preface to this work.
164   Printed in *P'eng Te-huai wen-t'i chuan-chi*, pp. 30, 33–4, 23. This was published in Hong Kong, but the passages in question seem authentic.
165   See bibliography under T'an Cheng-pi and Chi Fu-hua.
166   Ch'ü Shui-yüan (2). Stephen Owen's *Poetry of the Early T'ang* contains a good deal of information relevant to this chapter, particularly concerning the T'ang attitudes toward Six-Dynasties literature. Unfortunately, the Owen book appeared too late for detailed citation here.

Chapter 3   'The Lament for the South'

1   In the following, the right-hand column is a very loose paraphrase intended to guide the reader through the complexities of the 'Lament'. Originally intended as an imitation of Coleridge's glosses on 'The Rime of the Ancient Mariner', the paraphrase has since expanded so much that the model would no longer be recognizable in it. On the other hand, because of its scope, it has made it unnecessary in the commentary to belabor either Liang history or the specific terms of reference of the many allusions. The left-hand column contains a fairly literal rendering of the Chinese original; even here, I have supplied whatever seemed clearly implied by Yü Hsin's text, such as pronouns and logical connections ('but', 'therefore', 'now', and so on).

Chapter 4   Commentary

1   *Ch'u tz'u* 9.19b, trans. Hawkes (1), p. 109.
2   Hawkes (1), p. 102. For Ch'ü Yüan as the would-be savior of a doomed state, see Hawkes (1), pp. 11–15.
3   Yü is, in effect, calling himself another Ch'ü Yüan; see Chapter 2.
4   Legge (1), I, 297.
5   The tenth month was November 16–December 15, 548. For date conversion I have used Ch'en Yüan (1); all dates are according to the Julian calendar. On the use of the Dipper as a natural calendar, see John Chambers in Legge (1), III, (93–4).
6   Kao Pu-ying quotes some of the arguments about the identity of this Mount Hua (or Hua-yang); they need not concern us here. For similar conventional references to Hua-yang, see *Ch'üan Han wen* 54.3a5 and *Works* 13.54a, 13.73a.
7   According to the *Tso chuan*, Shu-sun Ch'o was seized in the twenty-third year of Duke Chao of Lu, later lodged in Chi while his companion was sent elsewhere, and finally returned to Lu in the twenty-fourth year; Legge (1), V, 698a–b, 702a. The imprisonment at Chi (or an earlier period of separation) would satisfy the requirement for a 'detached lodging', but Shu-sun was detained for only a year or so, not Yü's three years. Yü may have confused this with another *Tso chuan* story; his friend Hsü Ling complains of his own detention by the Northern Ch'i, 'You have transferred the minister to a separate lodging in Chi, imprisoned Master Yüeh *for three years* (*Ch'üan Ch'en wen* 7.8b9–10, cf. 10.3a11, also by Hsü, where the syntax is clearer). Hsü's first line clearly refers to Shu-sun Ch'o. Master Yüeh is Yüeh Ch'i, an ambassador from Sung detained by Chin; the three-year term of his detention is pointed out in the *Tso chuan*, Legge (1), V, 763b, 768b–769a.

8   Professor William Hung's ingenious rendering 'Self Introduction' would allow for both senses of the phrase, (1), p. 20 n. 30.

9   For Huan T'an, see *Pei-t'ang shu-ch'ao* 55.5b11 and Timoteus Pokora, p. 41. For Tu Yü, Lu Fan-ch'ao points out *Pei-t'ang shu-ch'ao* 97.1a3.

10 For P'an Yüeh, see Ting Fu-pao, p. 373 (Wang); for Lu Chi, *Yi-wen lei-chü* 20.11b–12a (Wang). The phrase 'ancestors' deeds' may have been taken from another work by Lu Chi; cf. Fang (2), p. 531, couplet 5.

11 *Ch'un-ch'iu ching-chuan chi-chieh* 6.7a (hereafter *Ch'un-ch'iu CCCC*).

12 For the story of Ching K'o's departure, see J. R. Hightower (4), pp. 224–9.

13 *Li T'ai-po shih chi* 17.3a.

14 Ni Fan and several others, failing to recognize the Ching K'o reference in the line, have taken it as an announcement of Yü Hsin's hypothetical writing of his 'Song of Yen' ('Yen ko hsing', *Works* 5.14a–17a) on the occasion of his departure. Yü presumably has in mind here the feelings he shared with Ching K'o, not the fact that both wrote poems. In fact, there is no apparent connection between Ching K'o's song and the numerous poems to the ballad title 'Song of Yen', the latter here more of a red herring than anything else.

15 'Written at the Tomb of the Prince of Lu-ling', *WH* 23.21a (Yeh), trans, J. D. Frodsham (2), I, 140.

16 *Li T'ai-po shih chi* 25.25b–26a. Of course, the syntax of all these passages does not strictly require that the old man be *from* Ch'u, but only that he be associated with that state.

17 *Lieh-nü chuan* 2.15a. If *yü*[c] (literally 'to wish') in this passage is not a misprint, it must indicate the future tense, as in my translation. The last thing this panther wants is conspicuous spots; as *Chuang tzu* says (20/7/13), 'Tigers and leopards are hunted because of their patterned [fur].'

18 *Hsieh Hsüan-ch'eng chi chiao-chu*, p. 237.

19 Trans. D. C. Lau (2), p. 123; bracketed matter added. With lines 25–6, compare a similar passage on a life in retirement in the rhapsody 'A Journey to North Mountain' by Wang Chi (*Wen-yüan ying-hua* 97.9b8): 'Agreeing to the admirable retirement to the North Sea, Consenting to a refusal to serve as on South Mountain.' The allusions here are the same as in Yü, except for the reference to Po-yi's North Sea rather than T'ai-kung's eastern one.

20 I have generally avoided arguing line after line against Ni Fan's interpretation, but his approach to this line has been rather widely accepted. The commentary is unfortunately too long to translate (354 words on lines 25–6, *Works* 2.3b–4a). The gist is that, having observed the Western Wei's abdication (*jang*) in favor of the Northern Chou, Yü Hsin nevertheless consented to take office under this new dynasty. Since it was called the Chou, he was eating the grain of the Chou. It should be sufficient to point out that *jang* ('yield, decline') here has nothing to do with abdication; that to Yü Hsin, a Southerner, it made little difference which alien state he served, since both were to the same extent the conquerors of his *Liang* dynasty; and that any such treasonable comment on the Western Wei abdication would have got Yü beheaded. The Ssu-k'u editors singled out for particular praise Ni's explanations of the contemporary references in the 'Lament'; this is, unfortunately, the sort of thing they had in mind.

21 Hightower (4), p. 133.

22 Watson (3), p. 109, n. 4, explains the anecdote.

23 As in the preface to Liang Su's (late 8th century) elegy 'On Visiting My Old Garden' (*Wen-yüan ying-hua* 130.5a8): 'So I wrote a *fu* to record the matter' (*sui tso fu chi shih*). Liang's use of a different radical for *chi* may be of comfort to others who confuse the two characters.

24 A contemporary had described as 'words of fear and suffering' (*wei k'u chih yü*) a memorial protesting the Liang decision to give refuge to the fugitive Hou Ching in 548 (*Ch'üan Liang wen* 24.3a8).

25 Line 35 had earlier served as the defense of Wu Tzu-hsü when he was criticized for digging up and beating the corpse of his former ruler, *Shih chi* 66.12. For both Wu and Yü Hsin, the phrase means 'Time is running out'; aside from that, the earlier use of the phrase is irrelevant.

26 *Jen-chien chih shih p'iao-hu chi ho* (*Chin lou tzu chiao-chu*, p. 261).

27 Hightower (4), p. 226.

28 *Shuo yüan* 13.5a (Wu). Wei-kung looks like a posthumous title ('Duke Wei'), but cannot be, as Yeh Chia-ying points out. He is not a ruler himself, since he goes on to complain of the conduct of his ruler. *Shih chi* 71.8 mentions another native of Lower Ts'ai, a rather obscure state.

29 *Shih-shuo hsin-yü* BB.40a.

30 J. R. Hightower (5), p. 109, n. 1, notes that the double line predominates in the parallel-prose 'Preface to *New Songs from the Tower of Jade*', by Yü Hsin's contemporary Hsü Ling (507–83). About a fourth of the Preface to the 'Lament' is in double lines, but in the 'Lament' proper only 4 out of 260 couplets are so constructed (lines 1–2, 335–6, 339–40, 519–20). Suzuki Torao (1), pp. 115–16, rather overstates the rarity of such double lines in *fu* proper before Yü Hsin; they can be found at least as early as Hsieh Ling-yün's *fu* 'Record of a Journey', (*Ch'üan Sung wen* 30.5a11–12), and occur occasionally in other *fu* of the fifth and sixth centuries.

31 For the Yellow and Lo Rivers, see Legge (1), III, 117. Legge, *loc. cit.*, note on paragraph 54, points out that Mount Hua is sometimes described as belonging to Yü-chou. Mount Sung, about thirty miles east of Loyang, appears slightly later under the name Wai-fang; Legge (1), III, 130, and 131b, note on paragraph 2.

32 *Ch'un-ch'iu ching-chuan yin-te* 16/Yin 8/2 *Kung* (Kao).

33 The earliest surviving source, *Shih chi* 84.19–20, says only that Sung Yü was a native of Ch'u and a literary follower of Ch'ü Yüan. Even a writer as late as Li Shan (d. 689) can add nothing to this in his commentary on *WH* 13.1b.

34 The first king of Lin-chiang seems to have been Kung Ao, who was given that position by Hsiang Yü (*Shih chi* 7.39, trans. Chavannes, II, 290). The kingdom still existed under the Han (*Han shu* 26.25b10, 35.1b3), and one of the rulers appears below in line 460.

35 This has been the traditional interpretation of the line, though individual commentators disagree on the exact allusion involved. For this reading, the most suitable is probably the occasion when two men moved their couches outdoors beneath a tree to escape the heat and spent the day in 'pure conversation'; this story, pointed out by Hu Wei-sheng, is quoted in P'ei Sung-chih's commentary, *San-kuo chih* 29.20a.

36 Yü Chien-wu continued to serve Hsiao Kang after he became Emperor, but both here and in lines 321–6 below, Kang is treated only as a Crown Prince. Kang's reign as a puppet of Hou Ching was politically awkward; Hsiao Yi, for obvious reasons, refused to recognize his brother as Emperor, and continued to use the last reign-period of the late Emperor Wu until taking the throne himself.

37 The source of the Yangtze and Han is probably the 'Tribute of Yü' rather than the *Tso chuan* passage; see commentary on line 57.

38 *Juan pu-ping Yung-huai shih chu*, p. 78; trans. Holzman, p. 51.

39 Ni Fan claims to have found Lan-ch'eng recorded as a child-name for Yü Hsin in the *Hsiao ming lu*, by Lu Kuei-meng (d. 881). Ni may have been quoting from an encyclopedia. I have been unable to find the story in the Pai hai edition; this

Ming dynasty *ts'ung-shu* is the source of all existing editions of the *Hsiao ming lu*.
On the Liang examination system, see Teng Ssu-yü, pp. 58–60. Yü-wen Yu
mentions Yü Hsin's successful completion of the examination in his preface to
the collected works, 6b4. He uses the same term as in line 42 (*she ts'e*), but this
is probably not significant; the Liang Emperor Wu had also used the term in
an edict of 505, *Tzu-chih t'ung-chien*, p. 4546.

40   Yü Hsin's contemporary Wang Pao says in one place: 'The Imperial Crown
Prince . . .' and immediately quotes the two *Yi ching* tags (*Ch'üan Hou-Chou
wen* 7.3b13); Wang also pairs the two tags in a memorial urging the appointment
of a Crown Prince (*Ch'üan Hou-Chou wen* 7.1a13). Emperor Yüan of the Liang
also uses the two phrases to describe the Crown Prince (*Ch'üan Liang wen* 18.5a4).
It is conceivable, in the case of Hexagram 30, that the association arose from the
Crown Prince's position in relation to the Emperor, analogous to a second, or
replacement, sun in the heavens; Yü Hsin mentions this idea twice, in connection
with Hexagram 30, in *Works* 7.23a–b.

41   Wu Chao-yi points out a similar line in an untitled *shih*-poem by Liu Chen:
'Square banks enclose sparkling water; In it there are ducks and geese' (*WH*
29.13b, trans. von Zach, p. 526). The Liu Chen poem, about a desire to get away
from it all, does not help much here, nor does a social quatrain by Yü Hsin 'On
the Assigned Topic: Geese in the Lake' (*Works* 4.65a): 'They still remember the
water in the square banks; This autumn they have already come back.'

42   See Herrmann, p. 25.

43   There was a good deal of secret diplomacy, and a better understanding of it might
help explain some of the vagaries of Liang history. Emperor Yüan, for example,
tried to keep secret his alliance with the Northern Ch'i against Hou Ching, and the
simultaneous Northern Ch'i and Western Wei embassies to Chiang-ling in 554
must have been embarrassing for him.

44   *San Ch'i lüeh-chi*, quoted in *Yi-wen lei-chü* 6.7a (Wu).

45   *Ti-wang shih-chi*, quoted in *Yi-wen lei-chü* 11.12b (Wu).

46   Yü could have given his own catalogue, of course; a variety of tribute actually
presented is listed in *Liang shu* 54, the chapter on foreigners.

47   By Tso Ssu, in the preface to his 'Rhapsody on the Three Capitals', *WH* 4.12a–
13b. The passage is translated in Watson (2), pp. 115–17.

48   *Pan Ch'ao wei Ting-yüan chih hou¸ Wang Hsi wei ho-ch'in chih shih*.

49   Legge (1), III, 293, cf. II, 480. For another interpretation of the phrase, see
D. C. Lau (2), p. 195.

50   *Ti-wang shih chi*, quoted in *Shih chi* 4.42, line 8 commentary (Wu).

51   *Pen, hai, k'uei, chi*. Kao Pu-ying's *ch'ing* ('pure') is simply a misprint. Except in
this line, variants in the 'Lament' fall generally into one of two categories: (1)
obvious corruptions, as in people's names; (2) differences so slight that it scarcely
matters which reading one follows, for example a different word-order or a
different particle. For this reason, I have seldom mentioned variants.

52   *T'ai-p'ing yü-lan* 888.1b, citing the *Pao-p'u tzu*. As Kao notes, the present text of
the *Pao-p'u tzu* (8.5b11–12) omits the apes and insects. It also fails to mention
King Mu.

53   *Ch'un-ch'iu CCCC* 11.8a (Wu).

54   Quoted in *Ching-tien shih-wen*, *Erh-ya yin-yi* AB.25b (Kao).

55   Cf. Karlgren (1), p. 4 (Wu). Karlgren, following the rationalistic tradition, makes
the *hsüan-chi* simply an astronomical instrument; in the original, as he recognizes,
Shun seems to be *controlling* the heavenly bodies.

56   Hou Ching himself may be referring to this same allusion when he says that the
Liang 'wore my/our animal patterns' (*p'i wo shou wen*) and gave him rank in return

(*Ch'üan Liang wen* 70.5b2–3). 'Animal patterns' should mean patterned furs in this context.

57 *Yi ching-lu tao chin liu-li nao chiu . . . kung yin hsüeh meng'*. Ying Shao's explanation of *ching-lu* as the name of a knife is plausible enough. That of *liu-li* as a rice-scoop is less so, and sounds like a guess. Even Yü Hsin would surely think twice before using *chin* to mean 'to cut up gold'. Unfortunately I can find no occurrence of the *Han shu* phrase *liu-li*[a] not based on this passage. One suspects that in the original story, the white horse was killed with the *ching-lu* knife, and that a golden *liu-li*[a] (meaning uncertain, probably a foreign word) was then used to mix the blood with the wine which the covenanters drank, thus explaining the 'blood-draught oath'.

58 Chang Ch'ien's bamboo canes came from a non-Chinese part of Szechwan and were therefore 'foreign', but this may not be the correct allusion for the line.

59 *WH* 51.1a: *yi k'uei Chou shih*. As suggested in the 1971 *Chou shu*, p. 747, note 17, I have adopted the variant *chien* (from the Po-na *Chou shu*), instead of Ni's *wen* ('hear'); the latter would make no sense here.

60 After being deposed, Hsiao Cheng-te is supposed to have written a letter, intercepted by Hou Ching, which led to his death. Ni took this as the reference in line 132; he is surely wrong. That letter could hardly be described as 'model words', and Ni's interpretation would require advancing the plot almost a year, to a date several months after the fall of Chien-k'ang and a death at which Yü Hsin could only have rejoiced.

61 It occurs in the midst of a fishing scene in Chang Heng's *fu* 'Returning to the Fields', trans. Hightower (2), pp. 215–16.

62 *Shih chi* 74.6–7 (Wu); see Fung Yu-lan, I, 160–1.

63 *Shui-ching chu* 24.13a (Wang), *Shih chi* 1.43 commentary. See also Legge (1), III, Proleg., 116 n. 8.

64 Wu Chao-yi, who correctly identified the allusion, has been ignored in favor of Lu's story of T'ao K'an sharing grain with another general during a rebellion. Hsiao Yi did send ships loaded with grain partway to the capital during the rebellion, but this is not implied in line 157.

65 It may have originated in the *Ssu-ma fa*, quoted by Li Shan in *WH* 40.2a.

66 *Ch'üan Liang wen* 15.5a13. Hsiao Yi also uses the phrase *wo ch'iang* ('to topple walls').

67 He has no biography in the *Liang shu*, and only a short one in *Nan shih* 38.14b5–16b. There are scattered references to him in the *Tzu-chih t'ung-chien*, and some additional anecdotes quoted in Ssu-ma Kuang's *k'ao-yi* only to be rejected as false.

68 'Yin ma ch'ang-ch'eng k'u hsing'. The most famous is that by Ch'en Lin (d. 217), text in Ting Fu-pao, p. 182; trans. Watson (1), pp. 56–7.

69 Yü evidently accepted Tu Yü's interpretation of *ts'e* as 'to bury', *Ch'un-ch'iu CCCC* 17.12a. Tu's gloss on *hsia ch'e* as 'chariots buried with the dead' is amply justified by archaeological evidence of Shang and Chou burial practice.

70 My interpretation; cf. Kristofer Marinus Schipper, pp. 130–2 and p. 21 of Schipper's appended Chinese text (Wu).

71 The traditional interpretation of *chin ku* is as a clapperless bell and a drum (Morohashi, 40152/375), and Watson therefore translates (and glosses) the original passage, 'bearing in his hands the gong and drum with which he signaled the advance or retreat of his troops' (6), I, 484. In some cases the two words clearly do mean two different objects, for example in *Hsün tzu* 10.7b9: 'When the army hears the sound of the drums (*ku*), it advances; when it hears the sound of the bells (*chin*), it retreats', trans. Watson (5), p. 67. In line 334, I prefer to take it as a single object, because of the parallel with 'engraved axe', and also because it seems to me that

a man with a clapperless bell in one hand and a drum in the other would find both useless except perhaps for juggling. There is a large Shang drum made of bronze in the Sumitomo collection in Japan. One notes also that Tu Yü, a third-century general, when confronted with the phrase *chin ku* in the *Tso chuan*, ignores the *chin* and comments only on the reason for beating drums; this suggests that Tu Yü also analyzed the phrase as adjective–noun rather than noun–noun.

72 According to *Nan shih* 53.16b10, something struck Lun's ship and almost over-turned it when he was headed for Chien-k'ang to attempt to relieve the siege (Lu). As Kao points out, the story does not mention a dragon; neither is the ship sunk. Chang Jen-ch'ing, who says that 10–20% of Lun's men and horses were drowned, has fused two stories; the supposed mass drowning is a different event occurring sometime later, *Nan shih* 53.17a1–2. On line 345, see Appendix VI.

73 Line 372 refers to an obscure passage in the *Mencius*, and incidentally provides a useful gloss on it: Someone comes to Mencius and tells him of another man's observation that *Shih ching* 197 is 'plaintive' (and therefore not an edifying poem). Mencius tells a parable to justify the song, which, as he concludes, 'deals with a major wrong . . . committed by one's parent', trans. D. C. Lau (2), p. 173. It is important to realize that the song was supposed to be about a wrong done by a parent to a child, not to some outsider; for example, see Mencius's paraphrast Chao Ch'i, *Meng tzu cheng-yi* 24.7a. Yü Hsin is talking about fratricide; so is Yen Chih-t'ui, in a closely related passage in his *fu* 'Contemplation of my Life' ('Kuan wo sheng fu'), which was written in imitation of the 'Lament'. Yen says of Hsiao Yi's behavior toward his brothers: 'One would smile at a passer-by drawing back his bow, but weep at the killing of flesh and blood' (*Yen-shih chia-hsün hui-chu*, p. 139b). Both Legge (1), II, 427 and D. C. Lau have taken the *Mencius* parable as involving three characters: one shooting, one being shot at, and one either trying to stop the shooting (Legge) or telling the story afterward (Lau). I would suggest that there are only two characters involved, the intended victim later telling the story himself. This would yield the following modification of Lau's translation; it is certainly the way Yü and Yen read the passage, and it seems to me to make better sense anyway: 'Here is a man. If a man from Yüeh bends his bow and takes a shot at him, he [the intended victim] can recount the incident in a light-hearted manner. The reason is simply that he would feel no concern for the man from Yüeh. If it had been his own elder brother who did this, then he would be in tears while recounting the incident.' One is more willing to accept the amusement of a man telling about an attack on himself (war stories, or some-thing of the sort) than about an attack on a third person. The narrator, after all, has in this case obviously survived the attack. Tears also seem more appropriate from a man whose brother has tried to kill him, even though he has failed; the fact that it was his own brother does make a difference. If the tears are only at the knowledge that one's brother has committed a crime against a third person, then we are placed in the disagreeable position of accepting amusement at crimes committed by outsiders. Interpreted this way, however, the parable means that ill treatment by one's relatives is bound to cause greater resentment, and that the resentment expressed in *Shih ching* 197 is justified because of the circumstances.

74 I have not had access to Yen Shu's encyclopedia, but Kao Pu-ying locates the passage in *chüan* 32, 'Similes'. Yen quotes a 'Lament' commentary several times, but apparently never identifies the author, so that one cannot even tell whether his source is one work or several. Kao points out two lost commentaries on the 'Lament' listed in the 'Essay on Bibliography', *Hsin T'ang shu* 60.13b10–11. One was by Chang T'ing-fang, the other by Ts'ui Ling-ch'in (*fl.* 742–56 and 756–62 respectively, according to *Tōdai no sambun sakka*, pp. 15, 33). The *Shih tzu* survives now only in editions reconstructed from fragments; in view

of the rarity of Yen Shu's encyclopedia, the absence of such passages from modern texts is not surprising.

75 C. Martin Wilbur, pp. 436, 438 plates 1–2, explains the functioning of one Chinese repeating crossbow. As Wilbur says, it 'is illustrated as early as . . . 1621, but it is probably much older'.

76 Edward Schafer, p. 68, identifies the bamboo as *Phyllostachys puberula* var. *boryana*.

77 *Hu yen* also occurs only once in the *Tso chuan*: because of the actions of the tyrants Chieh and Chou, 'their ruin was swift' (*ch'i wang yeh hu yen*) cf. Legge (1), V, 87, 88b. Tu Yü treats *hu yen* and *hu chu* as synonymous and glosses both as 'quick, sudden, swift'; Karlgren ((3), p. 16, Tso G1. 55; p. 57, Tso G1. 204) agrees with Tu about *hu yen* but suggests that *hu* in the phrase *hu chu* has the sense 'to destroy', as in a Mao gloss on *Songs* 241. Yü Hsin follows Tu Yü, and in doing so he could claim P'an Yüeh as a precedent; P'an had written, 'The sacrifices to Chung-yung ended abruptly' (*Chung-yung chih ssu hu chu*, WH 10.9a).

Appendix I Historical and biographical sources

1 The officials commanded by the Emperor to prepare an edition of the *Ch'en shu* in 1061 found it difficult to obtain a complete copy of that work or several of the other separate histories of the dynasties covered by the *Nan shih* and *Pei shih*; see Chang Shun-hui, p. 110. There are very useful detailed discussions of the *Liang shu*, *Chou shu*, *Nan shih*, and *Pei shih* in Hsü Hao, pp. 103–8, 129–56.

2 Liu Chih-chi, 17.7b–8a. On Liu, see William Hung (1).

Appendix II Yü Hsin's career

1 This information appears only in Yü-wen Yu's preface (6a4). The wording is not as clear as one might wish: *shih Liang Tung-kung chiang-tu*. This has misled some into making Yü a tutor of the Crown Prince. While it is true that either *shih-chiang* or *shih-tu* was a possible title for a tutor during the Liang, the combination *shih-chiang-tu* was not a Liang title. It seems most unlikely that a 26-year-old Crown Prince, then compiling the *Wen hsüan*, would have accepted a 14-year-old boy as a tutor. Four years later, the post of *shih-tu* was held by Hsü Ling's father Ch'ih (*Tzu-chih t'ung-chien*, p. 4810). Hsü Ch'ih was 60 years old at the time (Hsiao Yi says that he was 64 *sui* in 534, *Ch'üan Liang wen* 17.12b4); this is the sort of age we would expect for someone in that position. Yü-wen Yu later says that the post of Acting Military Consultant was the first government office that Yü ever held (Preface 6b8); his phrase *shih . . . chiang-tu* is apparently analogous to *shih-yin*, etc., and means only that Yü was studying in the company of a superior, the Crown Prince in this case. Yü-wen Yu, a Northern Chou prince, seems to have known very little about Liang institutions; there are a number of problems in his account of Yü's career in the South.

2 See commentary on line 42 of the 'Lament' proper.

3 There was a separate system for military officials. Where possible, I have supplied the level of each position according to Hu San-hsing's account of the Liang hierarchy, *Tzu-chih t'ung-chien*, pp. 4576–80.

4 The phrase *t'ung-chih* prefixed to official titles changed its meaning with time. Under the Chin, it meant 'with direct access', and adding it to a title amounted to a promotion; the Chin Emperor Hui (*reg.* 290–306), noting that a certain Grand Counselor (*san-chi ch'ang-shih*) needed more direct access to the throne, added *t'ung-chih* to his title, *Ch'üan Chin wen* 7.5a8–9. It is apparently with this sort of thing in mind that Albert E. Dien (1), p. 31, translates *t'ung-chih* 'with Direct Access'. By the Liang, the situation was exactly the opposite. Now the meaning was 'equivalent to' or 'honorary', and adding it to a title would have

    meant a demotion. A Grand Counselor ranked on the twelfth level; a *t'ung-chih* Grand Counselor, only on the eleventh (see *Tzu-chih t'ung-chien*, p. 4577, lines 1–2). I have therefore adopted the translation 'Surrogate' from Albert E. Dien (2), p. 43, a later work.

5   Ni Fan's *nien-p'u* (6a) contains a statement, purportedly quoted from the *Wei shu*, that in the third year of Wu-ting (545) 'The Liang sent the *san-chi ch'ang-shih* Hsü Chün-fang and the *t'ung-chih ch'ang-shih* Yü Hsin [on an embassy to us]. In the tenth month, [we] sent the *chung-shu she-jen* Wei Chin on an embassy to the Liang.' The first half of this is Ni Fan's own fabrication. What the *Wei shu* (12.14a) actually says for that date is, 'Hsiao Yen (= Liang Wu-ti) sent an envoy/ envoys to come to court and present tribute. Winter, the tenth month, [we] sent the *chung-shu she-jen* Wei Chin on an embassy to Hsiao Yen.' Because of this sort of thing, I have for the most part ignored Ni Fan's *nien-p'u.*

6   Yü-wen Yu's preface (8a) at this point gives Yü a post with which I am not familiar, *Tung-kung ling-chih*; according to the same source, Yü was also assigned control of the Crown Prince's troops.

7   The date when Hsiao Shao was assigned a post in Chiang-hsia, *Tzu-chih t'ung-chien*, p. 5070. On the quarrel, see note 28 to Chapter 1.

8   Hu San-hsing gives a useful summary of the nine-command system, *Tzu-chih t'ung-chien*, pp. 5108–10. I have also used *Chou shu* 16.14b–17a, 24.2b–5b; *Pei shih* 30.27b–31a; *T'ung tien*, pp. 221a–223c; *T'ung-chih*, p. 2538a–c; and *Sui shu* 27.20b–21b.

9   Yü-wen Yu makes him Duke of Yi-ch'eng.

10   When the Chou Emperor Hsüan took the throne, *Chou shu* 7.1b2. The position of Middle Grandee (*chung ta-fu*), which had been abolished in 573, was restored by Emperor Hsüan, *Chou shu* 24.2a9–2b2.

Appendix III   Editions and commentaries

1   *Ssu-k'u ch'üan-shu tsung-mu t'i-yao* 29.24 (3112). The first edition, according to Yü-wen Yu's preface (14a), included only works written in the North, between 554 and 579. On the other hand, Ni Fan's, which may be taken as representative of the editions now in circulation, contains a poem on the T'ung-t'ai Monastery, Liang Wu-ti's great foundation at Chien-k'ang, which was certainly written in the South (*Works* 3.26a), and also two grave inscriptions containing dates corresponding to 676 and 682 (*Works* 16.41b5, 45b1–2)! Ni Fan points out that these two inscriptions cannot conceivably have been written by Yü (*Works* 16.36a), but they had earlier been included without reservation in the Ming edition reprinted in the Ssu-pu ts'ung-k'an (16.12b–18a). Other evidence, particularly of pre-554 works, could be given, but this should be sufficient to prove that the present collection is not that of Yü-wen Yu.

2   For example, the two grave inscriptions in note 1 above.

3   Ni Fan received the *chü-jen* degree in 1705, according to *Ssu-k'u ch'üan-shu tsung-mu t'i-yao* 29.24 (3112).

4   Date provided by *Shu-mu ta-wen pu-cheng*, p. 165.

5   Reprinted in *Erh-shih-wu shih* (Hong Kong: Wen-hsüeh yen-chiu she, 1959), 2325c–26b.

6   3 vols. (Peking: Chung-hua shu-chü, 1971), pp. 734–42.

Appendix V   Yü Hsin and Ssu-ma Ch'ien

1   In his *Shih-ch'i shih shang-ch'üeh* of 1787, quoted in the 'Shiki sōron' appended to Takigawa's edition of the *Shih chi*, p. 30.

BIBLIOGRAPHY

This list contains, with few exceptions, only works actually cited in the body of the book or in the notes; it is intended only to identify the editions used.

Bear, Peter M. 'The Lyric Poetry of Yü Hsin'. Unpublished doctoral dissertation, Yale University, 1969.

Birch, Cyril, ed. *Anthology of Chinese Literature: From Early Times to the Fourteenth Century*. New York: Grove Press, 1965.

Bodde, Derk. *China's First Unifier: A Study of the Ch'in Dynasty as Seen in the Life of Li Ssu 280?–208 B.C.* Leiden: Brill, 1938.

Chan-kuo ts'e 戰國策 . Kuo-hsüeh chi-pen ts'ung-shu edition.

Chang Jen-ch'ing 張仁青 , ed. *Li-tai p'ien-wen hsüan* 歷代駢文選 . Taipei: Chung-hua shu-chü, 1963.

Chang Shun-hui 張舜徽 . *Chung-kuo li-shih yao-chi chieh-shao* 中國 歷史要籍介紹 . Wu-han: Hu-pei jen-min ch'u-pan she, 1956.

Chang Tun-yi 張敦頤 . *Liu-ch'ao shih-chi pien-lei* 六朝事迹編類 . Chin-ling Chang shih 金陵張氏 , 1840.

Chao-tai ts'ung-shu 昭代叢書 . Ch'en-yung t'ang 沈鑣堂 , 1919.

Chao Yeh Chia-ying. 'The Ch'ang-chou School of *Tz'u* Criticism', *HJAS* 35 (1975), 101–32.

Ch'ao-yeh ch'ien-tsai 朝野僉載 . Pao-yen t'ang mi chi 寶顏堂秘笈 edition.

Chao Yi 趙翼 . *Nien-erh shih cha-chi* 廿二史劄記 . 2 vols., Peking: Chung-hua shu-chü, 1963.

Chavannes, Edouard, trans. *Mémoires historiques de Se-ma Ts'ien*. 5 vols., Paris: Adrien-Maisonneuve, 1967.

Ch'en Ch'ü-ping 陳去病 . *Tz'u-fu hsüeh kang-yao* 辭賦學綱要 . 2 vols. in 1, Taipei: Wen-hai ch'u-pan she, 1971.

Ch'en En-liang 陳恩良 . *Lu Chi wen-hsüeh yen-chiu* 陸機文學研究 . (Hong Kong?): Kuang-hua shu-chü, 1969.

Ch'en shu 陳書 . Po-na edition.

Ch'en Yin-k'o 陳寅恪 . (1) *Sui T'ang chih-tu yüan-yüan lüeh-lun kao* 隋唐制度淵源略論稿 . Reprinted in *Ch'en Yin-k'o hsien-sheng lun chi* 先生論集 . (Institute of History and Philology, Academia Sinica, Supplement 3) Taipei: Academia Sinica, 1971, pp. 1–104.

— (2) 'Tu Ai Chiang-nan fu' 讀哀江南賦 . *Ch'ing-hua hsüeh-pao* 13 (1941), 11—16.

Ch'en Yüan 陳垣 . (1) *Erh-shih shih shuo-jun piao* 二十史朔閏表 . Peking: Chung-hua shu-chü, 1962.

— (2) *T'ung-chien Hu-chu piao-wei* 通鑑胡注表微 . Peking: K'o-hsüeh ch'u-pan she, 1958.

Chien-k'ang shih-lu 建康實錄 . 1902 edition.

Chin lou tzu chiao-chu 金樓子校注 , ed. Hsü Te-p'ing 許德平 . Taipei: Chia-hsin shui-ni kung-ssu wen-hua chi-chin hui, 1969.

Chin shu 晉書 . Po-na edition.

Ching-tien shih-wen 經典釋文 . 1869 edition.

Ching-ting Chien-k'ang chih 景定建康志 . 1261, reprinted 1801.

Chou Fa-kao 周法高 . (1) 'Yen Chih-t'ui Kuan wo sheng fu yü Yü Hsin Ai Chiang-nan fu chih kuan-hsi' 顏之推觀我生賦與庾信哀 江南賦之關係 . *Chung-kuo yü-wen lun-ts'ung* 中國語文論叢 (Taipei, 1963), pp. 240—9.

— (2) ed. *Yen-shih chia-hsün hui-chu* 顏氏家訓彙注 . Taipei: Academia Sinica, 1960.

Chou shu 周書 . Po-na edition.

Chou-yi yin-te 周易引得 . (Harvard—Yenching Institute Sinological Index Series, Supplement 10) Taipei, 1966.

Ch'u-hsüeh chi 初學記 . Peking: Chung-hua shu-chü, 1962.

Ch'u tz'u 楚辭 . SPTK.

Chuang tzu. See *Chuang tzu yin-te*.

Chuang tzu yin-te 莊子引得 . (Harvard—Yenching Institute Sinological Index Series, Supplement 20) Cambridge, Mass., 1956.

Ch'un-ch'iu CCCC. See *Ch'un-ch'iu ching chuan chi-chieh*.

Ch'un-ch'iu ching chuan chi-chieh 春秋經傳集解 . SPTK.

Ch'un-ch'iu ching chuan yin-te 春秋經傳引得 . (Harvard—Yenching Institute Sinological Index Series, Supplement 11) Peiping, 1937.

Ch'un-ch'iu Kung-yang ching chuan chieh-ku 春秋公羊經傳解詁 . SPTK.

Chung-kuo shih-hsüeh shih 中國史學史 . 1944, reprinted Taipei: Shang-wu yin-shu kuan, 1969.

Ch'ü Shui-yüan 瞿蛻園 . (1) *Chung-kuo p'ien-wen kai-lun* 中國駢文概論 . Reprinted Taipei: Ch'ing-liu ch'u-pan she, 1971. In the Taipei reprint the author's name is given as Ch'ü Tui-chih 兌之 , and the word *kai* is omitted from the title.

— (2) ed. *Han Wei Liu-ch'ao fu hsüan* 漢魏六朝賦選 . Peking: Chung-hua shu-chü, 1964.

Ch'üan Ch'en wen. See Yen K'o-chün.

Ch'üan Ch'i wen. See Yen K'o-chün.

Ch'üan Chin wen See Yen K'o-chün.

Ch'üan Han wen. See Yen K'o-chün.

Ch'üan Hou-Chou wen. See Yen K'o-chün.

Ch'üan Hou-Han wen. See Yen K'o-chün.

Ch'üan Hou-Wei wen. See Yen K'o-chün.

Ch'üan Liang wen. See Yen K'o-chün.

Ch'üan San-kuo wen. See Yen K'o-chün.

Ch'üan Sui wen. See Yen K'o-chün.

Ch'üan Sung wen. See Yen K'o-chün.

Combined Indices to Hou Han-shu and the Notes of Liu Chao and Li Hsien. (Harvard—Yenching Institute Sinological Index Series 41) Taipei, 1966.

Couvreur, S., trans. *Tch'ouen ts'iou et Tso tchouan*. 3 vols., Ho kien fou, 1914.

Crump, J. I., trans. *Chan-kuo ts'e* (Oxford Library of East Asian Literatures) Oxford, 1970.

Dien, Albert E., trans. (1) *Biography of Yü-wen Hu* (Chinese Dynastic Histories Translations No. 9) Berkeley and Los Angeles: Univ. of California, 1962.

– (2) *'Pei Ch'i shu* 45: Biography of Yen Chih-t'ui'. Unpublished monograph.

Diény, Jean-Pierre. *Aux Origines de la poésie classique en Chine* (Monographies du T'oung pao vol. VI) Leiden: Brill, 1968.

Dubs, Homer H., trans. *History of the Former Han Dynasty*. 3 vols., Baltimore, 1938, 1944, 1955.

Eberhard, Wolfram. *A History of China.* Third edition, Berkeley and Los Angeles: Univ. of California, 1969.

Erh-shih-wu shih 二十五史 . Wu-ying tien edition, reprinted Hong Kong: Wen-hsüeh yen-chiu she, 1959.

Erh-shih-wu shih pu-pien 二十五史補編 . 6 vols., Peking: Chung-hua shu-chü, 1955.

Erh-ya 爾雅 . SPTK.

Fang, Achilles, trans. (1) *Chronicle of the Three Kingdoms.* (Harvard—Yenching Institute Studies VI) 2 vols., Cambridge, Mass., 1952, 1965.

– (2) 'Rhymeprose on Literature: The *Wen-fu* of Lu Chi', *HJAS* 14 (1951), 527—66.

Frankel, Hans H. (1) 'The Chinese Ballad "Southeast Fly the Peacocks"', *HJAS* 34 (1974), 248—71.

– (2) *The Flowering Plum and the Palace Lady: Interpretations of Chinese Poetry*. New Haven and London: Yale University Press, 1976.

Frodsham, John David. (1) trans. *An Anthology of Chinese Verse: Han Wei Chin and the Northern and Southern Dynasties*. (Oxford Library of East Asian Literatures) Oxford, 1967.

– (2) *Murmuring Stream: The Life and Works of the Chinese Nature Poet Hsieh Ling-yün (385–433), Duke of K'ang-Lo*. 2 vols., Kuala Lumpur: Univ. of Malaya, 1967.

Fung Yu-lan. *History of Chinese Philosophy*, trans. Derk Bodde. 2 vols.,
    Princeton, 1952, 1953.

Gaspardone, Emile, trans. 'Le Discours de la perte du Wou par Lou Ki',
    Sinologica 5 (1958), 189–225.

Goodrich, Chauncey S., trans. *Biography of Su Ch'o*. (Chinese Dynastic
    Histories Translations 3) Berkeley and Los Angeles: Univ. of California,
    1961.

Graham, A. C., trans. *The Book of Lieh-tzu*. London: John Murray, 1960.

Graham, William T., Jr. 'Yü Hsin and "The Lament for the South"', *HJAS*
    36 (1976), 82–113.

Han Fei tzu 韓非子 . SPPY.

Han Shih wai chuan. See J. R. Hightower (3).

Han shu 漢書 . Po-na edition.

Han Wei Liu-ch'ao pai-san chia chi 漢魏六朝百三家集 , ed. Chang
    P'u 張溥 (1602–41). Hsin-shu t'ang 信述堂 edition, 1879.

Hawkes, David. (1) trans. *Ch'u Tz'u: The Songs of the South, An Ancient
    Chinese Anthology*. Oxford, 1959.

    – (2) 'The Quest of the Goddess', *Asia Major* N.S. 13 (1967), 71–94.

Herrmann, Albert. *Historical Atlas of China*. Second edition, Edinburgh,
    1966.

Hervouet, Yves. (1) trans. *Le Chapitre 117 du Che-ki (Biographie de Sseu-
    ma Siang-jou)*. (Bibliothèque de l'Institut des Hautes Etudes Chinoises,
    Vol. XXIII) Paris, 1972.

    – (2) *Un poète de cour sous les Han: Sseu-ma Siang-jou* (Bibliothèque de
    l'Institut des Hautes Etudes Chinoises, Vol. XIX) Paris, 1964.

Hightower, James R. (1) 'Allusion in the Poetry of T'ao Ch'ien', *HJAS* 31
    (1971), 5–27.

    – (2) 'The *Fu* of T'ao Ch'ien', *Studies in Chinese Literature*, ed. John L.
    Bishop. (Cambridge, Mass., 1965), pp. 45–106.

    – (3) trans. *Han Shih wai chuan*. (Harvard–Yenching Institute Monograph
    Series, Vol. XI) Cambridge, Mass: Harvard Univ. Press, 1952.

    – (4) trans. *The Poetry of T'ao Ch'ien*. (Oxford Library of East Asian
    Literatures) Oxford, 1970.

    – (5) 'Some Characteristics of Parallel Prose', *Studies in Chinese Literature*,
    ed. John L. Bishop (Cambridge, Mass., 1965), pp. 108–39.

    – (6) *Topics in Chinese Literature*. (Harvard–Yenching Institute Studies,
    Vol. III) Cambridge, Mass., 1965.

    – (7) 'The *Wen hsüan* and Genre Theory', *HJAS* 20 (1957), 512–33.

Ho Peng Yoke, trans. *The Astronomical Chapters of the Chin shu*. Paris:
    Mouton, 1966.

Holzman, Donald. *Poetry and Politics: The Life and Works of Juan Chi
    A.D. 210–263*. (Cambridge Studies in Chinese History, Literature
    and Institutions) Cambridge, London, New York, and Melbourne:
    Cambridge Univ. Press, 1976.

Hou-Han shu 後漢書 . Po-na edition.

Hsiao ching 孝經 . SPPY.

Hsiao-ming lu 小名錄 . Pai hai 稗海 edition.

Hsieh Hsüan-ch'eng chi chiao-chu 謝宣城集校注 , ed. Hung Shun-lung 洪順隆 . Taipei: T'ai-wan Chung-hua shu-chü, 1969.

Hsieh K'ang-lo shih chu 謝康樂詩注 , ed. Huang Chieh 黃節 . Taipei, 1967.

Hsin hsü 新序 . SPTK.

Hsü Hao 徐浩 . *Nien-wu shih lun-kang* 廿五史論綱 . Hong Kong: Nan-hsing shu-chü, 1964.

Hsü Hsiao-mu ch'üan chi 徐孝穆全集 . Pao-han lou edition.

Hsü Shih-tseng 徐師曾 . *Wen-t'i ming-pien hsü-shuo* 文體明辨序說 . Hong Kong: T'ai-p'ing shu-chü, 1965.

Hsün tzu 荀子 . SPPY.

Hu-pei hsien-cheng yi-shu 湖北先正遺書 . 1923 edition.

Huai-nan tzu 淮南子 . SPTK.

Hummel, Arthur W., ed. *Eminent Chinese of the Ch'ing Period*. 2 vols., Washington: United States Government Printing Office, 1943–44.

Hung, William. (1) 'A T'ang Historiographer's Letter of Resignation', *HJAS* 29 (1969), 5–52.

— (2) *Tu Fu: China's Greatest Poet*. 1952, reprinted New York: Russell and Russell, 1969.

Johnson, David. 'The Last Years of a Great Clan: The Li Family of Chao-chün in Late T'ang and Early Sung', *HJAS* 37 (1977), 5–102.

Juan pu-ping Yung-huai shih chu 阮步兵詠懷詩註 , ed. Huang Chieh 黃節 . Peking: Jen-min wen-hsüeh ch'u-pan she, 1957.

K'ang-ts'ang tzu 亢倉子 . Chu-ts'ung pieh lu 珠叢別錄 edition.

Kao Pu-ying 高步瀛 . 'Ai Chiang-nan fu chien' 哀江南賦箋 , *Shih-ta yüeh-k'an* 14.103–32, 18.234–55, 26.63–82.

Karlgren, Bernhard. (1) trans. *The Book of Documents*. Stockholm, 1950.

— (2) trans. *The Book of Odes*. Stockholm, 1950.

— (3) 'Glosses on the *Tso chuan*', *BMFEA* 41 (1969), 1–157.

— (4) *Grammata Serica Recensa*. Stockholm, 1957.

Knechtges, David R. (1) *The Han Rhapsody: A Study of the Fu of Yang Hsiung (53 B.C. – A.D. 18)*. (Cambridge Studies in Chinese History, Literature and Institutions) Cambridge, London, New York, and Melbourne: Cambridge Univ. Press, 1976.

— (2) 'Two Studies on the Han *Fu*', *Parerga*, I (1968), 5–61.

Knechtges, David R. and Jerry Swanson. 'Seven Stimuli for the Prince: the *Ch'i-fa* of Mei Ch'eng', *MS* 29 (1970–1), 99–116.

Ku-chin chu 古今注 . Ku-chin yi-shih edition, Shanghai: Shang-wu yin-shu kuan, 1937.

Ku Yen-wu 顧炎武 . *Jih-chih lu* 日知錄 . References are to the *Jih-chih lu chi-shih* 集釋 , SPPY.

Kuo yü 國語 . SPPY.

Lau, D. C., trans. (1) *Lao tzu: Tao te ching.* Harmondsworth and Baltimore: Penguin, 1967.

   – (2) *Mencius.* Harmondsworth and Baltimore: Penguin, 1970.

Legge, James, trans. (1) *The Chinese Classics.* Third edition, in 5 vols., Hong Kong: Hong Kong Univ. Press, 1960.

   – (2) 'Hsiao King', *Sacred Books of the East,* III, 447–88.

Li chi cheng-yi 禮記正義 . SPPY.

Li Hsiang 李詳 . 'Yü Tzu-shan Ai Chiang-nan fu chi-chu' 庾子山哀江 南賦集注 , *Kuo-ts'ui hsüeh-pao* 7.1 (1911), 7a–14a.

Li T'ai-po ch'üan chi 李太白全集 . 1912 blockprint.

Li T'ai-po shih chi 李太白詩集 . SPPY.

Li Tzu 李荻 , ed. *Chung-kuo li-tai san-wen hsüan* 中國歷代散文選 . Vol. I, Hong Kong: Hsiang-kang Shang-hai shu-chü, 1964.

Liang shu 梁書 . Po-na edition.

Liao, W. K., trans. *Complete Works of Han Fei Tzu.* 2 vols., London: Probsthain, 1959.

Lieh-hsien chuan 列仙傳 . Ku-chin yi-shih edition, Shanghai, 1937.

(Ku) Lieh-nü chuan 古列女傳 . SPTK.

Lieh tzu chi-shih 列子集釋 . Hong Kong, 1965.

Liu-ch'ao shih-chi pien-lei. See Chang Tun-yi.

Liu-ch'ao ssu chia ch'üan chi 六朝四家全集 . Facsimile of 1870 edition, Taipei: Hua-wen shu-chü, 1968.

Liu-ch'ao wen-chieh 六朝文絜 , comp. Hsü Lien 許槤 (preface dated 1825). References are to the *Liu-ch'ao wen-chieh chien-chu* 箋注 , with commentary by Li Ching-kao 黎經誥 . Peking: Chung-hua shu-chü, 1962.

Liu Chih-chi 劉知幾 . *Shih t'ung* 史通 . Peking: Chung-hua shu-chü, 1961.

Liu K'ai-yang 劉開揚 . 'Lun Yü Hsin chi ch'i shih fu' 論庾信及其詩賦 , *Wen-hsüeh yi-ch'an tseng-k'an* 7 (1959), 58–78.

Lü-shih ch'un-ch'iu 呂氏春秋 . SPTK.

Lü Ssu-mien 呂思勉 . *Liang-Chin Nan-Pei-ch'ao shih* 兩晉南北朝史 . 2 vols., Hong Kong: T'ai-p'ing shu-chü, 1962.

Mao Shih Cheng chien 毛詩鄭箋 . SPPY.

Mao Shih yin-te 毛詩引得 . (Harvard–Yenching Institute Sinological Index Series, Supplement No. 9) Repr. Tokyo, 1962.

Marney, John. (1) 'Emperor Chien-wen of Liang (503–551): His Life and Literature'. Unpublished doctoral dissertation, University of Wisconsin, 1972.

   – (2) '"Yen-ming nang fu" (Rhymeprose on the Eye-Brightening Sachet) of Emperor Chien-wen of Liang: A Study in Medieval Folklore', *JAOS* 97.2 (April–June 1977), 131–40.

Mather, Richard B., trans. *Shih-shuo Hsin-yü: A New Account of Tales of*

the World, by Liu I-ch'ing with Commentary by Liu Chün. Minneapolis:
    Univ. of Minnesota Press, 1976.

Meng tzu cheng-yi 孟子正義 . SPPY.

Morino Shigeo 森野繁夫 . 'Ryōsho no bungaku shūdan' 梁初 の文
    學集團 , Chūgoku bungaku hō 21 (1966), 83—108.

Morohashi Tetsuji 諸橋轍次 . Dai Kan-Wa jiten 大漢和辭典 . 13 vols.,
    Tokyo, 1955—60.

Mou Jun-sun 牟潤孫 . 'T'ang-ch'u nan-pei hsüeh-jen lun-hsüeh chih yi-
    ch'ü chi ch'i ying-hsiang' 唐初南北學人論學之異趣及其
    影響 ('The Differences of Academic Approach between the Northern and
    Southern Scholars in the Early T'ang Period, and their Influence'), The
    Journal of the Institute of Chinese Studies of the Chinese University
    of Hong Kong, I (September, 1968), 50—88.

Mu t'ien-tzu chuan 穆天子傳 . SPTK.

Nan-Ch'i shu 南齊書 . Po-na edition.

Nan shih 南史 . Po-na edition.

Okazaki Fumio 岡崎文夫 . Gi Shin Nambokuchō tsūshi 魏晉南北朝
    通史 . Tokyo, 1932, reprinted 1936.

Owen, Stephen. (1) 'Hsieh Hui-lien's "Snow Fu": A Structural Study', JAOS 94
    (1974), pp. 14—23.
    — (2) The Poetry of the Early T'ang. New Haven and London: Yale
    University Press, 1977.

Pao-p'u tzu 抱朴子 . SPPY.

Pei-Ch'i shu 北齊書 . Po-na edition.

Pei shih 北史 . Po-na edition.

Pei-t'ang shu-ch'ao 北堂書鈔 . Taipei: Wen-hai ch'u-pan she, 1962.

P'eng Te-huai wen-t'i chuan-chi 彭德懷問題專輯 , ed. Ting Wang 丁望 .
    Chung Kung wen-hua ta ko-ming tzu-liao hui-pien 中共文化大革
    命資料彙編 , Vol. 3. Hong Kong: Ming-pao yüeh-k'an she, 1969.

P'ien-t'i wen-ch'ao 駢體文鈔 , ed. Li Chao-lo 李兆洛 . 2 vols., Taipei:
    Kuang-wen shu-chü, 1963.

Po-wu chih 博物志 . Kuang Han-Wei ts'ung-shu edition.

Pokora, Timoteus. 'The Life of Huan T'an', Archiv Orientalni 31 (1963),
    1—79, 521—76.

Rogers, Michael C., trans. The Chronicle of Fu Chien: A Case of Exemplar
    History. (Chinese Dynastic Histories Translations, 10) Berkeley and
    Los Angeles: Univ. of California, 1968.

des Rotours, Robert, trans. Traité des fonctionnaires et traité de l'armée.
    2 vols., Leyden: Brill, 1947.

San-kuo chih 三國志 . Po-na edition.

Schafer, Edward H. The Divine Woman: Dragon Ladies and Rain Maidens
    in T'ang Literature. Berkeley, Los Angeles, and London: Univ. of
    California, 1973.

Schipper, Kristofer Marinus, trans. L'Empereur Wou des Han dans la légende taoiste: *Han Wou-ti nei-tchouan*. (Publications de l'Ecole Française d'Extrême-Orient, Vol. LVIII) Paris, 1965.

Shan-hai ching 山海經 . References are to the *Shan-hai ching chien-shu* 箋疏 . SPPY.

Shang shu 尚書 . SPTK.

Shen-hsien chuan 神仙傳 . Kuang Han-Wei ts'ung-shu edition.

Shih chi. See Takigawa Kametarō.

Shih ching. See *Mao Shih yin-te.*

Shih-shuo hsin-yü 世說新語 . SPTK.

Shih tzu 尸子 . Chekiang 1877 edition.

Shih-yi chi 拾遺記 . Ku-chin yi-shih edition, Shanghai, 1937.

Shu-mu ta-wen pu-cheng 書目答問補正 , comp. Chang Chih-tung 張之洞 ; revised and enlarged by Fan Hsi-tseng 范希曾 . Taipei: Hsin-hsing shu-chü, 1962.

Shu-yi chi 述異記 . Kuang Han-Wei ts'ung-shu edition.

Shui-ching chu 水經注 . SPTK.

Shuo-wen chieh-tzu ku-lin 說文解字詁林 . Taipei, 1959.

Shuo yüan 說苑 . SPTK.

Sou-shen chi 搜神記 . (1) Shanghai, 1928.

— (2) Han-Wei ts'ung-shu edition, Lien-chiang Wang-shih Shu-ku shan-chuang 練江汪氏述古山莊 , 1880.

Ssu-k'u ch'üan-shu tsung-mu t'i-yao 四庫全書總目提要 . Wan-yu wen-k'u hui-yao edition.

Sui shu 隋書 . Po-na edition.

(*Sung pen shih-yi chia chu*) *Sun tzu* 宋本十一家注孫子 . Peking, 1961.

Sung shu 宋書 . Po-na edition.

Suzuki Torao 鈴木虎雄 . (1) *Fushi daiyō* 賦史大要 . Tokyo, 1936.

— (2) 'Jo Yu no bunshō' 徐庾の文章 , *Shinagaku* 10.3 (1941), 331–58.

T'ai-p'ing kuang-chi 太平廣記 . Facsimile of Ming blockprint, Peking: Wen-yu t'ang, n.d.

T'ai-p'ing yü-lan 太平御覽 . Peking: Chung-hua shu-chü, 1960.

T'an Cheng-pi. See T'an Cheng-pi and Chi Fu-hua.

T'an Cheng-pi 譚正璧 and Chi Fu-hua 紀馥華 , ed. *Yü Hsin shih fu hsüan* 庾信詩賦選 . Shanghai: Ku-tien wen-hsüeh ch'u-pan she, 1958.

(*Chiu*) *T'ang shu* 舊唐書 . Po-na edition.

Tao te ching 道德經 . SPTK.

Teng Ssu-yü 鄧嗣禹 . *Chung-kuo k'ao-shih chih-tu shih* 中國考試制度史 . Taipei: Hsüeh-sheng shu-chü.

Teng Ssu-yü and Knight Biggerstaff, comp. *An Annotated Bibliography of Selected Chinese Reference Works.* (Harvard–Yenching Institute Studies, 2) Revised Edition, Cambridge, Mass.: Harvard Univ. Press, 1950. The entry cited does not appear in the 1971 third edition.

Ting Fu-pao 丁福保 , ed. *Chüan Han San-kuo Chin Nan-pei-ch'ao shih* 全漢三國晉南北朝詩 . 2 vols., Peking: Chung-hua shu-chü, 1959.

Tōdai no sambun sakka 唐代の散文作家 , comp. Hiraoka Takeo 平岡武 夫 and Imai Kiyoshi 今井清 . (T'ang Civilization Reference Series No. 3) Kyoto: Kyoto Univ., 1954.

Tu shih yin-te 杜詩引得 . (Harvard–Yenching Institute Sinological Index Series, Supplement No. 14) 3 vols., Taipei, 1966.

T'ung chih 通志 . Shih t'ung edition, Taipei: Hsin-hsing shu-chü, 1958–9.

T'ung tien 通典 . Shih t'ung edition, Taipei: Hsin-hsing shu-chü, 1958–9.

(*Hsin chiao*) *Tzu-chih t'ung-chien chu* 新校資治通鑑注 . Peking, 1957; reprinted in 16 vols., Taipei: Shih-chieh shu-chü, n.d. Cited as *Tzu-chih t'ung-chien*.

Van Gulik, R. H. *Hsi K'ang and His Poetical Essay on the Lute*. Second edition, Tokyo and Rutland, Vermont, 1969.

Waley, Arthur. (1) trans. *The Analects of Confucius*. London: Allen and Unwin, 1938.

– (2) trans. *Chinese Poems*. London: Unwin, 1961.

– (3) *The Life and Times of Po Chü-i, 772–846 A.D.* London: Allen and Unwin, 1949.

– (4) trans. *170 Chinese Poems*. 1918, repr. London and New York, 1939.

Wang Hsien-ch'ien 王先謙 , ed. *Han shu pu-chu* 漢書補注 . 1900 edition.

Wang K'ai-yün 王闓運 . *Hsiang-ch'i lou wen-chi* 湘綺樓文集 . Taipei: Hsin-hsing shu-chü, 1956.

Wang Li 王力 , ed. *Ku-tai Han-yü* 古代漢語 . Peking: Chung-hua shu-chü, 1962.

Wang Li-ch'ing 王禮卿 . 'Yü Tzu-shan Ai Chiang-nan fu ping hsü p'ing-yi' 庾子山哀江南賦并序評釋 , *Jen sheng* 333 (September, 1964), 12–16; 334 (October, 1964), 11–16; 335 (November, 1964), 13–19.

Wang Yao 王瑤 . 'Hsü Yü yü p'ien-t'i' 徐庾與駢体 , *Chung-ku wen-hsüeh shih lun-chi* 中古文學史論集 (Shanghai: Shanghai ku-tien wen-hsüeh ch'u-pan she, 1956), pp. 154–78.

Wang Yü-ch'üan. 'An Outline of the Central Government of the Former Han Dynasty', *HJAS* 12 (1949), 134–87.

Watson, Burton. (1) *Chinese Lyricism*. New York and London: Columbia Univ. Press, 1971.

– (2) trans. *Chinese Rhyme-Prose*. New York and London: Columbia Univ. Press, 1971.

– (3) trans. *Complete Works of Chuang Tzu*. New York and London: Columbia Univ. Press, 1968.

– (4) *Early Chinese Literature*. New York and London: Columbia Univ. Press, 1962.

— (5) trans. *Hsün Tzu: Basic Writings*. New York and London: Columbia Univ. Press, 1963.

— (6) trans. *Records of the Grand Historian of China*. 2 vols., New York and London: Columbia Univ. Press, 1961.

— (7) *Ssu-ma Ch'ien, Grand Historian of China*. New York and London: Columbia Univ. Press, 1958.

Wechsler, Howard J. 'Factionalism in Early T'ang Government', in Arthur F. Wright and Denis Twitchett, eds., *Perspectives on the T'ang* (New Haven and London: Yale Univ. Press, 1973), pp. 87—120.

Wei shu 魏書. Po-na edition.

Wen hsüan 文選. Hupeh: Ch'ung-wen shu-chü, 1869 reprint of Hu K'o-chia 胡克家 edition.

Wen-yüan ying-hua 文苑英華. Taipei: Hua-wen shu-chü, 1965 reprint of Ming edition.

WH. See *Wen hsüan*.

Wilbur, C. Martin. 'The History of the Crossbow, Illustrated from Specimens in the United States National Museum', *Annual Report*, Smithsonian Institution, 1936, pp. 427—38.

Works. See *Yü Tzu-shan chi*, ed. Ni Fan.

Wu-Yüeh ch'un-ch'iu 吳越春秋. Taipei: Shih-chieh shu-chü, 1967.

Yang Lien-sheng. (1) 'Schedules of Work and Rest in Imperial China', *Studies in Chinese Institutional History* (Harvard—Yenching Institute Studies XX, Cambridge, Mass.: Harvard Univ. Press, 1963), pp. 18—42.

— (2) 'Toward a Study of Dynastic Configurations in Chinese History', *Studies in Chinese Institutional History*, pp. 1—17.

Yao Wei-yüan 姚薇元. *Pei-ch'ao Hu hsing k'ao* 北朝胡姓考. Peking: K'o-hsüeh ch'u-pan she, 1958.

Yeh Chia-ying. See Chao Yeh Chia-ying.

Yen K'o-chün 嚴可均 (1762—1843), comp. *Ch'üan Shang-ku San-tai Ch'in Han San-kuo Liu-ch'ao wen* 全上古三代秦漢三國六朝文. Facsimile of first edition of 1887—93, in 4 vols. + 1 vol. index, Peking: Chung-hua shu-chü, 1958.

Yen-shih chia-hsün hui-chu. See Chou Fa-kao (2).

Yen-t'ieh lun 鹽鐵論. SPTK.

Yi Chou shu 逸周書. Ts'ung-shu chi-ch'eng, first series.

Yi-li 儀禮. T'ang shih Shih-san ching 唐石十三經 edition, Taipei: Shih-chieh shu-chü, 1953.

Yi-wen lei-chü 藝文類聚. Facsimile of blockprint of period 1131—62, Peking: Chung-hua shu-chü, 1959.

Yü Tzu-shan chi 庾子山集. SPTK.

Yü Tzu-shan chi, ed. Ni Fan 倪璠. Hu-pei hsien-cheng yi-shu facsimile of first edition of 1687. Cited as *Works*.

Yüan-ho hsing tsuan 元和姓纂. Chin-ling shu-chü, 1880.

Yüan-ho hsing tsuan ssu-chiao chi 四校記. Shanghai, 1948.

von Zach, Erwin. *Die Chinesische Anthologie: Ubersetzungen aus dem Wen hsüan* (Harvard–Yenching Studies XVIII) 2 vols., Cambridge, Mass.: Harvard Univ. Press, 1958.

CHARACTER GLOSSARY

'Ai Chiang-nan fu' 哀江南賦
an-nan fu hsing ts'an-chün 安南府行參軍
Ch'ang-an 長安
Ch'ang-ch'eng hsüeh ying an 長城雪應閣
Chang Ch'ien 張騫
Ch'ang-chou 長洲
Chang Heng 張衡
Chang Hua 張華
Chang Hui-yen 張惠言
Chang Jung 張融
ch'ang ku 暢轂
ch'ang-shih 常侍
Chang Shou-chieh 張守節
Chang T'ing-fang 張庭芳
Chang Tsai 張載
Chang Tsan 張纘
Chang Ying 張英
Chao Ch'i 趙岐
ch'ao-chuan hsüeh-shih 抄撰學士
'Chao hun' 招魂
chen 貞
Ch'en Pa-hsien 陳霸先
Ch'en She 陳涉
Ch'en Shih 陳寔
chen-tung chiang-chün 鎮東將軍
Ch'en Wan 陳完
cheng[a] 正
cheng[b] 征
Cheng Hsüan 鄭玄
'Cheng hui fu' 正會賦
cheng liu ming 正六命
cheng-yüan lang 正員郎
Chi 冀

'Ch'i fa' 七發
'Ch'i hsi fu' 七夕賦
Ch'i Liang 杞梁
ch'i pei wei ma 騎背為馬
'Ch'i pu fu' 奇布賦
chi shih 記事
Chi-sun Yi-ju 季孫意如
ch'i wang yeh hu yen 其亡也忽焉
'Chia feng shih' 家風詩
Chia Yi 賈誼
Ch'iang 羌
Chiang-chou 江州
Chiang-hsia 江夏
Chiang-ling 江陵
Chiang-tung 江東
ChiangTzu-yi 江子一
'Chiang-wu fu' 講武賦
Chiang Yen 江淹
'Chiao chü fu' 郊居賦
Chiao-hsi 膠西
'Chiao-liao fu' 鷦鷯賦
Chieh 鶪
chieh 劫
chieh chou tsa yü ku ch'u 胥囿匜於故處
'Chieh fu' 櫛賦
Ch'ien-ch'iu t'ing 千秋亭
Chien-k'ang 建康
chien shou 儉收
Ch'ien Ta-hsin 錢大昕
'Ch'ien-tu fu' 遷都賦
Chien-yeh 建業
Ch'ih-chang Man-chih 赤章蔓枝
'Ch'ih pi fu' 赤壁賦
Chih Yü 摯虞
Chin Cho 晉灼
'Chin ch'un fu' 金錞賦
Ch'in-huai 秦淮
Chin Mi-ti 金日磾
ch'in wang 勤王
'Chin yu fu' 近遊賦
ch'ing 清
Ching-chou 荊州
Ch'ing-chou 青州
'Ching fu' 鏡賦

Ching-hsing 井陘
Ching K'o 荆軻
ch'ing liu 清流
'Ching lun' 鏡論
Ch'ing Pu 黥布
'Ch'ing t'ai fu' 青苔賦
Ching-wei 精衛
Ching Wei hsiang luan 涇渭相亂
'Ch'ing ying fu' 青蠅賦
'Chiu fu' 鳩賦
'Ch'iu hsing fu' 秋興賦
chiu ming 九命
'Chiu te sung' 酒德頌
'Ch'iung-chu chang fu' 邛竹杖賦
cho liu 濁流
chou ching 州睘
chou hsing 周星
Chou kuan 周官
Chou wang feng Cheng fen; Ch'u hou chih Ch'in yüan 周王逢鄭忿
　　　楚后怨秦宛
'Chu chang fu' 竹杖賦
Ch'u-ch'iu 楚丘
chu hou 諸侯
Chu-ko K'o 諸葛恪
Chu-ko Liang 諸葛亮
Ch'u-shih 處士
Chu Yi 朱异
'Chuan-cheng fu' 撰征賦
'Ch'uan fu' 船賦
'Ch'un fu' 春賦
ch'ung che 衝車
'Chung-hsing fu' 中興賦
Chung-yung chih ssu hu chu 仲雍之祀忽諸
Ch'ü Yüan 屈原
'Ch'üan-nung fu' 勸農賦
chün 郡
Chün-shan 君山
'Erh ching fu' 二京賦
Feng ku Liang hsi 豐故梁徙
Feng Yi 馮異
fu 'rhapsody' 賦
fu 'talisman' 符
Fu Hsien 傅咸
Fu Hsüan 傅玄

'Fu-niao fu' 鵩鳥賦
'Hai fu' 海賦
'Han-shih san fu' 寒食散賦
Han-tan 邯鄲
Han-tan Ch'un 邯鄲淳
Han Wu-ti nei-chuan 漢武帝內傳
'Hen fu' 恨賦
Ho-fei 合肥
Ho Hsiu 何休
hou 侯
Hou Ching 侯景
Hsi Han 嵇含
Hsi ho 西河
Hsi K'ang 嵇康
hsi piao 繫表
hsi tz'u 繫辭
Hsia-cha 下溠
hsia ch'e 下車
Hsia-Chiang ping 下江兵
Hsia-hou Hsüan 夏侯玄
'Hsiang ching' 象經
Hsiang-chou 湘州
'Hsiang hsi fu' 象戲賦
Hsiang Hsiu 向秀
Hsiang-tung 湘東
Hsiang Yü 項羽
Hsiao Ch'a 蕭詧
Hsiao Cheng-te 正德
Hsiao Chi 紀
Hsiao Chien 堅
Hsiao Chih 躓
Hsiao Ch'üeh 確
Hsiao Fang-teng 方等
Hsiao Feng 鋒
Hsiao Hsü 續
Hsiao Kang 綱
Hsiao Lun 綸
Hsiao Shao 韶
Hsiao Ta-hsin 大心
Hsiao Ta-yüan 大圜
Hsiao Tsao 慥
Hsiao T'ung 統
Hsiao Tzu-hui 子暉
Hsiao Tzu-lung 子隆

Hsiao Yen 衍
Hsiao Yi 繹
Hsiao Yü 譽
Hsiao Yüan-ming 淵明
Hsieh Chuang 謝莊
Hsieh Hui-lien 惠連
Hsieh Ling-yün 靈運
Hsieh T'iao 朓
hsien 縣
Hsien Chen 先軫
hsien chü 閒居
hsien-ma 洗馬
Hsien-pei 鮮卑
'Hsin kung fu' 新宮賦
Hsin-yeh 新野
hsing 行
hsing ching 硎穽
hsing chou yü t'ien 星周於天
Hsing-ku 硎谷
Hsing Shao 邢劭 / 邵
'Hsiu po fu' 修栢賦
Hsiung-nu 匈奴
Hsü Ch'ih 徐摛
Hsü Chiung 徐州
Hsü Ling 徐陵
hsüan 縣
hsüan chih jen-shou; T'ien-tzu wan nien 懸之仁壽天子萬年
'Hsüeh fu' 雪賦
'Hsüeh Liang wang T'u-yüan fu' 學梁王兔園賦
hsüeh ssu Hu sha an 雪似胡沙暗
hsün meng 尋盟
Hsün-yang 尋陽
Hu San-hsing 胡三省
Hu Tsung 胡綜
Hu Wei-sheng 胡渭生
'Huai fu' 淮賦
Huan T'an 桓譚
Huan Wen 桓溫
'Huang lung ta ya fu' 黃龍大牙賦
Huang-ti chan-chün chüeh 黃帝占軍決
'Huang yin fu' 豐瘖賦
hui 回
'Hui fu' 悔賦
Hung-nung 弘農

jen-chien chih shih p'iao hu chi ho 人間之世飄忽幾何
'Jen-chien shih' 人閒世
Jen Fang 任昉
Jen Yüeh 任約
Juan Chi 阮籍
jung-chao chiang-chün 戎昭將軍
k'ai-fu 開府
k'ai-kuo 開國
'Kan-liang fu' 感涼賦
Kan Pao 干寶
kan pu pen wen kuan shou 敢不奔問（＝問）官守
Kao Huan 高歡
Kao Yün 高允
Keng Kung 耿恭
Keng-shih 更始
Ku 蠱
'K'u shu fu' 枯樹賦
ku wen 古文
'Kua fu' 瓜賦
K'uai-chi 會稽
kuan 館
Kuan-chung 關中
'Kuan wo sheng fu' 觀我生賦
Kuan Yü 關羽
Kuei Chuang 歸莊
'Kuei hun fu' 歸魂賦
'K'un-je fu' 困熱賦
kung 公
Kung Ao 共敖
K'ung Jung 孔融
Kung Sheng 龔勝
Kung-sun Hung 公孫弘
Kung-sun Lung 公孫龍
K'ung Sung 孔嵩
Kuo P'u 郭璞
Lei yao 類要
Li Ch'ien 李鶱
Li Hsieh 李諧
Li Kuang 李廣
Li Ling 李陵
'Li-pieh fu' 離別賦
Li Po 李白
'Li sao' 離騷
Li Shan 李善

Li Shang-yin 李商隱
Li Shao-chün 李少君
Li Shih-min 李世氏
Li Yen-shou 李延壽
Li Yung 李顒
Liang-chou 涼州
Liang Hung 梁鴻
Liang Su 梁肅
'Lien chu' 連珠
lien nu 連弩
Lin-chiang wang chi ch'ou-ssu chieh-shih ko-shih ssu p'ien 臨江王
　　及愁思節士歌詩四篇
Lin-chih hsüeh-shih 麟趾學士
Lin-ch'ing 臨清
Lin Hsiang-ju 藺相如
ling Chien-k'ang ling 領建康令
Ling-hu Te-fen 令狐德棻
Ling-kuang k'uei-jan tu ts'un 靈光巋然獨存
Liu Chen 劉楨
Liu Ching-kung 劉敬躬
Liu Chung-li 柳仲禮
Liu Hsieh 劉勰
Liu Hsüan 劉玄
liu-li[a] 留黎
liu-li[b] 琉璃
Liu Ling 劉伶
Liu Ssu-chen 劉思真
Liu Yüan 劉淵
Lo Hsien 羅憲
lo hsing 落星
Lu Chao-lin 盧照鄰
Lu Chi 陸機
Lu Fa-ho 陸法和
Lu Fan-ch'ao 陸繁詔
Lu Kuei-meng 陸龜蒙
Lu Nü-sheng pieh chuan 魯女生別傳
Lu Yün 陸雲
lü p'in 廣聘
Ma Yüan 馬援
Mao Sui 毛遂
'Mei-hua fu' 梅花賦
Mei Sheng 枚乘
Meng K'ang 孟康
Mi Heng 禰衡

'Mi-hou fu' 獼猴賦
ming liang tso li 明兩作離
Mo-tu 冒頓
mou 敏
Mu Hua 木華
'Nan cheng fu' 南征賦
Nan-chün 南郡
'Nan tu fu' 南都賦
Nan-yang 南陽
nien-p'u 年譜
O-fang 阿房
Pa-ling 巴陵
pai yi 白衣
Pan Ku 班固
P'an Yüeh 潘岳
Pao Chao 鮑照
P'ei Po-mao 裴伯筏
P'ei Sung-chih 裴松之
'Pei tu fu' 北都賦
pen, hai, k'uei, chi 賁海潰積
Pi-kan 比干
pi-shou 匕首
p'i wo shou wen 被我默文
p'iao 溧
p'iao-chi ta chiang-chün k'ai-fu yi-t'ung-san-ssu 驃騎大將
　　軍開府儀同三司
'Pieh fu' 別賦
Pieh Hsü-yang fu wu p'ien 別棚楊賦五篇
Pien Ho 卞和
Pien Lan 卞蘭
Pien Pin 卞彬
'P'in chia fu' 貧家賦
'Ping fu' 餅賦
'P'ing-Wu sung' 平吳頌
Po Ch'i 白起
Po-teng 白登
Po-yi 伯夷
pu ssu hu chu 不杞忽諸
pu yu fei yeh, chün ho yi hsing 不有廢也君何以興
san-chi ch'ang-shih 散騎常侍
San Ch'i lüeh chi 三齊略紀
san kung 三公
'San tu fu' 三都賦
'San yüeh san jih Hua-lin yüan ma-she fu' 三月三日華林園馬射賦

'Shan fu' 肩賦
Shan-yü 單于
'Shang-hsin fu' 傷心賦
'Shang-lin fu' 上林賦
shang pin yü Ti so 上賓於帝所
'Shang-shih fu' 傷逝賦
shang-shu lang 尚書郎
shang-shu tu-chih lang-chung 尚書度支郎中
Shen Chiung 沈炯／洞
Shen Yüeh 沈約
Shih chi cheng-yi 史記正義
Shih-ch'i shih shang-ch'üeh 十七史商攉
shih-chiang 侍講
shih ch'ih-chieh chü-chi ta chiang-chün yi-t'ung-san-ssu 使持節車
    騎大將軍儀同三司
shih ch'ih-chieh fu-chün chiang-chün 使持節撫軍將軍
'Shih-ch'ing fu' 釋情賦
shih Liang tung-kung chiang-tu 侍梁東宮講讀
Shih-t'ou ch'eng 石頭城
shih-tu 侍讀
shih-yin 侍飲
'Shiki sōron' 史記總論
Shu ching 書經
Shu Hsi 束皙
'Shu-shen fu' 述身賦
Shu-sun Ch'o 叔孫婼
ssu-hsien chung ta-fu 司憲中大夫
'Ssu-hsüan fu' 思玄賦
ssu-k'ung 司空
Ssu-ma 司馬
Ssu-ma Ch'ien 司馬遷
Ssu-ma fa 司馬法
Ssu-ma Hsiang-ju 司馬相如
Ssu-ma Kuang 司馬光
Ssu-ma T'an 司馬談
'Ssu-shih fu' 四時賦
ssu-shui hsia ta-fu 司水下大夫
ssu-tsung chung ta-fu 司宗中大夫
Su Ch'o 蘇綽
Su Chün 蘇峻
Su Shih 蘇軾
Su Wu 蘇武
Sui-ch'ang 遂昌
Sui chün 隨郡

sui tso fu chi shih 遂作賦紀事
Sun Ch'o 孫綽
Sun Ch'u 孫楚
Sun Ch'üan 孫權
sung 頌
'Sung po fu' 松柏賦
Sung Yü 宋玉
Ta 大
'Ta jen fu' 大人賦
Ta-liang 大梁
Ta ti 大帝
ta tu-tu 大都督
T'ai-ch'ing chi 太清記
T'ai-kung 太公
T'ai-shih Tz'u 太史慈
T'ai-po 太伯
t'ai-shou 太守
'Tai tu fu' 代都賦
'Tan-sha k'o hsüeh fu' 丹砂可學賦
'Tang-tzu fu' 蕩子賦
T'ao Ch'ien 陶潛
T'eng 滕
'Teng fu' 燈賦
'Ti tu fu' 朴杜賦
Ti-wang shih-chi 帝王世紀
T'ien 田
T'ien Tan 田單
T'ien wang 天王
'T'ou-hu fu' 投壺賦
'Ts'ai-lien fu' 採蓮賦
ts'an hua 礬花
'Tsan-shu t'ai-tzu fu' 贊述太子賦
Ts'ao Chih 曹植
Ts'ao Kuei 曹劌
Ts'ao Mei 曹沫
Ts'ao P'i 曹丕
'Tsao shih fu' 蚤蝨賦
Ts'ao Ts'an 曹參
Ts'ao Ts'ao 曹操
Tseng tzu 曾子
Tso Fen 左芬
Tso Ssu 左思
Tsou Yen 鄒衍
Ts'ui Ling-ch'in 崔令欽

ts'ung-shu 叢書
Tu Chi 杜畿
tu-chih shang-shu 度支尚書
Tu Fu 杜甫
t'u hsüan jen-shou ching; k'ung chü Mao-ling shu 從懸仁壽鏡
　　空聚茂陵書
tu-kuan shang-shu 都官尚書
T'u Lung 屠隆
'Tu shu fu' 讀書賦
Tu T'ai-ch'ing 杜臺卿
Tu Yü 杜預
'Tui-chu fu' 對燭賦
t'ung-chih 通直
t'ung-chih cheng-yüan lang 通直正員郎
t'ung-chih san-chi ch'ang-shih 通直散騎常侍
Tung Cho 董卓
Tung-kung hsüeh-shih 東宮學士
Tung-kung ling-chih 東宮領直
Tung-o 東阿
T'ung-t'ai 同泰
Tzu-chü 子駒
Tzu-shan 子山
tz'u-shih 刺史
wang 望
Wang Ch'en 王沈
Wang Chi 王勘
Wang Ch'i 王琦
Wang Hui 王洄
Wang Hsü 王滑
Wang Mang 王莽
Wang Ming-sheng 王鳴盛
Wang Pao 王褒
Wang Seng-pien 王僧辯
Wang-tzu Ch'iao 王子喬
Wang Yen-shou 王延壽
Wang Yi 王逸
Wang Yi[a] 王廙
Wang Yin 王隱
Wei (River) 渭
Wei Cheng 魏徵
'Wei-ch'i fu' 圍棋賦
Wei Ch'ing 衛青
Wei Fang 韋欣
Wei Jui 韋叡

Wei Tan 魏澹
Wei Ts'an 韋粲
wei yu 偽遊
Wen Ch'iao 溫嶠
Wen Chung 文種
Wu-an 武安
Wu Chao-ch'ien 吳兆騫
Wu Chao-yi 吳兆宜
'Wu ch'eng fu' 蕪城賦
Wu-k'ang 武康
'Wu ma fu ying-chao' 舞馬賦應詔
Wu-ning 武寧
Wu Tzu-hsü 伍子胥
Yang Chien 楊堅
Yang Fu-chi 楊復吉
Yang K'an 羊侃
Yang Ku 陽固
'Yao ch'üeh fu' 鷁雀賦
Yao Ssu-lien 姚思廉
Yeh 鄴
'Yeh e fu' 野鵝賦
Yeh Shu-ch'ung 葉舒崇
Yen Chih-t'ui 顏之推
'Yen ko hsing' 燕歌行
Yen ko Yi shui pin 燕歌易水濱
Yen Shih-ku 顏師古
Yen Shu 晏殊
Yen Yen-chih 顏延之
Yi (River) 伊
Yi-ch'eng 義城
yi ch'i t'ou wei yin ch'i 以其頭為飲器
Yi ching-lu tao chin liu-li nao chiu . . . kung yin hsüeh meng 以徑路
　　刀金留犁撓酒......共飲血盟
Yi-chou 益州
'Yi feng fu' 儀鳳賦
yi hsing yi chou 一星已周
yi k'uei Chou shih 以窺周室
Yi-yang 義陽
yi yen ta ch'i ts'ai 以言達其才
Yi-yü-chou 乙羽周
Yin Chü 殷臣
'Yin ma ch'ang-ch'eng k'u hsing' 飲馬長城窟行
Ying 郢
Ying-chou pieh chia 郢州別篇

yüan 苑
Yüan Huang 袁黃
Yüan-k'ai 元凱
Yüan Shun 元順
yüan tu 怨讟
'Yüan-yang fu' 鴛鴦賦
'Yüan yu' 遠遊
Yüeh Ch'i 樂祁
'Yüeh ling' 月令
yün ch'uan 運船
yün-t'i 雲梯

INDEX